Family–School Collaboration in Multi-Tiered Systems of Support

The Guilford Practical Intervention in the Schools Series

Kenneth W. Merrell, Founding Editor
Sandra M. Chafouleas, Series Editor

www.guilford.com/practical

This series presents the most reader-friendly resources available in key areas of evidence-based practice in school settings. Practitioners will find trustworthy guides on effective behavioral, mental health, and academic interventions, and assessment and measurement approaches. Covering all aspects of planning, implementing, and evaluating high-quality services for students, books in the series are carefully crafted for everyday utility. Features include ready-to-use reproducibles, appealing visual elements, and an oversized format. Recent titles have Web pages where purchasers can download and print the reproducible materials.

Recent Volumes

Executive Function Skills in the Classroom:
Overcoming Barriers, Building Strategies
Laurie Faith, Carol-Anne Bush, and Peg Dawson

The RTI Approach to Evaluating Learning Disabilities,
Second Edition
*Joseph F. Kovaleski, Amanda M. VanDerHeyden,
Timothy J. Runge, Perry A. Zirkel, and Edward S. Shapiro*

Effective Bullying Prevention:
A Comprehensive Schoolwide Approach
Adam Collins and Jason Harlacher

Social Justice in Schools:
A Framework for Equity in Education
Charles A. Barrett

Coaching Students with Executive Skills Challenges,
Second Edition
Peg Dawson and Richard Guare

Social, Emotional, and Behavioral Supports in Schools:
Linking Assessment to Tier 2 Intervention
Sara C. McDaniel, Allison L. Bruhn, and Sara Estrapala

Family–School Success for Children with ADHD:
A Guide for Intervention
Thomas J. Power, Jennifer A. Mautone, and Stephen L. Soffer

School Crisis Intervention: An Essential Guide for Practitioners
Scott Poland and Sara Ferguson

Classwide Positive Behavioral Interventions and Supports,
Second Edition: A Guide to Proactive Classroom Management
Brandi Simonsen and Diane Myers

Family–School Collaboration in Multi-Tiered Systems of Support
S. Andrew Garbacz, Devon R. Minch, and Mark D. Weist

Overcoming Test Anxiety:
Tools to Support Students from Early Adolescence to Adulthood
Alex Jordan and Benjamin J. Lovett

Family–School Collaboration in Multi-Tiered Systems of Support

S. ANDREW GARBACZ
DEVON R. MINCH
MARK D. WEIST

Foreword by Kelly Henderson

gp

THE GUILFORD PRESS
New York   London

Copyright © 2025 The Guilford Press
A Division of Guilford Publications, Inc.
www.guilford.com

Printed in the United States of America

This book is printed on acid-free paper.

Last digit is print number: 9 8 7 6 5 4 3 2 1

Library of Congress Cataloging-in-Publication Data is available from the publisher.

ISBN 978-1-4625-5660-1 (paperback)
ISBN 978-1-4625-5661-8 (cloth)

About the Authors

S. Andrew Garbacz, PhD, is Associate Professor in the Department of Educational Psychology at the University of Wisconsin–Madison. His work focuses on developing, testing, and scaling family–school–community partnership interventions in school and community settings to promote youth mental and behavioral health.

Devon R. Minch, PhD, is Implementation Specialist at the Frank Porter Graham Child Development Institute, University of North Carolina at Chapel Hill. She has served in various roles supporting the implementation of best practices for students and families, including as a school psychologist, professional learning specialist, and technical assistance provider. Dr. Minch's research focuses on the intersection of family–school collaboration and tiered systems of supports.

Mark D. Weist, PhD, is Professor of Clinical–Community and School Psychology at the University of South Carolina. His work focuses on advancing research, practice, and policy on effective school behavioral health programs involving mental health–education system partnerships.

Foreword

"Parenting is the hardest job you'll EVER have." We have all heard this, often offered up by experienced parents when a neighbor or relative is exhausted, knee-deep in diapers and toddler tantrums. While those early childhood years are undeniably tough, the school-age years make very different demands on parents and caregivers. Family members, especially those raising children and youth with unique and intensive needs, may feel like they are engaging in a large-scale Whack-A-Mole arcade game, trying to simultaneously nurture and support their children's development and growth at home, in the community, and pervasively, at school.

For many parents and caregivers, that sweet combination of circumstances, skills, and resources needed to be in real partnership with schools is elusive. They face barriers to being "tuned in" to the school culture and understanding expectations of teachers and others with whom they have trusting and respectful connections, all while exercising opportunities to contribute meaningfully to the school enterprise through shared decision making and collaborative problem solving. This may be even more elusive for families who experience acute adversities and chronic traumas, those who have been historically underrepresented in effective school–family partnerships, and those who face significant communication and other access barriers.

In multi-tiered systems of support (MTSS), families and educators alike should find great opportunities to collaboration and support approaches that are positioned to identify and effectively address student, staff, and family needs. When brought to scale, the defining elements of MTSS—team-based leadership and coordination, evaluation of implementation fidelity, a continuum of evidence-based practices, continued data-based progress monitoring and decision making, comprehensive universal screening, and ongoing professional learning with coaching and local content expertise (McIntosh & Goodman, 2016)—provide a powerful framework for ensuring safe learning environments and boosting student success. Yet as ghosts of past education reform efforts prove, the success of MTSS relies on deep and sustaining buy-in from staff, implementation with fidelity, and the strong and authentic engagement of families. In a recent school MTSS leadership team meeting, an example of this authentic engagement took the form of the two family member participants sharing equally in examining recent social–emotional learning screener data. While school leaders were quick to attribute "low" scores on the social awareness measure to skill deficits, the family members drew on personal lived experiences to offer an alternative explanation. They shared that opportunities to practice and generalize social awareness competencies had been scarce due to specific community conditions. As a result, the team refocused and action planned to build more structured opportunities for applying social awareness skills and offer scaffolded feedback to students as they practiced and applied the skills that had simply been underexercised.

As a career special educator, I have taught in public schools, worked in special education policy and advocacy, conducted and managed federal research initiatives, and prepared special education teaching personnel at the university level. But nothing has as greatly influenced my perspectives on what really matters for student growth as becoming a parent, raising three children with a range of unique strengths and needs. I cringe a bit now when I reflect on my early teaching years, working with students identified with emotional and behavioral disabilities. My job was to teach children, not to deal with their even more challenging parents and caregivers. "Difficult" and "absent" parents were often an easy explanation for the significant challenging behaviors of their children. "Good parents" helped with parties and events and sent in supplies but did not ask too many questions about pedagogy or my classroom management approaches. When a parent failed to show or complete the daily report card, rarely did I consider alternative reasons for their distance, such as their own personal histories with school or their demanding and shifting work schedules. Over time and with the support of strong mentors and the opportunity to build relationships with parents and caregivers, my perspective shifted from one of blaming and shaming to one of collaboration and shared problem solving. Raising my own children with unique needs grounded me even further, as I became more familiar with the glare of disappointment, shock, or wonder sent my way when retrieving a son from another unsuccessful school activity or in another conference called by staff to lay out their concerns. I envied those who parented kids whose needs were met seamlessly at Tier 1. For those families raising "easy" kids, opportunities to engage with educators were plentiful and comfortable. True problem-solving partnerships were rare and precious. In those few occasions when educators embraced two-way dialogue, listened to me, and when I had opportunity to really hear them, the team could problem-solve tough issues by pulling on our individual strengths and experiences. Those opportunities for partnership were key to my children's success: When the team truly engaged, considering wider school and classroom factors and then narrowing to identify realistic, functional approaches for small-group and individual interventions, the growth for my children and their peers was clearly evident.

I now have the opportunity to reinforce family–school partnerships at a new level. I instruct graduate students who are in their early years of special education teaching.

The humbling opportunity to guide novice teachers through sound classroom management and behavioral intervention content, through the lens of strong collaborative relationships with families and students, is reinforcing and cathartic on many levels. I am also honored and privileged to direct a family-led resource center to support parents and caregivers of children, youth, and young adults with special needs. As the family partner to our state MTSS project, we see firsthand the potential for student, staff, and community growth toward stronger and safer school cultures and increased academic, behavioral, and social–emotional learning. We see this in family members serving in authentic ways on district and school MTSS leadership teams. We see families reinforcing practices and language consistent with their children's schoolwide expectations in their own homes. Local businesses and community- and faith-based organizations partner with schools and offer family events in diverse and accessible settings, outside of school hours, increasing opportunities for navigating resources and building shared knowledge. We see family members not only responding to surveys and other measures designed to mark progress but also partnering with school leaders to review, interpret, and use data to ground decision making about practices and policies.

Our experiences reinforce extant research that offers even more examples of the powerful role that families can play in supporting, implementing, and evaluating district and school systems of supports across tiers. Significant barriers, however, threaten the potential for wide-scale adoption of authentic family–school collaboration in MTSS. While we recognize that strong and authentic family engagement is essential and foundational to implementation, robust implementation benefits from guideposts along the journey. Happily, *Family–School Collaboration in Multi-Tiered Systems of Support* offers a rare opportunity to focus on why and how to leverage authentic family–school partnerships in a powerful framework for educational systems improvement.

The initial chapters of this book are intended to ground readers in the foundations of the family–school partnership within the context of MTSS. Core features of family–school collaborations are shared from a theoretical and an applied framework, and the evolution of MTSS—including response to intervention (RTI) and positive behavioral interventions and supports (PBIS)—is described in detail. The authors also offer a fresh and much-needed perspective that involves a long-awaited conceptual model to align and integrate family–school collaboration and practices within schools and districts adopting MTSS.

From here, core components of collaborative partnerships are explicitly addressed in a series of chapters that can serve as a roadmap for exploration, installation, and initial and full implementation of MTSS. Engaging families of diverse, historically underserved, and marginalized groups in school is a challenge, and authentic engagement in a layered, complex framework such as MTSS is even more difficult. With these challenges in mind, the authors offer strategies and resources for assessment of collaboration and use of data. Specific interventions, associated guides, and other resources to support schoolwide Tier 1, targeted Tier 2, and intensive Tier 3 systems are helpful to families and professional educators alike. A selection of case studies performed at both the district and school levels supplements these recommendations. Coauthored by those who are implementing strong family–school collaborations, these studies offer motivational examples of real-life practices built on "lessons learned." In a related vein, the authors also include a problem-solving dialogue between a family member and educator, highlighting challenges and some empirically validated strategies to successfully overcome related challenges. Chapters also provide reproducible worksheets and other resources that can be used by educators to meet specific school and family needs.

Finally, the text concludes by synthesizing the core elements of family–school collaboration topics. Recommendations for future research and practice offer readers a glimpse of the future opportunities for authentic partnership.

With the support of this text, practitioners and family members will find a path forward toward authentic, empowering family–school partnerships. With evidence-based approaches in place, school teams will be ready to affirm that indeed "fostering family–school partnerships is the hardest AND most valuable job your MTSS team will ever have!"

KELLY HENDERSON, PhD
Executive Director, Formed Families Forward
Fairfax, Virginia

REFERENCE

McIntosh, K., & Goodman, S. (2016). *Integrated multi-tiered systems of support: Blending RTI and PBIS*. Guilford Press.

Contents

1. **Core Features of Family–School Collaboration and Multi-Tiered Systems of Support**   1

    Overview of Family–School Collaboration and Multi-Tiered Systems of Support   1
        Theoretical Underpinnings   2
        Research Support for Family–School Collaboration   3
        A Logic Model to Define Family–School Collaboration in MTSS   3
        Multi-Tiered Systems of Support   5
        Promoting Uptake in Schools   7
        Family–School Collaboration   9
    Overview of the Book   11
        Key Themes across Chapters   11

2. **Equity in Family–School Collaboration**   14

    Theoretical Foundations   14
    Historical and Contextual Challenges for Family–School Collaboration   16
    Reimagining Family–School Collaboration   18
    Family–School Collaboration in Schools' MTSS   20
    Equitable Family–School Collaboration in MTSS   20
    Relationships and Communication   25
    Equitable Family–School Collaboration: Start with Families as Leaders   25
        Shared Decision Making and Family Voice   29
    Equitable Family–School Collaboration: Goals for Shared Responsibility   30
        Training and Support, Collaborative Goals, and Problem Solving   30
    Equitable Family–School Collaboration: Strategies and Approach   31
        Strategies: Relationships and Capacity Building   31
        Approach: Collective Inquiry and Action   32
    Summary   33

 3. **Fostering Equity-Oriented Family–School Collaboration toward Culturally Responsive MTSS**   **37**

    Aydin Bal, Dian Mawene, Dosun Ko, Aaron Bird Bear, Linda Orie, and Sophia Candida Ferreira Dodge

    Technical Approaches to Family–School–Community Collaboration   39
    Culturally Responsive PBIS   41
    Culturally Responsive: What Does It Mean in the Context of CRPBIS?   43
    Learning Lab Methodology   44
    Case Study: Conducting Learning Lab at a Rural High School with an
            American Indian Community   46
        Formation of the Learning Lab Team   46
        Problem Identification   47
        Problem Solving   49
        Reflection and Implementation Plan   50
    Closing Thoughts and Reflections   50

 4. **Assessment in Family–School Collaboration**   **52**

    The Family–School Partnership   53
    Family Reports of Student Performance and Well-Being   55
    Tools for Collecting Data   56
        Measuring the Family–School Partnership   56
    Collection, Management, and Use of Data   60
        Using Data to Improve Family–School Collaboration   61
        Family Perspectives to Inform Supports for Students   61
        Data Management and Use Infrastructure   62
    Case Study: Family–School Collaboration Data Collection and Use
            at Maxwell Elementary   63
    Summary   67

 5. **Building Family–School–Community Partnerships within Tier 1 of Schools' MTSS**   **69**

    Case Study: Shifting the Paradigm from Family/Student Involvement to Partnership   73
        Families and Youth as Collaborative Partners   74
    Summary   78

 6. **Embedding Family–School Collaboration in Tier 2 Systems and Practices**   **79**

    Sarah Fefer, Zack Santana, and Kimberli Breen

    What Is Tier 2 within MTSS?   80
    Multidimensional Approach to Family–School Collaboration in Tier 2   81
    Status of Collaboration in Tier 2   83
    Identifying Students in Need of More Support   84
    Where to Start? Simple and Adaptable Tier 2 Practices   88
        Check-In, Check-Out   88
        Positive Parent Contact   91
        A Continuum of Collaboration within Tier 2 Interventions   93
        Tier 2 Practices along the Continuum of Collaboration   96
    Case Examples   99
    Summary   101
    Acknowledgment   102

7. Family–School Partnerships at Tier 3   **106**

Development of Social, Emotional, and Behavioral Concerns   106
Research Supporting Family–School Partnerships   107
Chapter Orientation   107
Partnership-Centered Components   107
Problem-Solving Components   111
Schoolwide Systems to Support Implementation of Tier 3 Family–School Practices   114
Case Example: Alex's Attendance Story   118

8. Overcoming Challenges to Family Engagement and Leadership in Schools' MTSS   **120**

A "Counterfactual" or Nonexample of Family–School Collaboration Partnership   121
Moving Away from the Counterfactual toward Genuine Family–School
    Collaboration Partnerships   122
    Enhancing Family–School Collaboration at the School Building Level   122
    Enhancing Family–School Collaboration at the District Level   124
    Enhancing Family–School Collaboration at the State Level   125
Case Study: Family-Run Organizations—Partners in Schools' MTSS   125
    ROADSHOW in New Jersey   125
    Student Assistance Program in Steel Valley School District, Pittsburgh, Pennsylvania   126
    *Maryland Coalition of Families: The Family Leadership Initiative
        and Project AWARE*   126
    Mississippi Families as Allies: Making a Plan Team in Jackson, Mississippi   127
    Family Involvement Center in Arizona   127
    Common Themes across These Examples   128
Summary   128

9. District Considerations for Building Capacity to Increase Family–School Collaboration   **131**
Lindsay M. Fallon, Adam B. Feinberg, Katherine Meyer,
and Phylitia Jamerson

Importance of District Coordination of Family–School Collaboration   132
School Districts as Systems   136
Leadership Teaming   137
Executive Functions   137
    Stakeholder Engagement   138
    Funding and Alignment   138
    Policy   139
    Workforce Capacity   139
Implementation Functions   140
    Training   140
    Coaching   140
    Evaluation   141
    Local Implementation Demonstration   141
Case Study   142
    Training and Coaching   143
    Leadership Team and Evaluation   143
    Stakeholder Engagement   143
    Funding, Alignment, and Policy   144
    Local Implementation Demonstration   145
Summary   145

10. From Theory to Practice: Successful Family–School
    Collaboration in Schools   **150**
    Shelby Cook, Imad Zaheer, Julie Fogt, Laura Casey,
    and Misty Lewis
    Case Study: West Tennessee School, Tennessee   151
        School History and Demographics   151
        TBSP FACE Pilot Project   152
        FACE Team Development   153
        FACE Team Initiatives: Year 1   155
        Year 2 FACE Team Adaptations and Initiatives   158
        Next Steps   160
    Case Study: Penn School, Pennsylvania   161
    Summary   167

References   **179**

Index   **203**

Core Features of Family–School Collaboration and Multi-Tiered Systems of Support

OVERVIEW OF FAMILY–SCHOOL COLLABORATION AND MULTI-TIERED SYSTEMS OF SUPPORT

Family–school collaboration involves families and school personnel working as coequals in supporting the learning and social–emotional development of children and youth. Within the context of a multi-tiered system of support (MTSS) framework, family–school collaboration focuses on families and educators working together within and across the tiers of support to agree on educational and social–emotional supports for students and to connect school practices to home and community settings. At Tier 1, this involves sharing in the development of two-way (school–home) communication strategies, developing sustainable data systems to monitor family–school and student outcomes, examining school practices for disproportionate impact, and promoting a feedback loop with families and educators about school systems and practices. At Tier 2 and Tier 3, families and educators work together to design, implement, and evaluate academic and social–emotional supports for students experiencing targeted or intensive services. These core components are described in more detail in the sections that follow, after a review of theory and research that support family–school collaboration in MTSS.

Please note that editors of this book have developed the Family–School–Community Alliance (FSCA; see *https://fscalliance.org*) to promote ongoing change from the common scenario of very limited family engagement and leadership in schools to families and youth collaboratively co-creating the educational environment with educators and other staff. The FSCA followed the development of an e-book (Weist et al., 2017) on enhancing family engagement and leadership within positive behavioral interventions and supports (PBIS), with support from the national center on PBIS (see *www.pbis.org*). The vision of the FSCA is to

promote family, youth, and community engaged partnerships in research, practice, and policy to improve prevention and intervention in the systems and practices of positive behavioral interventions and supports and related multitiered systems of support toward improvement in valued outcomes. (FSCA, 2019)

The FSCA seeks to impact research, practice, and policy (and interconnections among these realms) to create genuine family engagement and leadership in schools toward improved social, emotional, behavioral, and academic outcomes for students and families. The current book builds from the work of the FSCA as well as research and collaborations to enhance family engagement/leadership within schools' MTSS. In the next section, we review theoretical underpinnings for this work, building toward recommended strategies for future policy, practice, and research directions found in this book.

Theoretical Underpinnings

Theoretical underpinnings for family–school collaboration and MTSS have shared and distinct areas of emphasis. Theoretical support for family–school collaboration is derived from theories that describe a set of overlapping ecological systems within which a child develops. Ecological systems theory includes proximal microsystems, such as home and school, that are primary influences on child development (Bronfenbrenner, 1979). The mesosystem refers to the connections between microsystems and is the primary system that captures parent and educator interactions. Extending out from the mesosystem, the exosystem includes neighborhoods and community organizations. Next, the macrosystem refers to the broader social and political context that influences systems and practices in the exosystem and microsystem. An ecological framework can also be applied to schools, where individual-level influences are proximal influences on child learning and development, and broader school-level factors, such as school climate, influence how systems and practices are implemented and experienced by students (Domitrovich et al., 2008).

Two other theories relevant to family–school collaboration are the multiple worlds typology and the phenomenological variant of ecological systems theory. Multiple worlds typology captures how messages within and across home, school, and community settings can influence child development. Multiple worlds typology specifically describes how different messages within settings can be challenging for students, particularly when messages in one setting, such as school, do not align with messages in their home and community settings (Phelan et al., 1991). This can be particularly problematic for students who come from minoritized communities and who are in schools that do not reflect their culture and experiences. The phenomenological variant of ecological systems theory has specific implications for adolescent identity formation by addressing the social, historical, and cultural context in which youth develop (Spencer et al., 1997). These principles are explored in more detail in Chapter 2.

MTSS is a prevention framework applied to education from public health (Walker et al., 1996). The MTSS framework has been refined over time and operationalized through frameworks such as PBIS. A focus on promoting social behavior within MTSS has been conceptualized as a systems-level application of applied behavior analysis (Horner et al., 2005). This behavioral orientation provides a context for applying a set of antecedents to support academic and social behavior, behavior teaching strategies to build skills, and consequent strategies to reinforce skill development. This scoped and sequenced approach to support academic and social behavior may at times be in conflict with family values and routines. Thus, an integrated approach to family–school collaboration within MTSS may require working with families at Tier 1 to identify ways to promote collaboration and partnership building in the context of a behavioral process that historically has been implemented within a specific scope and sequence.

Research Support for Family–School Collaboration

The influence of family–school connections on student outcomes has been studied for decades. A line of correlational research has examined associations between family educational involvement and student social behavior and academic achievement (Henderson & Mapp, 2002). This line of research has suggested that increased family educational involvement is associated with positive outcomes for students (e.g., attendance). These correlational studies conclude that family involvement in education matters for students, and the findings have been documented in primary studies as well as meta-analyses (Fan & Chen, 2001; Jeynes, 2012).

In addition to correlational studies, a line of more rigorous intervention research using randomized controlled trials has shown that students experience positive outcomes when their family participates in a family–centered or family–school partnership intervention (Sheridan et al., 2019). These findings are documented across elementary school and secondary school settings (Sheridan et al., 2012; Stormshak et al., 2011). These family-centered and family–school interventions typically include a consultant or school clinician working with a family and educator to support the design and implementation of home and school supports for an individual student. Findings from these studies suggest that students on average experience positive outcomes as a result of family and educator participation (Sheridan et al., 2017). In addition, positive impacts are documented for families, educators, and the family–school relationships. For example, parents and teachers who have a child with emotional and behavior concerns report improvements in the parent–teacher relationship, that improved relationship is partially responsible for improvements in student behavior (Sheridan et al., 2012).

> "I want teachers and administrators to know me by name, know that I really care, that I am not checked out. I feel like just showing up and being in the school, they know that I'm serious and I just feel like it's better for my kids when I do that."

A Logic Model to Define Family–School Collaboration in MTSS

A logical model for family–school collaboration in MTSS can be helpful in defining key systems and practices, along with proximal and distal variables to articulate how theoretical underpinnings can be combined with research findings to describe integration and impact on outcomes. Figure 1.1 depicts conditions, context variables, core variables, mechanisms, and outcomes. Conditions and context variables establish the conditions to support adoption and sustained implementation of core variables. Core variables have proximal impacts on mechanism, which in turn leads to improved outcomes.

Conditions	Context Variables	Core Variables	Proximal Mechanisms	Distal Mechanisms	Outcomes
Federal, state, and local emphasis on family–school collaboration and family leadership to support children and youth	District and school investment in promoting families as leaders	Family–school collaboration as foundational to school systems and practices	**Enhanced:** Family and teacher/staff efficacy, beliefs, and expectations	**Enhanced:** Family-youth and teacher/staff–youth relationships	**Enhanced:** School attendance
	Commitment to cultural responsiveness and anti-racism	Proactive systems and practices that consider flexibility, adaptation, and responsiveness to capacity and needs	Family–school collaboration and family–teacher/staff relationships	Youth self-regulation and peer relationships	Adaptive and problem-solving skills
	School atmosphere to support family–school collaboration	Support to school staff and families to develop and implement culturally responsive collaboration systems and practices			Social, emotional, and behavioral competencies
	Data systems to proactively screen and monitor student academics and behavior and family–school collaboration	Engaged interactions among educators, families, and youth			Academic performance
	Clear roles and bidirectional communication systems				Matriculation across grades and graduation
	Positive interactions and shared decision making among families and educators				

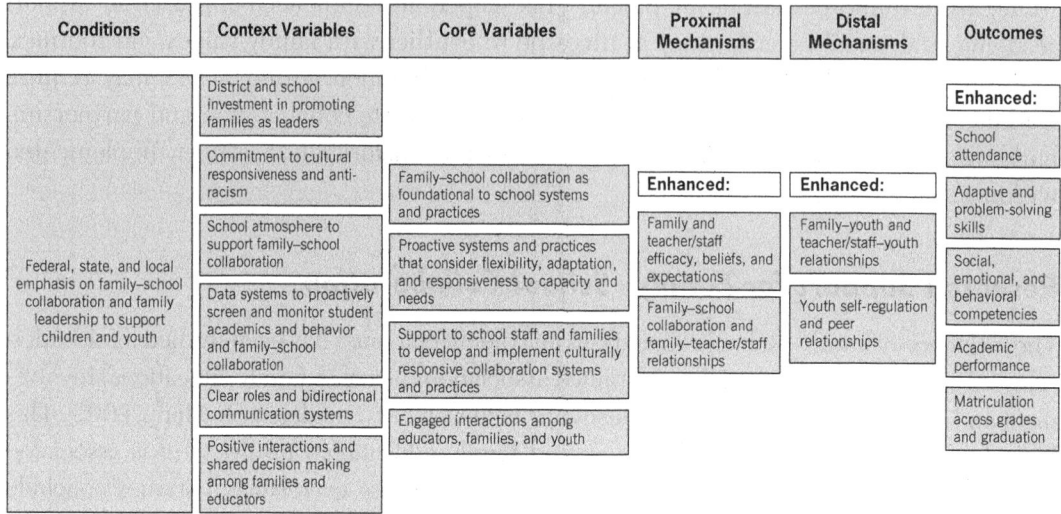

FIGURE 1.1. Conceptual model of family–school collaboration.

Figure 1.1 displays a conceptual model for family–school collaboration. We offer this conceptual model to organize the key variables associated with family–school collaboration and demonstrate key mechanisms of action to promote student well-being. This modeling approach has been used in education research (Horner, 2016), family-centeredness (Stormshak & Dishion, 2009), and family–school collaboration (Garbacz et al., 2017).

Figure 1.1 illustrates conditions, core variables, mechanisms, and outcomes. Conditions include the federal, state, and local emphasis on family–school collaboration that can set the stage for or facilitate family–school collaboration in schools. For example, federal education policy that mandates two-way communication among schools and families can be operationalized at the state and local levels to clarify and impact educators' work with families. Context variables can occasion specific family–school practices. As one example, a school atmosphere that is developed with families can create a welcoming, culturally responsive, inclusive, and supportive orientation to parents and help promote collaboration between families and educators to develop school systems and practices (Bal & Perzigian, 2013; Ishimaru, 2020). Alternatively, school atmospheres that are created by educators alone may be prone to reflect a narrower range of opportunities for families to be involved and limit involvement to tokenistic approaches. Turning from core variables to mechanisms, the key pathways to change become clearer. Research suggests that when parents and teachers collaborate to support a student's social, emotional, and behavioral competencies, collaborative process leads to improved parent–teacher relationships.

> "Even though educators are educators, parents know their children in a way that can make educators' jobs easier."

Through improvements in the parent–teacher relationship, students experience improved competencies (Sheridan et al., 2017). Thus, the parent–teacher relationship is a key mechanism to target within family–school collaboration to promote positive student outcomes.

Family–school collaboration is inherently a strengths-based process, focused on recognizing, identifying, celebrating, and encouraging family strengths, leveraging family strengths to empower and develop capacities of individuals and systems, and supporting families' use of their strengths to overcome challenges. However, education systems are often not developed in ways that recognize the strengths of minoritized families (Powell & Coles, 2021). In fact, institutional systems and practices have marginalized minoritized families, further separating schools and families and harming children (Williamson et al., 2005). The emphasis on family–school collaboration must integrate the necessary core variables of cultural responsiveness and anti-racism (Proctor et al., 2017). Thus, in the conceptual model, the outcomes, which reflect various dimensions of family, school, and student well-being, can only be realized when all families are included, and no one is excluded. Co-equal relationships among families and schools, where families are valued as leaders and key decision makers, benefit educators, families, and students. Figure 1.1 provides an overview of the key conditions and practices that drive implementation and sustainment.

❙ "Parents should be seen as allies, not just partners."

Multi-Tiered Systems of Support

Informed by public health approaches, education has shifted to tiered prevention and intervention systems intended to allow for efficient and effective use of resources aligned with and targeted to students' needs (Domitrovich et al., 2010). MTSS frameworks emphasize the proactive and integrated use of academic, behavioral, and social–emotional assessment and intervention strategies to improve related student learning outcomes. Various terms and frameworks under the MTSS umbrella have become associated with particular emphasis on students' academic, behavioral, or social–emotional needs, including response to intervention (RTI; Jimerson et al., 2016); positive behavioral interventions and supports (PBIS; Sugai & Horner, 2002a); and interconnected systems frameworks (ISF; Eber et al., 2019; Weist et al., 2018).

The key components of multi-tiered systems of supports can often be organized under three broad domains including data (i.e., screening, progress monitoring, fidelity), systems (i.e., multilevel prevention and intervention systems; teams), and practices (e.g., communication, collaboration; Bailey et al., 2020; McIntosh & Goodman, 2016). School leadership teams are organized to plan and implement screening and monitoring systems based on direct assessments of students' academic, behavioral, and social–emotional learning needs to inform interventions and supports that effectively address and improve student skills and performance outcomes.

Tiered prevention frameworks begin at the universal level (Tier 1), wherein student data are used to inform curriculum and instructional supports and strategies to maximize outcomes for *all* students. Through effective programming and regular monitoring of student progress using universal screening approaches and quarterly assessments, high quality instruction provided to all students at Tier 1 reduces proportion of students requiring supplemental interventions (Gibbons et al., 2019). Regular review of student progress proactively identifies students that may benefit from additional intervention and supports at the selected (Tier 2) level. At the Tier 2 level, student interventions are intensified by increasing the amount of time, repetition with skills, or direct instruction through smaller ratios of staff to student groups (Batsche et al., 2005). Some students who demonstrate the greatest need require intensive, individualized supports at the indicated (Tier 3) level. Through proactive and systematic monitoring of student learning data, schools can maximize the effectiveness of instruction and curriculum at Tier 1, and free-up resources and supports for students demonstrating elevated risk and the greatest need to ensure the success for all. Various systems and practices, such as professional development and coaching, teaming, and collaboration, are essential for schools to successfully implement tiered systems of support.

Core Domains of MTSS

Drawing from research on effective implementation of innovations and systems change, various measures and conceptual frameworks have been adopted to outline the core features of MTSS among schools, often including six domains: (1) leadership, (2) building capacity and infrastructure for implementation (e.g., master schedules), (3) communication and collaboration, (4) data-based problem solving, (5) tiered prevention and intervention frameworks, and (6) evaluation (e.g., self-assessment of MTSS implementation; Stockslager et al., 2016). These domains that advance MTSS can be operationalized at a school and district level. For example, each school builds capacity and infrastructure for implementing a certain innovation, such as PBIS, establishes processes for collaboration and communication, creates data-based problem-solving systems, and puts into place evaluation systems and practices. Similarly, these domains are operationalized at a district level as well. A key distinguishing feature of MTSS at a school and district is the level of implementation. For example, at a school level, capacity and infrastructure might support coaching of teachers to support implementation, teaming at the schoolwide as well as Tier 2 and Tier 3 levels, and procedures to screen and progress monitor data for all students in the school and students within certain groups (e.g., students at risk for serious emotional and behavior concerns). At the district level, implementation of an innovation would focus across schools and could include providing professional development (training and coaching) to schoolwide teams in adopting and implementing PBIS. At the district level, implementation data and student outcome data can focus across schools or within certain schools.

Research on MTSS

Research examining MTSS frameworks has investigated implementation and outcomes. In the context of the PBIS framework, factors influencing district adoption include district size and the geographic area of the district is located (Kittelman et al., 2019). Among school administers who were initially opposed to or not supportive of PBIS, administrators identified several factors as helping promote their implementation (McIntosh et al., 2016). These factors included learning from others, networking with implementing schools, talking with other administrators, and learning about how PBIS aligns with personal valuesIn terms of factors that might help schools sustain MTSS, school personnel in schools implementing PBIS noted school buy-in, administrator support, and consistency as factors that promoted sustainability (Pinkelman et al., 2015). Regarding outcomes, implementation of PBIS is associated with decreases in restraints and seclusions in alternative education settings (Grasley-Boy et al., 2020). In addition, findings suggest that implementation of PBIS is associated with reductions in school discipline and increased academic achievement (Lee & Gage, 2020). MTSS frameworks for promoting enhanced core reading instruction have also been examined (Smith et al., 2016). Findings associated with implementation of a framework that included Tier 1 and Tier 2 reading instruction and intervention suggest improvements on student literacy skills (Fien et al., 2021).

Promoting Uptake in Schools

Despite advances in evidence-based practices in K–12 education settings associated with improved student outcomes, the impact of the knowledge and research on student outcomes has yet to be realized. Furthermore, efforts to advance tiered prevention frameworks continue to articulate siloed areas of focus (e.g., behavior or mental health) while truly *integrated* MTSS implementation is less common in practice (McIntosh & Goodman, 2016). Within this chapter we provide an overview of key considerations for promoting uptake in schools. These principles are explored in more depth in Chapters 8, 9, and 10.

Growing interest and support for better understanding of the processes and mechanisms to select, implement, and scale-up evidence-based practices in schools has resulted in a growing support for implementation science to inform K–12 settings (George et al., 2018; McIntosh et al., 2013). To underscore the role of implementation science in adopting and implementing evidence-based practices with fidelity in educational settings, the term *usable innovations* (Fixsen et al., 2013) has been used interchangeably with evidence-based practices. Active implementation frameworks (Blase et al., 2012; Fixen et al., 2005; Fixen et al., 2013) and common implementation science frameworks for K–12 settings purport that implementation happens in discernable stages (i.e., exploration, installation, initial implementation, full implementation), and there are common components of successfully implemented programs (i.e., leadership, competency, organization). The drivers underscore the role of leadership in developing competency and organizational drivers to advance the system through implementation stages from exploration, adoption/installation, and initial implementation to full implementation resulting in improved practices and outcomes in schools. Active implementation methods incorporate best practices related to the stages of implementation and implementation drivers (Fixen et al., 2013).

Implementation Drivers

Competency drivers refer to the selection, training, coaching, and fidelity monitoring mechanisms that support staff efficacy and use of evidence-based practices. Organizational drivers refer to the leadership, communication and feedback loops, policy and procedural mechanisms, and external support mechanisms that uphold educational environments conducive to adoption of evidence-based practices (e.g., data systems for decision making).

Together, these drivers are often referred to as an organization's *capacity* for supporting implementation of evidence-based practices with fidelity (Horner et al., 2017).

Growing tiered prevention models advance evidence-based practices to improve student outcomes; however, these are often advanced as siloed frameworks affecting academic performance (e.g., RTI) or social behavior (PBIS). The ISF (Eber et al., 2019) interconnects social behavior support within PBIS and social–emotional supports to promote mental health for all. In addition, McIntosh and Goodman (2016) advanced an approach for improving integration of academic and social behavior supports. However, in practice truly integrated MTSS continues to be primarily aspirational. Furthermore, measures to support uptake and fidelity of evidence-based practices are often siloed, resulting in districts or schools requiring multiple yet similar assessments of similar components or features of implementation necessary for any evidence-based practice (e.g., coaching, data use). Efforts to advance integrated assessments of school-level capacity and fidelity are available (e.g., Tiered Fidelity Inventory [TFI]; Algozzine et al., 2014; McIntosh et al., 2016), yet the degree of specificity offered by these assessments to improve school practices requires additional information more specific to an evidence-based practice or framework (e.g., Benchmarks of Quality [BOQ] for PBIS; Reading TFI for literacy; Martin et al., 2015).

Given the role of district capacity in school-level fidelity and outcomes of implementing evidence-based practices (McIntosh et al., 2013; George et al., 2018), Ward and colleagues (2015) recently published findings on efforts to provide districts with a comprehensive assessment of their capacity for supporting implementation of evidence-based practices in schools). Their work provides a reliable, valid and efficient tool for districts to regularly assess capacity for supporting school's selection, scale-up, and sustained implementation of evidence-based practices (Ward et al., 2021). The District Capacity Assessment (DCA) is a 27-item measure completed by district leadership teams assessing features aligned with implementation drivers of the district's ability to support school-level implementation of evidence-based practices specific to a content area (e.g., behavior, literacy) in three broad domains (i.e., leadership, competency, and data systems). Results are then used to guide district planning and improvement efforts (Ward et al., 2021). At the time of this publication, authors of the DCA noted evolving nature of research and will update the tool once information on the validity of the DCA as an effective, valid tool to assess and improve district capacity for supporting implementation of usable innovations among schools becomes available.

Even with these recent advancements in district and school-level integrated assessments to determine capacities for supporting and implementing evidence-based practices, these decisions and input on the assessments are often limited to the perspectives of educational staff, with little to no input from families or communities. Furthermore, the degree to which family–school collaboration is a central component to MTSS implementation or scale-up varies across conceptual models and locations. Many times, states, districts, and schools wait to get their internal processes and practices sorted out before opening up conversations about MTSS with families. This contradicts research underlying the importance of educators and families in co-creating and co-implementing innovations and further reinforces family–school collaboration as an add-on component to implementation of MTSS. This has resulted in miscommunications and misunderstanding about the intent and purpose of MTSS implementation among families, with many feeling that the approach delays the support for students in need.

> "You [educators] might not be an expert in how the school works, but you're [parents] an expert in your child."

However, there have been efforts to advance family–school collaboration within MTSS and even fully developed tiered approaches to family–school collaboration that have resulted in the foundational research needed to better understand key systems and practices required for integration within MTSS.

Family–School Collaboration

MTSS frameworks include a clear set of systems and practices for establishing systems of support to promote academic performance, social behavior, and mental health. When implementing these frameworks, students experience positive outcomes (Fien et al., 2021; Lee & Gage, 2020). One limitation of common frameworks advanced within MTSS is a lack of or minimal attention to families and the family–school connection (Garbacz et al., 2016). Typically, family–school collaboration systems and practices are implemented in a siloed manner similar to academic frameworks, social behavior frameworks, and school mental health frameworks (Garbacz, McIntosh, et al., 2018). Aligning and integrating family–school collaboration within MTSS has several advantages (Weist et al., 2017). Integrating family–school collaboration within MTSS frameworks can help improve implementation of family–school collaboration systems (Garbacz, McIntosh, et al., 2018). Such integrated implementation can amplify outcomes for students. Indeed, research findings suggest that family–school interventions are associated with improved academic and social–emotional outcomes for students (Fan & Chen, 2001; Sheridan et al., 2019).

MTSS frameworks offer a useful set of organizing features (data, systems, practices) that can support implementation of family–school collaboration in the context of academic, social–behavioral, and mental health supports. Learning from active implementation frameworks and the stages of implementation, schools would be better equipped to implement contextually relevant family–school collaboration approaches by including families as true partners in the exploration stage. When exploring evidence-based practices to meet the needs of all students, partnering with families to explore the best approaches moving forward increases the chances for developing truly collaborative partnerships and ensures fit and feasibility for students' culture and context. Partnering alongside families and providing them with opportunities to voice perspectives and provide input throughout all stages of implementation can assist educational systems in partnering with families as competencies are developed and organizational mechanisms are adjusted to support implementation and outcomes.

Participatory Approaches within Family–School Collaboration

Family–school interventions often include a participatory component that emphasizes the voice and perspective of families when considering organizational change in schools (Bang &

Vossoughi, 2016; Ishimaru, 2019). Such an approach allows for a family-driven process that is responsive to contextual needs of the school and neighborhood. When used in the context of active implementation frameworks, participatory approaches hold promise for fundamentally reshaping the connections between families and schools within MTSS. These frameworks integrate collective learning from youth and families, allowing for improved beliefs and skills among educators to better partner with historically marginalized and excluded families (Bertrand & Rodela, 2018; Brooks et al., 2020; Lac & Cumings Mansfield, 2018). Continuing to investigate generalized design frameworks that center on local voices and contextual fit within the design and research process offers replicable family–school collaboration strategies that show promise for improving family–school relations particularly for historically marginalized families (Ishimaru, 2020).

When families are treated as equal partners throughout the stages of implementation, family voices are elevated, including the voices of historically marginalized and excluded families. Such perspectives are integrated within school systems and practices. Integrating family perspectives into school decision making can help reduce outcome disparities by race/ethnicity and improve school climate. Within an active implementation framework, continuous improvement cycles can be leveraged to advance continuous improvement in trial-and-error approaches alongside families and educators to advance family–school collaboration (Ishimaru, 2020).

Competencies and feedback loops are important components of active implementation framework drivers. Social capital, or the degree to which families have connections and relationships with others, is a predictor of student success (Goddard, 2003; Sheldon, 2002). Integrating family–school collaboration within MTSS holds promise for expanded connections with educators. In addition, family-to-family connections within an MTSS framework hold particular promise for improving social support and community connections, essential for promoting positive school climate. Future research should investigate the role of various forms of social capital for historically marginalized and excluded families including intergenerational relations between schools and families (Garcia, 2019) as well as relationships among families within the school. Creating accessible, respectful, and equitable opportunities for families to learn about family engagement behaviors from one another normalizes the challenges of parenting, supports student success and well-being, and reinforces the importance of these behaviors. Increasing equitable parental ties with other families of children enrolled at the school offers a potential strategy to increase equitable family–school collaboration (Goddard, 2003; Sheldon, 2002).

Moving toward Integration

Integrating family–school collaboration within MTSS requires study of the school and community context, as well as systems and practices germane to the specific MTSS framework. For example, a framework supporting instruction and intervention for literacy skills might focus family–school collaboration on shared book reading at home. In all instances, family–school collaboration emphasizes a consideration of family culture and values and integrating those cultures and values in the school community. In addition, integration of family–school collaboration emphasizes systems and practices at Tier 1, Tier 2, and Tier 3, differentiating family–school collaboration for prevention and early intervention, targeted approaches, and intensive support strategies. When these factors are considered within a school and district teaming process with school and district administrative support, one can expect improvements in implementation of family–school practices and enhanced valued outcomes (Garbacz, Hirano, et al., 2018).

OVERVIEW OF THE BOOK

In this book, we strive to provide multiple perspectives about advancing family–school collaboration in a scoped and sequenced manner. We hope that this book works as a guide for school teams in aligning and integrating family–school collaboration within their existing systems and practices. With that in mind, we acknowledge that each school is at different places in their implementation journey—with schoolwide frameworks like MTSS and family–school collaboration—hence this book works as a resource to read from cover to cover and each chapter can stand alone. For example, for a school that is newer to their family–school collaboration journey, it may be helpful to read the book from cover to cover. Other schools may choose to use different chapters as resources as they strengthen their Tier 1 systems and build their Tier 2 systems.

We have included Chapters 2 and 3 early in the book because equity and educational justice are critical to every facet of family–school collaboration. Chapter 2 provides a review of key principles and practices that underscore equity and justice; Chapter 3 provides an orientation to practical strategies teams can implement. After reviewing the key equity and justice considerations, the book moves to a discussion of assessments in family–school collaboration in Chapter 4, which provides foundational ideas and examples of assessments school teams can use to take stock of their practices (baseline) and monitor the impact of their work over time. Chapters 5, 6, and 7 address alignment and integration of family–school collaboration at Tier 1, Tier 2, and Tier 3, respectively. In Chapter 8, we include primary strategies or facilitators school teams can consider to overcome challenges to their work with families and communities. The book concludes with Chapters 9 and 10, which provide examples of district and school cases to clarify how principles and practices included across other chapters can advance in practice.

Key Themes across Chapters

Chapters within this book provide a comprehensive orientation to the key issues for promoting family–school collaboration within an MTSS framework. We identified five primary themes across chapters that are important to consider when adopting and integrating family–school collaboration practices.

Theme 1: Findings from Research Studies Support Family–School Collaboration

Research grounding family–school collaboration suggests that when families and school staff collaborate, there are benefits for families, students, and schools. These findings point to the importance of focusing on families' experiences and strength, and using those strengths as a primary way to support goal-directed change. In addition, strengthening the parent–teacher relationship is a primary avenue to support positive student outcomes.

Theme 2: There Are Challenges to Integrating Family–School Collaboration in School Practices

School staff and families experience challenges in their work together. School systems are often not set up to promote family–school collaboration. Moreover, school staff and families may not have had uniformly positive experiences working together. Indeed, some families and school staff may have had negative experiences with each other in the past. These challenges can be overcome by reaching out to families proactively to better understand their experiences and ideas and use those experiences and ideas when creating or refining school systems and practices. When problems arise, families and school staff can work together to develop a shared understanding for the nature of the problem, focusing on their shared interest in promoting student success to develop plans to address concerns.

Theme 3: Tier 1 Practices Promote Tier 2 and Tier 3

Strong Tier 1 family–school systems can promote Tier 2 and Tier 3 services. For example, family–school approaches to social–emotional support at Tier 1 can be integrated into Tier 2 and Tier 3 interventions plans to promote continuity across settings. In addition, family engagement in Tier 2 and Tier 3 can be promoted through clear communication systems at Tier 1. Incorporating family and student feedback into schoolwide practices is essential to advance Tier 1, Tier 2, and Tier 3 systems and practices.

Theme 4: Schoolwide Teaming Is Critical to Align and Integrate Family–School Collaboration

A schoolwide Tier 1 team can anchor family–school practices and support alignment and integration across systems. Schoolwide teaming should include multiple avenues for families and students to provide input on schoolwide systems and practices. Schoolwide teams should have a documented procedure for incorporating family and student feedback into school systems. School teams should also include community connections, building and strengthening community partnerships with youth- and family-serving organizations. School teams can use these connections to better understand family experiences and to establish collaborative relationships with families.

Theme 5: Training and Ongoing Coaching for School Staff Is Essential to Strengthen Family–School Systems and Practices

School staff often do not have explicit preparation or training in collaborating with families, but they do have well developed skill sets that can apply to family–school collaborative practices. School teams may find it useful to collect data on school staff attitudes and experiences about working with families. Teams can use these data to determine a training and coaching plan to support school staff in their work with families. For example, teams might organize a training to orient school staff to youth- and family-serving organizations in the area. In addition, teams can provide practical guidance to school staff about how to incorporate family ideas into their classroom practices, such as positive notes home to families about student social and behavioral successes at school. Ongoing coaching may be helpful to support school staff in problem solving their practices or adding depth to their plans for including families when building behavior support plans for students.

CHAPTER 2

Equity in Family–School Collaboration

In this chapter, we highlight important considerations for attending to culture, context, and racial equity within family–school collaboration in MTSS. First, we review theoretical foundations for research and practice followed by historical and contextual considerations to illustrate challenges to equitable family–school collaboration in MTSS. Finally, we align practical strategies for implementing the core features of family–school collaboration in MTSS (Family–School–Community Alliance, 2019) with best practices for equitable family–school collaboration (Ishimaru, 2020). A review of these areas informs a framework and process for advancing authentic collaboration with families. For example, key historical issues are helpful in better understanding of what has maintained inequities over time. A review of family–school collaboration in MTSS provides a framework for advancing alignment and integration. Practical strategies operationalize the framework to drive implementation.

THEORETICAL FOUNDATIONS

Family–school collaboration research and practice efforts focus on supporting children's healthy development and success in school and require consideration of culture, context, identity and ways these factors intersect within and across contexts (Garbacz et al., 2020). In this chapter, we extend Bronfenbrenner's ecological systems theory, including phenomenological variants of ecological contexts (Spencer et al., 1997) and critical theories (Kincheloe & Mclaren, 2011; Sabnis & Proctor, 2021). These theories increase focus and attention on race, equity, and social justice within overlapping spheres of influence, offering implications for equitable family–school collaboration research and practice (Garbacz et al., 2020; Holmes et al., 2020).

Phenomenological variants acknowledge lived experiences and ethnic-racial socialization processes for minoritized youth identity development, recognizing the historical, systemic, social, and cultural influences of racism and discrimination across time, contexts, and spheres of influence on youth development. Practice implications derived from these theoretical foundations include the importance of supporting congruent messages between home and school that empower youth of color, support racial pride, embrace lived experiences, and enable effective and equitable family–school partnerships (Hicklen House, 2020; Iruka et al., 2020). One example includes changes in school discipline and dress code policies that support congruent messages across home and school contexts, allowing for expressions of cultural and racial pride to support positive youth racial identify development (Bernadel, 2021; National Women's Law Center [NWLC], 2018a, 2018c, 2021).

Critical theory calls for the explicit examination of dominant (White) culture and influence (see Sabnis & Proctor, 2021, for a review of critical theory) and has been applied in various systems and contexts, with critical race theory (CRT) being a well-known application (Ladson-Billings & Tate, 1995). CRT offers a framework for understanding how racism operates in the United States as systemic and embedded in systems, policies, practices, and procedures to produce racial inequities (Pitre, 2021). CRT maintains several tenets, including (1) racism being embedded in systems; (2) interest convergence, referring to the act of giving up power only when it serves only those in dominant group; (3) race being a social construct that includes a hierarchy or label attached to who is inferior or superior by race; and (4) storytelling used as a counter narrative to inaccurate teaching of history (Pitre, 2021). Family–school collaboration efforts benefit from a critical examination of the systems, policies, and practices that produce racial inequities affecting youth outcomes, experiences, and family–school partnerships in schools. An example includes critically examining discipline and dress code policies based on dominant culture values and influences (i.e., White, middle-class) to identify policies that target, or disproportionality punish, students of color so that improvements can be made to produce equitable experiences and outcomes for all students (e.g., changes to policies that target or punish dress, haircut, or style; Bernadel, 2021). The vast misunderstandings and misuse of CRT in policy, legal proceedings, and media (Kaplan & Owings, 2021; Ray & Gibbons, 2021; Reilly, 2022) underscore the urgency of advancing approaches to family–school collaboration that examine influence of race, culture, and context within and across contexts for youth development (Schwartz, 2021).

Advancing these theoretical lenses enables research and practice focused on equitable family–school collaboration and student outcomes within schools. For example, questioning the status quo, or research as usual approach, to family–school collaboration calls into question decisions about what and how family–school collaboration practices are researched. This critical examination of dominant cultural influences creates opportunities for new, or nondominant perspectives, to be considered in decision-making processes for family–school collaboration research and subsequent practice in schools. Questioning the status quo, or typical school discipline and behavior policy on behavioral expectations for students, allows for examining dominant culture influences and creates opportunities for nondominant perspectives to be considered in school discipline and behavioral policies. Historical and contextual challenges for family–school collaboration in the United Staters are reviewed briefly in the next section to further underscore the urgent need to *reimagine* equitable connections between families and schools in the remaining sections of this chapter (Ishimaru, 2020).

HISTORICAL AND CONTEXTUAL CHALLENGES FOR FAMILY–SCHOOL COLLABORATION

Several historical and cultural challenges contribute to current barriers experienced in family–school collaboration. Racism in the United States continues to have an impact on educational laws and policies (e.g., zoning, funding, disciplinary policies) that undermine family–school collaboration (NWLC, 2018b). For decades, policies have maintain limited roles for families in education and unintentionally distanced historically marginalized and excluded families from schools by discouraging equal partnerships between families and schools in educating children (Adkins-Sharif, 2017; Gonzalez & Gabel, 2017). For example, school policies preventing families from observing in classrooms while encouraging families to serve as classroom volunteers assert educators as authorities above families in decisions about families' roles in schools. We further review these challenges below to illustrate the collective impact on perpetuating inequities in family–school collaboration and student outcomes.

Historically rooted and experienced presently (e.g., accumulation of/access to wealth/assets, healthcare, income, home and land ownership, and access to basic goods and services; Hedwig et al., 2020), the inequities in power, resources, exclusion, marginalization, and resources for racial and ethnic minoritized groups across the United States are paralleled within and across layers of the education systems evidenced by inequities in educational outcomes, opportunities, and resources among historically marginalized and excluded groups. Despite educational laws (e.g., *Brown v. Board of Education*, 1954) ending exclusion and separation of students of color from U.S. public education, these historic patterns of exclusion and separation continue today evidenced in disparate outcomes and policies that create inequities in educational resources and racially segregated schools and classrooms (e.g., zoning, funding, disciplinary policies, and outcomes; Proctor, 2016). Disparate outcomes and policies influence and reinforce efforts to advance family–school collaboration.

Educational policies shifted focus to implementation of evidence-based practices in schools (e.g., No Child Left Behind [NCLB], 2002). However, twenty years ago, there were limited studies investigating evidence-based practices conducted with racially diverse populations (Pogrow, 2017) and limited evidence these practices were effective, or evidence-based, for racially, culturally, and socioeconomically diverse populations (Schanding et al., 2021). Research supporting evidence-based practices is often conducted with populations and in contexts that do not match our classrooms and schools (Eppley & Shannon, 2017; Eppley et al., 2018). Therefore, limitations of evidence-based practices research and educational practice contribute to inequities in student outcomes. Educational outcomes for subgroups of students including Black, low-income, indigenous, LGBTQ, and especially those who belong to more than one of those groups (i.e., intersectional) experience disproportionate exclusionary discipline and are overrepresented in categories experiencing poor educational outcomes (National Association of School Psychologists, 2013; Proctor et al., 2017; Sullivan et al., 2020). Criteria used to determine student eligibility to receive special education services have historically resulted in overidentification of minoritized students (Sabnis & Proctor, 2021). Minoritized youth experience disproportionate exclusionary discipline for similar behaviors compared to their White peers (Rodriguez & Welsh, 2022). Families report feeling disrespected and begin to distrust educational systems that fail to acknowledge or make efforts to ameliorate disparate outcomes experienced by minoritized youth and their families (Baquedano-López et al., 2013; Hastings, 2018). The historical patterns of segregation and exclusion experienced by racially and ethnically marginalized families that continue in current educational contexts are further complicated for families that have been left out of the conversation about MTSS implementation. Siloed systems and initiatives within schools (e.g., academic improvement efforts separate from those focusing on student social–emotional–behavioral functioning) and across systems (e.g., school district program to reduce bullying and a parallel program of a mental health agency) persist in education, preventing meaningful improvement by creating role confusion and distrust among families. Allowing space for families and youth in designing *reimagined* educational systems holds promise for closing gaps in student achievement and discipline outcomes across racial subgroups and producing equitable outcomes for all students. Inviting historically marginalized and excluded families as co-equal collaborators in the design and implementation of schools' MTSS is needed to create equitable systems.

Despite law and policy calling for increased partnerships between families and educators (e.g., Individuals with Disabilities Education Improvement Act, 2004; NCLB, 2002), examples of families working alongside educators to co-design MTSS implementation efforts within schools have been limited. The exclusion of family perspectives and voice in the design and implementation of MTSS efforts has contributed to miscommunication about MTSS with families and has resulted in local educational systems fitting traditional, school-centric approaches and forms of family–school partnerships (e.g., reliance on written material from school to home, families as volunteers, PTA members, or fundraisers; Cooper, 2009) into tiered prevention frameworks. For example, MTSS does not require students to meet formal eligibility criteria to receive interventions, but concerns have been expressed that it can delay supports for students (Florida Problem Solving/Response to Intervention Project, 2011). The design and implementation of family–school collaboration in MTSS must begin with family voice and perspectives to improve partnerships, services, and address limitations of established evidence-based practices. Given the limitations of evidence-based practice, practice-based evidence or local evidence is especially important for historically marginalized and excluded students and families (Eppley & Shannon, 2017; Hrastinski, 2021; Yull et al., 2018). Intentional efforts that prioritize the experiences, outcomes, and perspectives of historically marginalized families and students in the design and implementation of educational services can reduce inequities in educational systems by ensuring services are responsive, flexible, and mindful of local needs and contexts (Amaro-Jimenez et al., 2021; Means et al., 2020; Sutherland et al., 2022). Including families as active participants in the design and implementation of MTSS allows educators *and* families to have a shared understanding of MTSS as a prevention and early intervention framework.

The traditional approaches to family–school collaboration are often fraught with challenges for educators and families alike (Pushor & Amendt, 2018; Smith et al., 2020). Generally, family–school collaboration and partnerships are approached through a default setting characteristic of prescribed, routine practices, behaviors, and activities, evidenced in district and school policies and in expectations around how educators and families interact (e.g., conferences, PTA, school-to-home information). Inherent in these traditional, routine approaches are values, norms, and expectations for interactions that favor White, middle-class families and the dominant culture within the United States and simultaneous marginalization of families who may not fit within the prescribed norms (Christianakis, 2011; Gillborn, 2005). For instance, during a back-to-school night, educators orient families to the ways of the school including expectations to attend the school during predetermined times (i.e., often business hours when many families would need to take unpaid leave from work) to listen, receive, and support information from educators about the school's policies, practices, and priorities (Park & Holloway, 2018). Further, these efforts have an implied purpose to encourage families' support of the school's efforts in predetermined ways (e.g., a message to families that they can partner with the school by participating in the PTA, volunteering, donating, and fundraising).

> "I'm one of the few special needs parents who has the time, support, and bandwidth, to leave my family and go to these meetings [PTA] in the evening."

Families are often expected to passively receive the information from educators and express support for the school's priorities and work in the identified approaches shared by educators rather than being asked what it looks like for them to support their child's education and how they would like to collaborate with school leaders and staff (Cooper, 2009; Jones, 2022). The underlying issues of power, voice, and authority are often inherent in these interactions that favor educators more than families. For example, educators have power to decide how and in what forms the partnership takes place and whose voices are included in those decisions. Traditional notions of family–school collaboration limit opportunities for all families to play a role in their child's education, including important family engagement activities that educators may not readily observe or benefit from yet are most important for historically marginalized and excluded families and youth (e.g., expressing high expectations for education, supporting their child's education at home; Ishimaru, 2020; Jeynes, 2010). Educators may perceive families' inability to participate in the prescribed ways as a lack of concern and disinterest, further perpetuating distrust and disengagement between home and school (Jeynes, 2010). Such attitude undermines, devalues, and divides schools and minoritized families' contributions and support (Ho & Cherng, 2018).

REIMAGINING FAMILY–SCHOOL COLLABORATION

Traditional approaches to family–school collaboration, such as family attendance at school PTA, volunteer, or fundraising events, perpetuate power imbalances between home and schools in terms of who decides priorities and solutions for the education of children in a school/community (Cooper, 2009). To create equitable outcomes and experiences, we need to *reimagine* family–school collaboration. *Reimagining family–school collaboration*, a phrase and an approach coined by Dr. Anne Ishimaru (2020), requires us to rethink our approaches to partnerships, even how we think about efforts to *increase* diversity, equity, and inclusion (DEI) within family–school collaboration. Limiting efforts to increasing DEI within our *existing* family–school collaboration approaches alone could result in invitations into broken systems and further marginalize the families we are attempting to include. Rather, we need to reconsider the existing approaches, as well as the systems and policies surrounding them. Questioning what we are inviting families into requires a fundamental shift to how we approach connections between families and schools. When inviting families into existing structures and approaches like student conferences or the PTA, rather than focusing only on increasing DEI in the families represented in those events, *reimagining* family–school collaboration calls us to work with families to rethink these structures and co-design opportunities for connection and collaboration from the ground up. Focusing on the function of a family–school collaboration activity rather than the form it takes can enable space for *reimagined* ways of connecting with families. For example, a parent–teacher conference is a common form of family–school collaboration. The function of the conference is to allow educators to share updates with families about classroom performance. Shifting attention to identifying ways for educators and families to share updates about student classroom performance rather than focusing only on how to improve families' attendance or engagement enables new forms and approaches beyond traditional parent–teacher conferences. Another common form of family involvement is the PTA. Rather than focusing on improving family participation or engagement in the PTA, shifting focus to identifying ways to connect families with one another to foster a sense of school community creates more possibilities and opportunities for reimagining family–school collaboration beyond traditional approaches. Using this approach, reimagining might involve the following steps:

- Take stock of school professional attitudes and beliefs about family partnerships.
- Learn about family experiences with the school over time.
- Invite families and students to join from the earliest possible stage, before plans have been developed.
- Elevate families into leadership positions in collaborative meetings (see Appendix 2.A).
- Emphasize systems and structures that promote multiple and varied ways for families to participate in decision making.
- Transparently review data with families and communicate the rationale for decisions.

> "I'm often thinking about inclusion . . . I feel like when I got to a PTA meeting or an event, you don't get people who don't speak English strongly, they don't feel comfortable to be part of those communities . . . I don't see a lot of diverse representation in the PTAs."

Aligned with recent calls for social justice and anti-racist practices (National Association of School Psychologists, 2020), we turn to highlighting strategies for schools to center those most impacted by educational inequities and leverage families' collective capacities, knowledge, and skills to successfully co-develop systems that produce equitable approaches and outcomes. Below we provide practical considerations, tools, and resources for co-designing equitable family–school collaboration with families in the context of MTSS.

FAMILY–SCHOOL COLLABORATION IN SCHOOLS' MTSS

Tiered prevention frameworks have defined essential components for implementing MTSS in schools that mention family–school collaboration (Algozzine et al., 2014). Although tiered frameworks provide a structure and process for enhancing collaboration with families (e.g., teaming structures, data collection and management), these frameworks are limited in depth or guidance for how to implement best practices in schools. The Family–School–Community Alliance (FSCA, 2019) developed a framework of family–school collaboration in MTSS (see Figure 2.1) and corresponding fidelity tool, the Tiered Fidelity Inventory—Family–School Collaboration (TFI-FSC; Garbacz, Minch et al., 2019; see Figure 2.2) to provide implementation and practice guidance for family–school collaboration in MTSS (Minch et al., 2019). Tables 2.1, 2.2, and 2.3 illustrate core practices of family–school collaboration in MTSS.

A primary way to advance family–school collaboration within MTSS is through the use of the TFI-FSC. School teams can use the TFI-FSC to examine their family–school systems and action plan enhancements. Then, school teams will complete the tool again yearly to monitor progress and create an action plan for the next year.

EQUITABLE FAMILY–SCHOOL COLLABORATION IN MTSS

In addition to FSCA's family–school collaboration in MTSS framework, Ishimaru (2020) offers a framework to guide schools' equitable family–school collaboration. Ishimaru's equi-

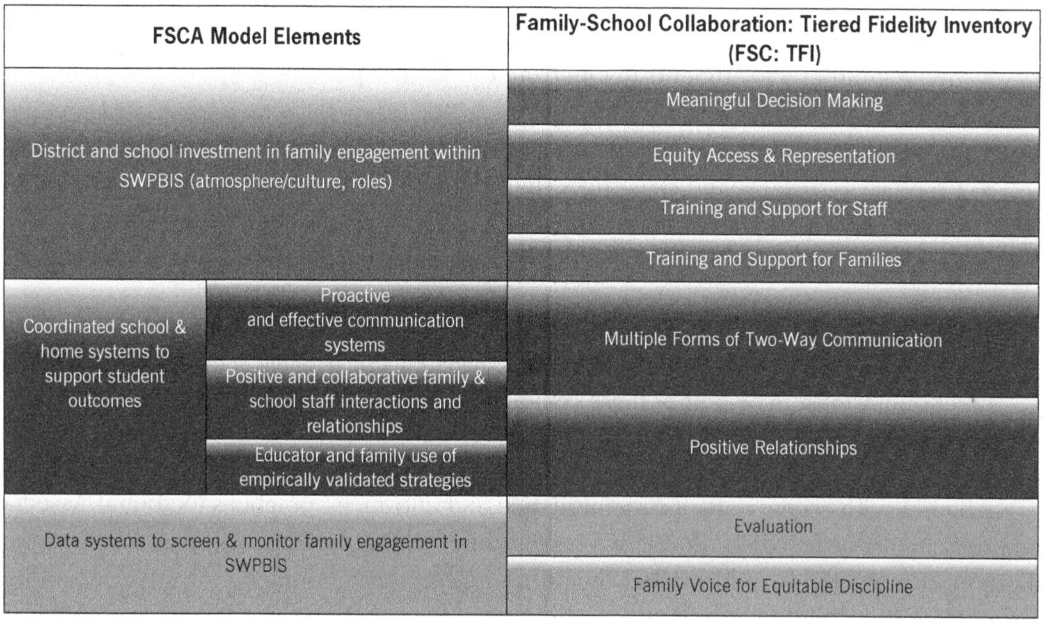

FIGURE 2.1. Family–school collaboration in MTSS model. From Family–School–Community Alliance (FSCA; 2019). Copyright © 2019 FSCA. Reprinted with permission.

Core Feature	Possible Data Sources	Scoring Criteria
F.1 Positive Relationships: The school makes proactive efforts to build and maintain positive, trusting relationships with families. The school collects data from both educators and families on their perceptions of home–school relationships.	• Family and educator surveys, such as the School Climate Survey, Family–School Relationship Scale, Parent Trust in School Scale • Focus groups • Family interviews/conferences	0 = The school does not obtain data on home–school relationships from both educators and families. 1 = The school obtains data on both family and educator perceptions of home–school relationships, but the data do not indicate that relationships are positive and trusting. 2 = School data indicates that both educators and families report positive and trusting home–school relationships.
F.2 Multiple Forms of Two-Way Communication: The school engages in ongoing, two-way communication with families. The school provides multiple avenues for families to receive regular information and provide constant feedback that reflects family preferences.	• Family surveys, interviews, or conferences • Focus groups • Home–school notes • Emails • Phone call logs • Social media data	0 = The school does not have multiple avenues in place for ongoing, two-way communication. 1 = The school utilizes multiple avenues for two-way communication, but not on an ongoing basis (only once or twice per year). 2 = The school utilizes multiple avenues for two-way communication on an ongoing basis, AND adapts communication strategies based on family preferences.
F.3 Meaningful Decision Making: The school provides a diverse range of opportunities for families to make shared decisions about PBIS systems and practices.	• Team minutes & agendas • School handbooks • Communication logs • Decision records	0 = The school provides no opportunities for families to make decisions about PBIS. 1 = The school provides some limited opportunities for families to make decisions about PBIS. 2 = The school provides a diverse range of opportunities for families to make decisions about PBIS and can provide evidence that there has been shared decision making between families and school staff about PBIS.
F.4 Equity Access and Representation: The school makes intentional efforts to obtain from families input and diverse perspectives proportional to enrollment subgroups. The team has a protocol for ongoing review of the effectiveness of their efforts to obtain family input and adjustments to PBIS implementation are made as needed.	• Team minutes & agendas • Team member roles and descriptions • Response rate and representation of family surveys/interviews (focus groups, etc.) proportional to enrollment subgroups[1]	0 = No protocol or evaluation of family representation/input takes place 1 = Input in sought but is not used or evaluate for effectiveness in shaping efforts or practices. 2 = Input is sought successfully; periodic evaluations of family representation/input proportional to enrollment subgroups[1] are conducted (at least annually); outcomes shared with staff and district leadership; and clear alterations for practices are in process.
F.5 Family Voice for Equitable Discipline: The school makes intentional efforts to obtain voice, input, full and diverse perspectives of families of students experiencing disproportionate rates of exclusionary discipline. The team has a protocol for ongoing review of family input, and adjustments to PBIS implementation are made as needed.	• Team minutes & agendas • Team member roles and descriptions • Response rate and representation of family surveys/interviews (focus groups, etc.); Proportional to enrollment subgroups	0 = No protocol or evaluation of input from families experiencing disproportionate rates of exclusionary discipline takes place 1 = Input is sought, but input is not used nor evaluated for effectiveness in shaping efforts or practices. 2 = Input is sought successfully, periodic evaluations of input from families experiencing disproportionate rates of exclusionary discipline are conducted (at least annually), outcomes are shared with staff and district leadership, and clear alterations for practices are in process.
F.6 Training and Support Options tor School Staff: A written process is followed for teaching all relevant staff how to collaborate with families about PBIS.	• Professional development calendar • Lesson plans for teacher trainings • School policy • Staff handbook	0 = No process for teaching staff in place 1 = Teaching process is informal 2 = Written process used to teach all relevant staff how to collaborate with families about PBIS
F.7 Training and Support Options for Families: A written process is followed for teaching families how to collaborate with school staff about PBIS.	• Family handbook • School website and social media accounts • School newsletters • Home matrix • lesson plans for home • School event calendar	0 = No process for teaching families in place 1 = Teaching process is informal 2 = Written process used to teach families how to collaborate with school staff about PBIS
F.8 Evaluation: Educators and families collaboratively develop and agree upon: • Comprehensive family–school collaboration goals/outcomes responsive to family and student needs across home, school, and community settings. • Strategies for monitoring progress towards goals (e g., surveys vs. text/social media polls) • Regular review of data used to monitor family–school collaboration goals and adjustments to strategic plans based on data.	• Strategic plans inclusive of explicit family–school collaboration goals • Data used to monitor family–school collaboration goals • Action plans illustrative of revisions and edits	0 = The school does not have goals or outcomes tor family–school collaboration identified or those goals/outcomes have not been co-developed with families. 1 = The school has goals/outcomes for family–school collaboration but they are not monitored with data 2 = The school has goals/outcomes of family–school collaboration, they monitor goals/outcomes with data, and adjust strategic plans based on regular review (at least annually) of data.

[1] Enrollment subgroups include (but are not limited to) gender, racial, ethnic, or cultural identification, socioeconomic status, physical or learning disabilities, language abilities, and school-assigned classifications (e.g. special-education students).
Scoring Criteria: 0=Not implemented; 1=Partially implemented; 2=Fully implemented

FIGURE 2.2. Tiered Fidelity Inventory—Family–School Collaboration (TFI-FSC; Garbacz et al., 2019).

TABLE 2.1. Tools and Considerations for Core Features 1 and 2 of Family–School Collaboration in MTSS

Family–School Collaboration in MTSS (FSCA, 2019)	TFI-FSC Item(s) Description
1. Positive Relationships	• The school implements strategies to build and maintain positive, trusting relationships with families. • The school collects data on both educators' and families' perceptions related to the effectiveness of their efforts to build positive and trusting home–school relationships.
2. Two-Way Communication	• The school conducts comprehensive assessments of families' preferences for two-way communication. • The school engages in ongoing, two-way communication with families. The school provides multiple avenues for families to receive information and provide feedback on a regular basis.

Getting Started	Considerations for Students Tiers 2 and 3
Before the year begins, staff are supported to organize meet and greets in students' neighborhoods or to make positive phone calls home to each student in homeroom/classroom within the first month of school.	As student needs increase, so too does the frequency and intensity of family–school collaboration efforts. More frequent or individualized efforts to build relationships and individualized communication efforts allow for nuanced strategies that support a positive relationship between home and school.
Initial relationship building opportunities are leveraged to gather input and feedback from families to design tiered communications systems and identify leadership roles with families.	
As families begin to see that their voice matters and that changes in the school occur because of their input, trust, and mutual respect. Reciprocity develops and strengthens the home–school partnership.	Staff make efforts to get to know families leveraging strengths and assets in the classroom. (Center on Culture, Race & Equity at Bank Street College, 2017).

table family–school collaboration framework outlines best practices including roles, goals, strategies, and approach described below.

- *Roles: Families as leaders.* Start with families' priorities, interests, concerns, knowledge, and resources to develop leadership roles for families within the system.
- *Goals: Shared responsibility for systemic transformation.* Develop shared goals and responsibility by *transforming power, reciprocity, and agency.*
- *Strategies: Positive relationships* and *capacity building* are central strategies for ongoing improvement efforts.
- *Approach: Collective inquiry* and *action* guide *transformative* educational change.

Whereas family–school collaboration in MTSS begins with developing positive relationships and two-way communication systems (FSCA, 2019; Minch et al., 2019), equitable family–school collaboration (Ishimaru, 2020) suggests starting with families to develop their

TABLE 2.2. Tools and Considerations for Core Features 3 and 4 of Family–School Collaboration in MTSS

Family–School Collaboration in MTSS (FSCA, 2019)	TFI-FSC Item(s) Description
3. Shared Decision Making	• The school provides a range of opportunities for families to make shared decisions about PBIS systems and practices. • The team has a clear and written process for ongoing review of the effectiveness of their efforts to obtain family input and makes adjustments to PBIS implementation and practices needed. • The school obtains from families input and diverse perspectives that are proportional to enrollment subgroups when making shared decisions about PBIS.
4. Family Voice in Disproportionate Discipline	• The school obtains voice, input, and full and diverse perspectives of students' families experiencing disproportionate rates of exclusionary discipline. • The school utilizes a clear and written process for ongoing review of input from families experiencing disproportionate discipline and adjusts PBIS implementation as needed.

Ideas for Getting Started	Considerations for Students Tiers2 and 3
Use tools below to empower families and educators to: • collaboratively define roles, goals, and strategies and change processes for equitable family school collaboration. • engage in shared decision making about improvements to FSC and supports for student:	For students with intensive or repeat behavioral offenses, families are invited to work with educators to co-create improvements to the discipline policy and behavior support systems within the school.
Tools: • The Spectrum of Family Engagement for Educational Equity (Gonzalez, 2020; see Figure 2.3) • Equity Impact Assessments (Race Matters Institute, n.d.)	Creating shared learning goals for students and empowering families to collaboratively discuss concerns and develop shared goals.

leadership roles. Integration of these two frameworks suggest schools start by designing two-way communication and positive relationship systems *with* family leaders (see Appendix 2.B). Shared decision making and family voice in equitable discipline systems, the two additional features of family–school collaboration in MTSS (FSCA, 2019; Minch et al., 2019), align with equitable family–school collaboration (Ishimaru, 2020) emphasizing reciprocity, agency, and transforming power to establish goals for shared responsibility between educators and families. The final features of family–school collaboration in MTSS (FSCA, 2019; Minch et al., 2019) include training and support, as well as collaborative goals and problem solving, which align with Ishimaru's equitable family–school collaboration (2020) components: capacity building, collective inquiry, and action to achieve transformative educational change.

The remaining sections of this chapter will illustrate connections between FSCA's family–school collaboration in MTSS framework (FSCA, 2019; Minch et al., 2019) and Ishimaru's Equitable family–school collaboration framework (Ishimaru, 2020) along with exam-

TABLE 2.3. Tools and Considerations for Core Features 5 and 6 of Family–School Collaboration in MTSS

Family–School Collaboration in MTSS (FSCA, 2019)	TFI-FSC Item(s) Description
5. Training and Support	• A written process is followed for supporting all faculty/staff on the components of family–school collaboration within PBIS implementation. • A written process is followed for supporting families on the components of family–school collaboration within PBIS implementation.
6. Collaborative Goals and Problem Solving	• Educators and families collaboratively develop and agree upon comprehensive family–school collaboration goals/outcomes responsive to family and student needs across home, school, and community settings. • Educators and families collaboratively develop and agree upon strategies for monitoring progress towards family–school collaboration goals (e.g., surveys vs. texts/social media polls). • The school regularly shares data used to monitor family–school collaboration goals with families and educators and adjusts strategic plans based on data.

Ideas for Getting Started	Considerations for Students Tiers 2 and 3
• Staff are supported in developing skills for connecting and building positive relationships with families (Appendix 2.B [U.S. Department of Health and Human Services, Administration for Children and Families, Office of Head Start, National Center on Parent, Family, and Community Engagement, 2018])	• Reducing the use of labels or emphasis on student deficits and maintaining a focus on shared goals for student learning and success creates opportunities for both partners to find value in their role in supporting positive student outcomes (Harry, 2008; Weist, Mellin, et al., 2019).
• Create opportunities for families and educators to develop capacity for bias awareness, cultural humility, competencies, and practices to increase perspective-taking, empathy, humility, and openness in family–school relationships.	• Enabling and empowering families' capacity for implementing strategies to support student learning goals in home and community settings and connecting families with community resources and supports as needed.
• Collaborative learning about the history of local community through the lens of various racial, ethnic, and cultural groups can create shared understanding and goals for collaboration and improvement. Supporting ongoing training and coaching to staff and families in ways that's responsive to local needs and school priorities (Minch et al., 2018).	

ples and tools to provide practical guidance to advance these practices in schools' MTSS implementation efforts. The features of family–school collaboration in MTSS (FSCA, 2019; Minch et al., 2019) are reviewed and integrated with Ishimaru's equitable family–school collaboration approach (Ishimaru, 2020) to bridge connections for schools and aid in their efforts to implement best practices. Table 2.4 illustrates the connections between the FSCA's framework for family–school collaboration in MTSS and Ishimaru's (2020) equitable family–school collaboration framework.

TABLE 2.4. Core Features of Family–School Collaboration in MTSS and Equitable Family–School Collaboration

Family–School Collaboration in MTSS (FSCA, 2019)	Equitable Family–School Collaboration (Ishimaru, 2020)
• Positive relationships • Two-way communication • Shared decision making • Family voice in disproportionate discipline • Training and support • Collaborative goals and problem solving	• Roles: start with families as leaders • Goals: shared responsibility through reciprocity, agency, and power sharing • Strategies: relationships and capacity building • Approach: collective inquiry and action

RELATIONSHIPS AND COMMUNICATION

The first two foundational components to FSCA's family–school collaboration in MTSS framework include positive relationships and two-way communication systems. These practices include educators' use of family preferences for designing two-way communication systems between home and school and prioritizing the development of positive relationships through intentional, responsive, and ongoing efforts. Developing systems that allow schools to regularly obtain family perspectives and voice to inform school priorities and practices is foundational to rethinking how families and educators interact. Rather than expecting families to engage and communicate in ways and frequencies that are preferred by educators, using family perspectives to inform the systems and practices for home–school communication ensures that resources are effectively allocated and invested in systems embraced by families and educators. At the beginning of the school year and regularly throughout the year, schools utilize multiple methods for obtaining family preferences, interests, and needs for engaging in two-way communication with educators. Prioritizing and centering the voice of families in the design of school systems and practices begins to shift the role of families as passive recipients to active leaders within the collaborative partnership wherein responsive systems empower and enable their participation. See Table 2.5 for a description of these core practices of family–school collaboration in MTSS along with tools and resources for implementation.

EQUITABLE FAMILY–SCHOOL COLLABORATION: START WITH FAMILIES AS LEADERS

Ishimaru's framework suggests starting with family leaders as a foundational feature for establishing equitable family–school collaboration (Ishimaru, 2020). Traditional leadership at every level of the system plays a key role in establishing priorities, allocating resources, and cultivating the development of systems, data, and practices that promote school cultures and conditions amenable to equitable family–school collaboration (Auerbach, 2009; Epstein et al., 2011; Ferguson et al., 2010; Sanders, 2011). Valuing families' perspectives, preferences, priorities, needs, strengths, and challenges sets a foundation that enables educators and family leaders

TABLE 2.5. Summary and Strategies for Reimagined Family–School Collaboration in MTSS

Equitable Family–School Collaboration	Family–School Collaboration in MTSS	Description	Strategies and Tools
Roles: Starting with Families as Leaders	Positive Family–School Relationship Building	The school implements strategies to build and maintain positive, trusting relationships with families. The school collects data on both educators and families' perceptions related to the effectiveness of their efforts to build positive and trusting home–school relationships.	Before the year begins, staff are supported to conduct meet and greets in students' neighborhoods (Southwest Educational Development Laboratory, 2005) At the beginning of the year, staff are supported in making positive phone calls home to each student in homeroom/classroom within the first month of school. Staff make efforts to get to know families leveraging strengths and assets in the classroom (Center on Culture, Race & Equity at Bank Street College, 2017).
	Two-Way Communication	The school conducts comprehensive assessments of families' preferences for two-way communication. The school engages in ongoing, two-way communication with families. The school provides multiple avenues for families to receive information and provide feedback on a regular basis.	Virtual family groups are supported, facilitating access to information and dialogue among families in each grade or class. Create connections among families who speak the same language or have children with similar needs (Teaching for Change, n.d.)
Goals: Shared Responsibility Strategies: Capacity Building	Shared Decision Making	The school provides a range of opportunities for families to make shared decisions about PBIS systems and practices. The team has a clear and written process for ongoing review of the effectiveness of their efforts to obtain family input and adjustments to PBIS implementation and practices are made as needed. The school obtains input and diverse perspectives from families that are proportional to enrollment subgroups when making shared decisions about PBIS.	Family leadership supports and information • Overview (North Carolina Partnership for Children Inc. (North Carolina Partnership for Children Inc. [NCPC], 2021a) • Empowering families as leaders (NCPC, 2021b) Checklist (NCPC, 2021c, see Appendix 2.A)

Equitable Family—School Collaboration	Family—School Collaboration in MTSS	Description	Strategies and Tools
	Family Voice in Discipline	The school obtains voice, input, and full and diverse perspectives of families of students experiencing disproportionate rates of exclusionary discipline.	See related tools and resources here: *https://youtu.be/ Fu231Y9x6yE* (Minch et al., 2018, see Figure 2.12).
		The school utilizes a clear and written process for ongoing review of input from families experiencing disproportionate discipline and adjusts PBIS implementation as needed.	
	Training and Support	A written process is followed for supporting all faculty/staff on the components of family-school collaboration within PBIS implementation.	Staff are supported in developing skills for connecting and building positive relationships with families (U.S. Department of Health and Human Services, Administration for Children and Families, Office of Head Start, National Center on Parent, Family, and Community Engagement, 2018, see Appendix 2.B)
Approach: Collective Inquiry and Action	Collaborative Goals and Problem Solving	Educators and families collaboratively develop and agree upon comprehensive family—school collaboration • goals/outcomes responsive to family and student needs across home, school, and community settings, • strategies for monitoring progress towards family-school collaboration goals (e.g., surveys vs. texts/social media polls). • data monitoring and use practices for ongoing improvement to family-school collaboration efforts	Initial Partnership Tool (Ishimaru, 2020, see Figure 2.11) Spectrum of Engagement for Educational Equity (Gonzalez, 2020, see Figure 2.10)

to co-create family—school collaboration efforts (Leverson et al., 2021; Ishimaru, 2020). Optimally, leaders establish a school identity that places families alongside educators as co-leaders in the business of educating students. Leaders demonstrate commitment and investment to equity and are clear on the importance and priority of anti-racism and social justice by investing in families as leaders and engaging in collective learning *with* families to ensure a positive school atmosphere supportive of family—school collaboration. This commitment is evidenced in resources, time, district, and school practices. Leadership acknowledges harm and makes efforts to repair injustices for families that have historically been excluded or marginalized in educational systems. For example, inviting families of students experiencing disproportionate rates of exclusionary discipline into listening sessions with educators to identify strategies to create equitable discipline practices helps repair trust and promote positive relationships by acknowledging inequities in the system and demonstrating commitment to improving outcomes for students. Efforts to repair systemic injustices experienced by families establishes mutual trust and respect among families and educators that will have a positive impact on subsequent outreach and communication efforts implemented (Minch et al., 2018; Sandomierski et al., 2021). Starting with family leaders to co-design positive relationships and two-way communication systems between families and educators enables equitable collaboration. Tables 2.6, 2.7, and 2.8 summarize alignment between Ishimaru's equitable family–school collaboration (2020) and FSCA's family–school collaboration in MTSS framework (FSCA, 2019;

TABLE 2.6. Alignment of and Tools for Core Features 1 and 2 of Family–School Collaboration in MTSS and A in Equitable Family–School Collaboration

Family–School Collaboration in MTSS (FSCA, 2019)	Equitable Family–School Collaboration (Ishimaru, 2020)	Example Strategies	Resources and Tools
1. Positive Relationships 2. Two-Way Communication	A. Roles: Start with Family Leaders	Redesign current structures to allow for collective family leadership that represents the school community in both formal and informal leadership roles.	Create connections among families who speak the same language or have children with similar needs (Teaching for Change, n.d.).
		Committees of subgroups of families within the school community (e.g., primary language, similar student needs [students with disabilities]) identify a group leader who creates connections across committees to form a *representative* family leadership group (e.g., PTA).	Family leadership supports and information • Overview (NCPC, 2021a) • Empowering families as leaders (NCPC, 2021b) • Checklist (NCPC, 2021c; Appendix 2.A)

TABLE 2.7. Alignment of and Tools for Core Features 3 and 4 of Family-School Collaboration in MTSS and B in Equitable Family–School Collaboration

Family–School Collaboration in MTSS (FSCA, 2019)	Equitable Family–School Collaboration (Ishimaru, 2020)	Example Strategies	Resources and Tools
3. Shared Decision Making 4. Family Voice in Disproportionate Discipline	B. Goals: Shared Responsibility through Reciprocity, Agency, and Power Sharing.	Families are invited to work with educators to co-create roles and goals for FSC and create a plan for collaborating on improvements to the discipline policy and behavior support systems within the school.	Use the family engagement for educational equity spectrum (Gonzalez, 2020; see Figure 2.3) to guide shared goals and shared responsibility in your school. The Initial Partnership Tool (Ishimaru, 2020)

TABLE 2.8. Alignment of and Tools for Core Features 5 and 6 of Family–School Collaboration in MTSS and C and D in Equitable Family–School Collaboration

Family–School Collaboration in MTSS (FSCA, 2019)	Equitable Family–School Collaboration (Ishimaru, 2020)	Example Strategies	Resources and Tools
5. Training and Support for FSC 6. Collaborative Goals and Problem Solving	C. Strategies: Capacity Building and Relationships D. Approach: Collective Inquiry and Action for Transformative Educational Change	Create opportunities for educators and families to repair harm and rebuild trust with historically marginalized and excluded families and communities (see Chapter 3 for additional examples) Use the family engagement for educational equity spectrum (Gonzalez, 2020; Figure 2.3) and equity impact assessments (Race Matters Institute, n.d.) guide shared goals and decision-making efforts in your school in your work.	Enable opportunities for shared learning with families within your school community and plan strategies for creating representative and welcoming schools (Appendix 2.B; U.S. Department of Health and Human Services, Administration for Children and Families, Office of Head Start, National Center on Parent, Family, and Community Engagement, 2018). Identify one priority of inequities and develop shared and collective responsibility through actionable strategies and commit to having two to four concrete changes implemented within the school year.

Minch et al., 2019) for starting with family leaders to co-design two-way communication and positive relationship efforts within MTSS along with example strategies, resources, and tools for schools.

Shared Decision Making and Family Voice

Asking and listening to families' input is fundamental to the next set of core practices of family–school collaboration in MTSS, including shared decision making and family voice for equitable discipline (FSCA, 2019; Minch et al., 2019). Shared decision making requires reciprocity, agency, and sharing power among families and educators (Ishimaru, 2020). Educators share power with families by allowing space for families to make decisions with educators about (1) *how, when,* and *for what purposes* they engage in collaborative efforts and (2) what *needs, ideas,* or *concerns* they may have regarding the educational system and about their child(ren). The family–school collaboration in MTSS framework emphasizes shared decision making between representative family groups and the school about discipline policies and practices to move beyond a compliance perspective to a focus on effectiveness of their family–school collaboration efforts. The practices described in the family–school collaboration in MTSS framework move schools beyond a focus on implementing a strategy (e.g., a family survey) to an emphasis on effectiveness of a strategy requiring ongoing improvements to ensure the strategy is working for families and educators (e.g., following up with families who didn't respond to the survey to discuss their perspectives over the phone). Finally, the family–school collaboration in MTSS framework describes the school's efforts to prioritize partnerships and shared decision-making opportunities with families of students who have received disproportionate exclusionary discipline to empower families in designing solutions alongside educators.

EQUITABLE FAMILY–SCHOOL COLLABORATION: GOALS FOR SHARED RESPONSIBILITY

Shared decision making within the family–school collaboration in MTSS framework aligns with Ishimaru's second component for equitable family–school collaboration which outlines the use of reciprocity, agency, and power-sharing to establish goals for shared responsibility among families and educators (Ishimaru, 2020). Creating opportunities for families and educators to align shared priorities and goals turns them into co-equal partners and collaborators and transforms power by enabling a shared responsibility in developing solutions. Developing and maintaining systems that regularly allow for shared decision making among families and educators should be central to the school's priorities and goals for both designing student services (e.g., decisions about Tier 1, 2, and 3 curriculum and instruction) *and* efforts to cultivate and support family–school relationships (e.g., decisions about what, when, who, and how of family–school collaboration). Sharing decision making involves giving equal weight and consideration to families *and* educators when making choices about programs and practices. This includes working *with* families to establish and maintain transparency about processes that reimagine power dynamics and ensure shared decisions between educators and representative subgroups of the student and family population (Murray & Curran, 2008; Murray et al., 2018). Trust and mutual respect are fostered through shared decision making, as well as acknowledgement of and efforts to repair harm with families who have been historically marginalized and excluded in school decisions and who experience disproportionate rates of poor outcomes.

Leaders play a critical role by enabling contexts for family–school collaboration through establishing shared responsibility and goals for systemic transformation among families and educators. Leaders establish commitment to redesign systems, data, and practices with those families and students who are most impacted by inequities and injustices within the school. Family leaders and educational leaders co-create clear roles, as well as approaches to collaboration, and establish equal power, authority, and capacity for shared decision making through bi-directional communication and accessible data systems. Together, families and educators collectively identify what is important, what matters and work to redesign data, evaluation, and assessment efforts in line with shared goals. This approach emphasizes reciprocity, agency, and power-sharing to facilitate for shared decision making and shared responsibility.

Training and Support, Collaborative Goals, and Problem Solving

The final core practices of FSCA's family–school collaboration in MTSS framework include training, support, collaborative goals, and problem solving. Training and support practices describe efforts to ensure plans for supporting families and educators. Such practices must be responsive to families' needs and encourage families and teachers to work together to support students. The core feature of collaborative goals and problem solving describe the importance of ongoing evaluation of family–school collaboration efforts to monitor effectiveness and outcomes of family–school relationships. Schools can support effective practices by collecting and using evidence of positive collaboration and relationships between families and staff. Evidence, or outcome data (e.g., family and educator beliefs and perspectives), should be regularly obtained and used to make improvements in the goals, strategies, and practices of family–school collaboration. Further, efforts to monitor and ensure all demographic subgroups of the local community and student population should be adequately represented and considered (given voice). Decades of research on family–school problem solving for individual students—also known as Teachers and Parents as Partners [TAPP; Sheridan, 2014a]—support the use of a general problem-solving approach to guide educators and families' work together for supporting student success (Conjoint Behavioral Consultation [CBC; Sheridan & Kratochwill, 2008]). The general problem-solving approach includes (1) identifying shared concerns and goals for student learning, (2) providing input on barriers and facilitators to the areas of concern and identified goals, (3) collaboratively planning by having educators and families clarify their roles in implementing strategies to support student progress, and (4) regularly convening to ensure the student is progressing toward goals and identified concerns are being addressed. The family–school collaboration in MTSS framework (FSCA, 2019; Minch et al., 2019) applies this general problem-solving approach to a system or schoolwide level to encourage teams of educators and families to collaboratively partner on priorities and solutions within schools (Bal et al., 2018). Effective partnerships are sustained overtime through responsive and flexible use of data to monitor family–school collaboration efforts and continuously improve to ensure equity and effectiveness (Leverson et al., 2021; Ishimaru, 2020).

EQUITABLE FAMILY–SCHOOL COLLABORATION: STRATEGIES AND APPROACH

The final two core features of the family–school collaboration in MTSS framework (FSCA, 2019), training and support for family–school collaboration and collaborative goals and problem solving, correspond to Ishimaru's (2020) last two features of the equitable family–school collaboration framework including strategies: relationships and capacity building and approach: collective inquiry and action for transformative change.

Strategies: Relationships and Capacity Building

Ishimaru's (2020) emphasis on capacity building in the context of support relationship describes opportunities for families and educators to engage in learning experiences to empower families and educators to support children and enable their collaboration. Leaders should focus on creating supportive environments and provide opportunities and coaching supports for educators and families to develop competencies and skills to implement best practices needed for advocating and partnering together to improve systems (Krijnen et al., 2022; Ishimaru, 2020). School teams can work to provide opportunities for families and educators to develop their individual and shared capacities offers the potential to improve awareness of culture and biases and supports a school community identity that acknowledges, embraces, and honors differences. Acknowledging and leaning into families' knowledge and expertise, particularly in areas where students are not experiencing success, increase families' reciprocity and begin to repair relationships to improve equity in family–school collaboration systems and practices.

Approach: Collective Inquiry and Action

Collective inquiry and action refers to the ongoing assessment and adaptation of practices that allow for *reimagined* partnerships with families and centers families as co-equal partners in improving services and outcomes for students. Establishing and prioritizing opportunities to engage in collective inquiry and action with families affected by these outcomes and acting on that input demonstrates value and respect and is described in greater detail in

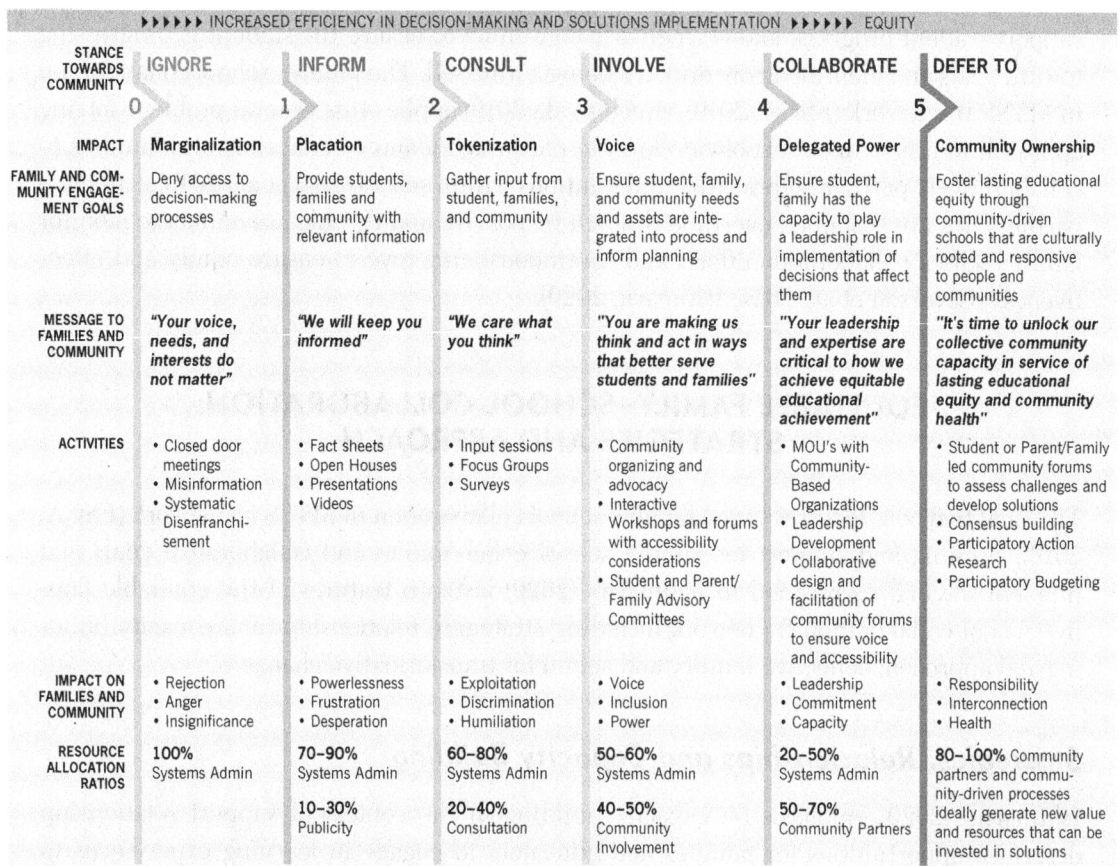

▶▶▶▶▶▶ INCREASED EFFICIENCY IN DECISION-MAKING AND SOLUTIONS IMPLEMENTATION ▶▶▶▶▶▶ EQUITY

STANCE TOWARDS COMMUNITY	IGNORE 0	INFORM 1	CONSULT 2	INVOLVE 3	COLLABORATE 4	DEFER TO 5
IMPACT	Marginalization	Placation	Tokenization	Voice	Delegated Power	Community Ownership
FAMILY AND COMMUNITY ENGAGEMENT GOALS	Deny access to decision-making processes	Provide students, families and community with relevant information	Gather input from student, families, and community	Ensure student, family, and community needs and assets are integrated into process and inform planning	Ensure student, family has the capacity to play a leadership role in implementation of decisions that affect them	Foster lasting educational equity through community-driven schools that are culturally rooted and responsive to people and communities
MESSAGE TO FAMILIES AND COMMUNITY	*"Your voice, needs, and interests do not matter"*	*"We will keep you informed"*	*"We care what you think"*	*"You are making us think and act in ways that better serve students and families"*	*"Your leadership and expertise are critical to how we achieve equitable educational achievement"*	*"It's time to unlock our collective community capacity in service of lasting educational equity and community health"*
ACTIVITIES	• Closed door meetings • Misinformation • Systematic Disenfranchisement	• Fact sheets • Open Houses • Presentations • Videos	• Input sessions • Focus Groups • Surveys	• Community organizing and advocacy • Interactive Workshops and forums with accessibility considerations • Student and Parent/Family Advisory Committees	• MOU's with Community-Based Organizations • Leadership Development • Collaborative design and facilitation of community forums to ensure voice and accessibility	• Student or Parent/Family led community forums to assess challenges and develop solutions • Consensus building • Participatory Action Research • Participatory Budgeting
IMPACT ON FAMILIES AND COMMUNITY	• Rejection • Anger • Insignificance	• Powerlessness • Frustration • Desperation	• Exploitation • Discrimination • Humiliation	• Voice • Inclusion • Power	• Leadership • Commitment • Capacity	• Responsibility • Interconnection • Health
RESOURCE ALLOCATION RATIOS	100% Systems Admin	70–90% Systems Admin 10–30% Publicity	60–80% Systems Admin 20–40% Consultation	50–60% Systems Admin 40–50% Community Involvement	20–50% Systems Admin 50–70% Community Partners	80–100% Community partners and community-driven processes ideally generate new value and resources that can be invested in solutions

FIGURE 2.3. The spectrum of family engagement for educational equity. From Gonzalez (2020). Copyright © 2020 Movement Strategy Center. Reprinted with permission.

Chapter 3 (Bal et al., 2016, 2018). Collective learning among educators and families regarding strengths and needs of individuals and systems enables action and ownership agency among educators and families. Both Ishimaru and FSCA's frameworks for family—school collaboration refer to the important practice of engaging in ongoing evaluation, assessment, and collaborative problem solving of family—school collaboration efforts to ensure ongoing improvements as the final element of both frameworks. The prerequisite features in both frameworks (e.g., positive relationships, shared goals) establish supportive environments, strategies, and approaches that enable collective learning among educators and families to achieve transformative change. Collective learning and action that center the voices of families, especially those that have been historically marginalized, enable reimagining of family—school collaboration in ways that rebuild trust, repair harm, and address systems that have perpetuated inequities and injustices. Through awareness and acknowledgement of harm, healing, and mutual respect, family—school collaboration enables learning together rather than from unequal places of power and authority (Pham et al., 2021). These foundational shifts in power and authority contribute to systems that produce equitable experiences and outcomes for all (Leverson et al., 2021). Figure 2.3 provides a spectrum of approaches to family—school connections.

SUMMARY

Incorporating theoretical frameworks in research and practice that mitigate challenges created by educational systems for developing equitable family—school collaboration requires centering families' voices and perspectives in the discussions and decisions about problems and solutions in education. The values, principles, and practices reviewed in this chapter can be used to begin *reimagining* family—school collaboration with MTSS.

Family Leadership Tool Checklist
Family Leadership & Engagement

PURPOSE

This tool is intended to provide a quick reference checklist of items to consider in pre-planning and budgeting efforts.

HOW TO USE THIS TOOL

This checklist highlights important considerations that can shape planning and budgeting decisions. This checklist is not intended to be used with family leaders, but to provide organizations with suggestions for internal discussion and action.

ORGANIZATIONAL SUPPORT AND STAFF CAPACITY

☐ Have you met with staff and board to build organization-wide shared understanding of and commitment to the value of family leadership and engagement?

☐ Have you discussed how your organization's work will be different with meaningful family leadership?

☐ Have you budgeted staff time for family leadership recruitment, coaching, and support, and have you designated a staff person to fill that role?

☐ Have you budgeted for administrative, technology, and other program support and discussed how those staffing needs will be met?

☐ Have you ensured that your staff have a shared understanding of and commitment to equity and dismantling White supremacy culture?

_____

_____

_____

POLICIES

☐ Have you developed a partnership agreement that lays out what is expected of the family leader, and what they can expect from the organization?

☐ Have you established a policy and process for how you will provide stipends and ensured the policies meet IRS guidelines and follow best practices in terms of amounts and distribution methods?

(continued)

☐ Have you addressed whether the stipend will also address child care and transportation needs or if those will be handled separately?

_____

_____

_____

RESOURCES

☐ **Stipends:** Have you developed a policy and process for stipends with clear guidelines that are the least burdensome possible? Have you included funding for stipends in your budget?

☐ **Transportation:** Have you decided how transportation needs will be met and developed any needed policies and procedures? Included this in your budget and made plans to assess the needs of your family leaders?

☐ **Child care:** Have you decided how child care needs will be met and developed any needed policies and procedures? Have you included this in your budget and made plans to assess the needs of your family leaders?

☐ **Printing and mailing:** Have you budgeted for printing and mailing? Have you made plans to assess the needs of your family leaders?

☐ **Communication:** Have you identified communication tools/resources and developed policies to support regular effective family communication? Have you reviewed your materials to ensure that they are appropriate in terms of literacy levels?

☐ **Translation:** Have you included both simultaneous and materials translation in your budget and made plans to assess the needs of your family leaders? Have you explored translation options in your community to ensure translation is available at the beginning of the program if needed?

☐ **Technology:** Have you considered what technology needs your families might face and budgeted for potential needs and staff support? Have you made plans to assess the needs of your family leaders?

☐ **Equity training:** Have you budgeted and built in time for equity training? Have you explored who might be best suited to provide this training?

_____

_____

_____

_____

Relationship-Based Competencies to Support Family Engagement
Professional Development Assessment for Teachers and Child Care Providers

SELF-AWARE AND CULTURALLY RESPONSIVE RELATIONSHIPS
Respects and responds appropriately to the cultures, languages, values, and family structures of each family

Knowledge, Skills, and Practices for Teachers and Child Care Providers	I have a solid understanding and skills and continue to grow in this area.	I am making progress in my understanding, skills, and growth in this area.	I need support to learn more and grow in this area.	I would like to focus on this area in my professional practice.	Notes
Knowledge					
Understands that each family has unique strengths and resilience	☐	☐	☐	☐	
Understands how families' cultures influence caregiving practices and shape children's early development	☐	☐	☐	☐	
Understands and respects variations in families' cultures, experiences, expectations, and child-rearing beliefs and practices	☐	☐	☐	☐	
Understands one's own beliefs, values, experiences, ethics, and biases to increase self-awareness about how they may affect work with children and families	☐	☐	☐	☐	
Understands how to help parents navigate differences in cultures between home and school	☐	☐	☐	☐	

Fostering Equity-Oriented Family–School Collaboration toward Culturally Responsive MTSS

Aydin Bal, Dian Mawene, Dosun Ko, Aaron Bird Bear,
Linda Orie, and Sophia Candida Ferreira Dodge

In this chapter, we describe key principles underlying equity-oriented family–school collaboration and propose an approach for operationalizing equity-oriented family–school collaboration. We first provide background to this area and then describe a framework for student–family–school–community collaboration. We end with a case study that describes how principles and practices occur in action.

The United States is a nation built on settler colonialism, slavery, and capitalism. Unlike the popular belief that education is a great equalizer, formal education has served and reproduced the power, privilege, and interests of the dominant groups, namely White, able-bodied, and cisgender. Fifty-three percent of students enrolled in U.S. public schools are Black, Indigenous, and People of Color (BIPOC; National Center for Education Statistics, 2021). The changes in student demographic compositions have generated new challenges

Aydin Bal, PhD, is Professor in the Department of Rehabilitation Psychology and Special Education at the University of Wisconsin–Madison.

Dian Mawene, PhD, is Professor in the Department of Rehabilitation Psychology and Special Education at the University of Wisconsin–Madison.

Dosun Ko, PhD, is Professor in the School of Education and Counseling Psychology at Santa Clara University.

Aaron Bird Bear, MS, was Professor, Assistant Dean, and inaugural Director of Tribal Relations at the University of Wisconsin–Madison.

Linda Orie, Ed-GRS Fellow, is a doctoral candidate in the School of Education at the University of Wisconsin–Madison.

Sophia Candida Ferreira Dodge, PhD, is a licensed psychologist at Journey Mental Health Center in Madison, Wisconsin.

and opportunities pertaining to inequities in schools. BIPOC students, in particular Black, Latinx, and American Indian students, have faced significant disparities in academic, social, and behavioral opportunities and outcomes (Artiles, 2019; Darling-Hammond, 2015). A long-standing educational crisis is the disproportionate representation of BIPOC students in special education programs for high incidence disabilities (e.g., learning disabilities and emotional disturbance) and in exclusionary school discipline (e.g., suspension and expulsion; Donovan & Cross, 2002; Dunn,1968).

Disproportionality presents significant challenges for BIPOC students, parents, and community members, as well as educators, education leaders, and the society as a whole. In the 2015–2016 academic year alone, students who received exclusionary discipline missed a total of 11 million days of instructional time (Losen & Martinez, 2020). Exclusionary discipline often becomes a pipeline for students to become involved in the juvenile justice system (Bacher-Hicks et al., 2019; Gregory, et al., 2010). Racial disproportionality severs relationships between the school and BIPOC students, families, and communities (Bal et al., 2018; Ko et al., 2021). Educators are forced to be adaptive in managing behavioral problems across settings and to be responsive to BIPOC students' diverse social, emotional, behavioral, and academic needs, interests, and goals in the ever-changing social, political, and economic contexts of their local education systems (Lewis et al., 2017).

For local educational agencies, once cited for significant racial disproportionality in special education and discipline of students with disabilities, it is difficult to exit citation through race-neutral, technical, or procedural compliance efforts without deep consideration of culture, racial relations, and power in shaping racialized opportunity to access to resources and intervention services (Kramarczuk Voulgarides et al., 2014). When districts are cited for significant racial disproportionality, they must reallocate 15% of special education funds to reduce special education identification and the office discipline referral of BIPOC students with disabilities. Despite its detrimental impacts on all stakeholders, racial disproportionality in special education and discipline remains a persistent conundrum.

As an enduring injustice, racial disproportionality in special education and disciplinary practices requires bold and sustained systemic interventions to design inclusive, culturally responsive, positive, and supportive systems in response to cultural resources, histories, and interests of BIPOC students and families. Addressing racial disproportionality demands systemic analysis of taken-for-granted school practices that have been historically grounded in the cultural practices, interests, and goals of the dominant groups. For the last several decades, education leaders and educators have been urged to collaborate with families and community members. Various state and federal laws deem family–school–community collaborations as essential (Grant & Ray, 2019; Miller, 2019). The Every Student Succeeds Act (ESSA, 2015) mandates local education agencies receiving federal grants to collaborate with parents. Particularly pertaining to special education, the 2004 reauthorization of the Individuals with Disabilities Education Act (IDEA) also requires local education agencies to partner with multiple stakeholders including parents. Procedural safeguards ensure family involvement in every stage of the special education process. The Standards for Professional Practice of the Council for Exceptional Children (CEC) further mandate partnership with parents and families built on cultural responsiveness (CEC, 2015). Reciprocal and sustained family–school–community relationships help leverage rich cultural and linguistic resources, practices, ideas, and support from multiple stakeholders, particularly BIPOC communities who have been impacted by disproportionality yet are often excluded from school decision-making activities (Bal, 2018; Ishimaru, 2020). Despite the legislative mandates and their potential positive and restorative impacts, collaborations with the BIPOC family and community remain challenging. Miscommunication, distrust, cultural mismatch, and other accumulating contradictions (e.g., deficit-oriented racial ideologies, bureaucracy) in siloed and hierarchical school systems hamper collaboration among multiple stakeholders—even among educators (Bal, 2011; Harry, 2008).

In this chapter, we introduce a framework for building capacity in schools for effective and sustained student–family–school–community collaborations and examining and addressing racial disparities in response to the unique social, emotional, behavioral, and academic needs, interests, and resources of local school communities: *culturally responsive positive behavioral interventions and supports* (CRPBIS). The CRPBIS framework has been tested and expanded by practitioners in urban, suburban, and rural school districts since 2012 (Cakir, 2020; Ko, 2020). CRPBIS takes racial disproportionality as a critical opportunity to examine and transform schools through reciprocal and sustained family–school–community partnerships to address disparities in behavioral outcomes. Before delving into CRPBIS, we will provide a review of the existing approaches to racial disparities and family–school–community collaboration through an MTSS, in particular, positive behavioral intervention and supports (PBIS). In this section, we will highlight the opportunities and challenges of the current approach and how CRPBIS leverages the existing MTSS structure to facilitate reciprocal partnerships with BIPOC students, families, and community members.

TECHNICAL APPROACHES TO FAMILY–SCHOOL–COMMUNITY COLLABORATION

Schools, policymakers, and researchers have been investing in school–based teams and maintaining the active involvement of students and families for several decades (Epstein, 1996). However, the depth of partnership ends at so-called parent education and inconsequential and unsustainable family involvement rather than active, reciprocal, and consequential collaboration to design and implement responsive and adaptive school systems (Bal, 2011; Christenson et al., 1992; Garbacz, McIntosh, et al., 2018). Involvement means the participation of families and community members in their children's learning activities, decision making, and advisory committees, whereas collaboration implies cooperation between home and school to support the social and academic growth of children. Family–school–community collaboration implies parents' involvement, yet such involvement does not always mean collaboration, where there is a shared responsibility and collaborative agencies and distribution of knowledge for working toward a shared goal and systemic transformation (Christenson et al., 1992; Fullan, 2007; Snow, 2016).

> "I feel comfortable walking into a school because I have a master's degree. I can speak the language, I have transportation, and I can help my children with homework, so I have very few barriers . . . I've always thought about the people that didn't have those."

Addressing inequities became one of the goals of PBIS and other MTSS models (McIntosh et al., 2018, 2021). PBIS scholars define collaborations as responsibilities shared between families and educators, starting from schoolwide planning to problem solving and evaluation (Garbacz et al., 2016). The purpose of the collaboration is to turn families and schools into equal partners (Garbacz, McIntosh, et al., 2018). PBIS is a robust systemic intervention model that emphasizes team-based problem solving, early intervention, and data-driven decision making (Sugai & Horner, 2006). Vincent and Tobin (2011) stated that PBIS implementation does not provide ample room for family–school–community collaboration especially for those with BIPOC backgrounds. Scholars identified the potential barriers to collaborations that may hinder family–school–community collaboration: First, parents' involvement remains in roles such as volunteer, fundraiser, and homework helper (Christenson & Sheridan, 2001). While these involvements are important, there is a need to move beyond those roles to tap into the voices of family, specifically those who are from minoritized communities.

Second, family–community members may diverge in values about learning and human development. Third, there is a power gap between family/community members and school personnel (Harry, 1992, 2008; Harry & Klingner, 2014). Parents delegate decision making to schools, or are reluctant to get involved, because they feel inferior to knowledgeable educators (Harry, 2008). Often, the power imbalance is also perpetuated by everyday interactions wherein parents feel that their experiential knowledge about their children's behaviors is undermined or ignored by the knowledgeable others (Rao & Kalyanpur, 2002). Especially pertaining to immigrant and refugee parents, linguistic barriers restrict their ability to collaborate (Kalyanpur & Harry, 1999). These differences often contribute to misunderstanding and distrust between parents, community members, and school staff. Another critical barrier that hinders family–school–community collaboration is the lack of structural arrangements. Although PBIS has been implemented for years, some schools report having no formal structures to link the school's desire to reach families with school and community service systems (Warren et al., 2003). To be able to meaningfully engage with BIPOC students, family, and community members, it is necessary for school leaders to intentionally provide opportunities, such as infrastructure of collaboration (e.g., designating staff time and support for family and community outreach, presenting school data with families and students during the monthly assemblies, and including family and community members and students on MTSS and other school-based problem-solving and decision-making teams; Bal, 2011, 2018).

Scholars recognized that while PBIS has put forth efforts to encourage family–school–community collaboration, there is a lack in the infrastructure of how to engage parents in the first place: "Although several investigations have noted the strengths associated with family involvement within positive behavior support, typical universal (i.e., schoolwide) PBIS implementation underemphasize formal, comprehensive systems for engaging families" (Garbacz et al., 2016, p. 62). As a result of the lack of systemic efforts, the extent to which families are meaningfully involved remains underutilized. The focus on BIPOC families continues to be unaddressed albeit scholars' recommendation to meaningfully address the rich diversity of students and families served by PBIS schools (Fallon et al., 2021).

CRPBIS offers a theoretically robust yet practical framework to facilitate and nurture coordination, collaboration, and communication between schools, districts, students, families, and community members, particularly in working with BIPOC students and families, those whose experiential knowledge has been historically placed at the periphery of school decision making. Leveraging the existing PBIS infrastructure (e.g., PBIS teams, data collection tools), CRPBIS presents Learning Lab as a process-oriented problem solving and systemic transformation methodology to enable family–school–community–school stakeholders to work collectively as equal partners and agents who will design the future of their schools (Bal, 2011, 2018). In CRPBIS, family–school–community collaboration is conceptualized as follows:

> School–family partnerships within CRPBIS function toward creating school cultures that: (a) from the start, position families as equal partners with school practitioners in determining the goals, activities, and desired outcomes for local CRPBIS implementation; (b) center voices and perspectives of students and families as crucial conduits for building safe and inclusive schools; and (c) attend explicitly to institutional structures that have hindered such partnerships in the past and seek to remediate them through collaborative inquiry. (King-Thorious et al., 2014, p. 2)

Research has suggested a need to reimagine school–family partnership (Miller, 2019). However, the filed needs research studies that have translated the theoretical framework of reimagining school–family–community collaboration into practical tools. Local education agencies and school communities can use and adapt research-based tools every day to address diverse social, economic, and material contexts of the school communities and ever-changing systemic issues that they face. CRPBIS addresses this gap in practice.

CULTURALLY RESPONSIVE PBIS

CRPBIS is the first framework to operationalize cultural responsiveness in the context of PBIS (Bal, 2011). The CRPBIS framework is a theoretical and practical framework developed as a response to the two-lingering conundrum: overrepresentation of the BIPOC students in special education and exclusionary school disciplinary practices and struggles of schools to collaborate with students, families, and communities, particularly, with those who have been marginalized in/through education systems, those whose experiences, interests, and goals have been ignored, and those who have been excluded from decision-making activities (Bal, 2011).

In the United States, BIPOC communities have been placed at the periphery of decision making (hooks, 1989). Indigenous scholars, for example, have criticized educational institutions as a White settler-colonial apparatus to eradicate, pathologize, punish, and criminalize Indigenous communities' ways of being, knowing, and behaving (McKinley & Brayboy, 2005; Tuck, 2009). Overrepresentation of BIPOC students in behavioral outcomes illustrates how schools operate within the mindset of settler colonialism, anti-Blackness, and ableism functioning as sites of oppression and everyday suffering—what Pierre Bourdieu called *la petite misère* (Dumas, 2014). CRPBIS centers knowledge system(s), histories, and collective struggles of historically marginalized community members and leverages rich knowledge(s), experiences, and histories as a resource for schools to adapt and adopt their systems to become inclusive, sustainable, and just.

CRPBIS is an ethical response to research and practice wherein scholars and educators work collectively *with*—not for— the community (Bal, 2011; Bang et al., 2016). CRPBIS creates an inclusive and productive decision-making group wherein family–community members, educators, and students all have an equal voice and power over the process. While reducing racial disproportionality in academic and behavioral outcomes is the ultimate end goal of the equity interventions informed by the CRPBIS framework, CRPBIS invests in the process to transform school cultures: foregrounding educators and other stakeholders' lived experiences in the existing system, unearthing the root causes of behavioral problems and outcome disparities, and (re)thinking solutions to those problems from the ground-up through critical dialogues and collective agency among local stakeholders.

Student–family–school–community collaboration in the CRPBIS framework takes a historicized and situated lens to understand racial disproportionality within the specific cultural, historical, geographical, and political contexts of the community where schools locate (Artiles, 2013; Bal, 2017). Rather than having a one-fits-all list of solutions prescribed to school and families, CRPBIS provides a platform for productive and sustained family–school–community collaborations and facilitates critical dialogue and collective agency among educators, administrators, families, students, and local civic organizations (e.g., YMCA, Urban League) to identify their unique local problems and collectively identify solutions.

Overrepresentation of BIPOC students is inseparable from race relations in the community, its historical patterns and evolution, and ways race relations permeate and take shapes in that community. Racial disproportionality is only a symptom of systemic, structural inequities lived every day by BIPOC students and families (Bal, 2017). It goes beyond the inability of certain racial ethnic/economic/linguistic groups of students and families to adhere to the rules and cultures of schools. In CRPBIS, we shift the focus of intervention from individual students with perceived behavioral problems to the interacting systems (e.g., school, school district, families) as the unit of analysis. Instead of fixing individual behaviors, CRPBIS aims to transform the system that produces and maintains inequitable outcomes, distrust, and deficits. Collaboration becomes necessary when the unit of analysis is the interacting systems instead of individual people and their thoughts and acts (e.g., increasing awareness among White educators). Acknowledging and challenging whiteness as a system and how it operates within the school are fundamental steps to building a culturally responsive system, building trust, and establishing an alliance with family and community members.

Grounded in critical pragmatic pedagogies of Vygotsky (1978), Dewey (1997), Freire (1978), and critical race theory in education (Ladson-Billings & Tate, 2006), CRPBIS is asset-based and preventive. Instead of waiting for the problems to occur as a "prerequisite" for collaborations, CRPBIS prevents such behavioral problems by first collaborating with families to unpack the challenges and potentials of the existing school system and collectively provide solutions. Student–family–school–community collaboration takes place at the universal level, meaning that collaboration is the prerequisite of locally meaningful, efficient, and sustainable systemic changes.

CULTURALLY RESPONSIVE: WHAT DOES IT MEAN IN THE CONTEXT OF CRPBIS?

There is no one universal solution to racial disproportionality whose patterns and predictors change from one community to another at the intersection of race, gender, sexual orientation, geographical locations, and district policies (Bal, 2011). In the CRPBIS framework, interventionists do not impose a predetermined checklist for a culturally responsive system. Instead, it provides a research-based process, *Learning Lab*, through which local stakeholders examine the problem and design a culturally responsive system in response to unique histories, needs, interests, and goals of their local contexts. CRPBIS challenges existing practices wherein school or school districts fall short in inviting external experts or working with technical assistance centers to inform or train educators on cultural responsiveness. While external experts are trained in their specific field, they might be less knowledgeable about specific sociocultural, political, and historical contexts of the community that shape inequities such as racial disproportionality.

CRPBIS honors and expands the knowledge, goals, experiences, and critical feedback from BIPOC families and community members. Cultural responsiveness in the framework of CRPBIS requires a paradigm shift in perceiving the units of intervention as well as the roles of students, families, and community members. Instead of focusing on individuals, CRPBIS focuses on the system that mediates individuals' perceptions, actions, and interactions. What CRPBIS examines is the social and historical milieus influencing relationships in school, behavioral expectations, consequences, and circumstances within which problematic behaviors and their consequences are contested. For example, in a CRPBIS implementation at a rural high school serving students from Anishinaabe tribal nation and non-Indigenous students in northern Wisconsin, we critically consider the historical conflicts over the rights to spearfish. The tension along with other cumulated settler-colonial practices deeply impacts trust and relationships between educators and American Indian students and families in the school community. Addressing racial disproportionality in this community requires addressing the broken relationship stemming from treaty rights (Bal et al., 2021). In another CRPBIS effort at a middle school in a suburban district, we delved into the history of urban design to understand how a community through their city engineers ensures that people of color, especially those from low-income backgrounds, are located separately from the middle-class Whites (Mawene, 2021; Mawene & Bal, 2020). These geographical and temporal backgrounds inform how the notion of different as deviants permeate in civic organizations including schools. Focusing on discrete individual behaviors hinders educators from holistically examining cultural assumptions that are (re) produced and shape school climate and day-to-day practice.

CRPBIS challenges the existing notion of the roles of parents and community members in collaboration. School discipline systems (e.g., procedures), for example, are typically redesigned by outside experts (e.g., consultants and technical assistant centers) *for* the school community. Parents and community members have little to no room in the redesign process. This practice assumes school systems as acontextual, ahistorical, and acultural systems. BIPOC family and community members are passive recipients of the system. In general, schools rarely engage in a transformative process wherein all stakeholders collectively unpack the problems, unleash tension and contradictions, and inclusively develop their own locally meaningful solutions.

> "Working with us would be helpful when we have concerns about equity issues, and I really think sharing data would make me feel better—if I could see that it wasn't disproportionate, or if it is disproportionate, if there are groups that are being disproportionality impacted by discipline or suspension, I think that we need to come together, look at the data and try to institute policies that change that."

Instead of being passive recipients of the expert's knowledge, CRPBIS positions BIPOC family and community members as the expert of their local problems, their contexts, and locally meaningful solutions. For a meaningful transformation, systemic changes need to take place from the bottom-up *with* the local stakeholders with an outside-in support from district, states' education agencies, civic organizations, and universities (Bal, 2018). CRPBIS invests in building a coalition and collective agency that positions the experience and perspectives of stakeholders, including BIPOC students, family, and community members as a fundamental source of knowledge.

LEARNING LAB METHODOLOGY

To address the critical gap in the literature, the CRPBIS framework offers a specific methodology, *Learning Lab*, to facilitate reciprocal, productive, and sustained student–family–educators–community partnerships wherein local stakeholders such as parents, community members, students, teachers, and school administrators represent diverse voices within the school community come together as a team to examine the existing school system and develop a new system in response to their social, historical, and geographical contexts, and available local resources (Bal, 2011). Learning Lab is a formative intervention methodology (Engeström, 2011; Engeström & Sannino, 2010). Each locality has its own specific needs and solutions and CRPBIS through Learning Lab honors that heterogeneity and diversity. Learning Lab is not a focus group discussion but is a working group with a clear division of labor and goals to design and implement an efficient and equitable system. Learning Lab consists of three phases: design, implementation, and sustainability phase. This book chapter focuses on the design phase of Learning Lab.

One important aspect every Learning Lab needs to secure before embarking on the process is leadership support. The support from school leadership is critical in Learning Lab because any systemic changes would be successful only with the commitment from school leaders such as principals, assistant principals, and dean of students. Learning Lab includes 12–15 members (e.g., BIPOC students, families, educators, principal, and PBIS coach) who meet monthly or biweekly to engage in the inclusive problem-solving process. If resources allow, we highly recommend biweekly meetings as holding them enables continuous work. We have successfully conducted six Learning Labs (ending at design phase) in six public schools (two elementary, two middle, and two high schools) in three school districts (urban, suburban, and rural) in Wisconsin between 2012 and 2021. In addition, five public middle

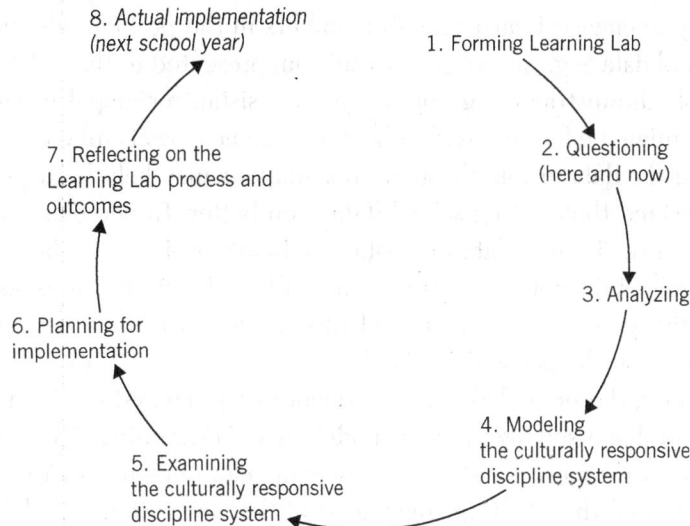

8. Actual implementation
(next school year)

1. Forming Learning Lab

2. Questioning
(here and now)

7. Reflecting on the
Learning Lab process and
outcomes

3. Analyzing

6. Planning for
implementation

4. Modeling
the culturally responsive
discipline system

5. Examining
the culturally responsive
discipline system

FIGURE 3.1. The cycle of change in Learning Lab's design phase. From Bal (2016). Copyright © 2016 Springer Nature. Reprinted with permission.

schools in an urban school district in Florida, one public middle school in Kansas, and one special education school in Rio, Brazil, have implemented Learning Labs. Learning Lab follows the cycle of change (Bal, 2016; see Figure 3.1) to design a new, culturally responsive support system by allowing Learning Lab members to engage in structured meetings.

Each Learning Lab session has its unique agenda and objective(s); all cumulatively lead to the end product: a new culturally responsive system. The Learning Lab embarks with the formation of an inclusive problem-solving team that represents diverse perspectives and voices within the school community. Learning Lab can consider the demographic balance of the school community (e.g., race, gender, economic class, immigration status, ability differences, and gender expressions) and reach out to school staff, families, and community members to expand its membership. At the end of the meeting, the facilitator can use a question of whose voices or perspectives are missing in the problem-solving space to identify potential members with expertise and rich experiential knowledge related to racial disproportionality. It is possible to allocate the first two to three Learning Lab meetings to form the team. Child care, transportation, interpretation services, food, and beverages are provided during the meeting.

After the team is formed, members engage in a problem identification process: questioning and analyzing. Learning Lab members map out the existing school disciplinary practices, rules, and division of labor. One way to conduct this process is to have school leadership present the school's existing system and have Learning Lab members identify what works and what does not; how and why they do and do not engage in each system component. We used a printed version of a school (middle school) discipline system. In this process, members revisited their practices as teachers, administrators, and parents to identify what part of the system was missing (e.g., what happened when a student was sent to the front office). We also provided Learning Lab members with post-it notes, papers, and markers so they can map out the school discipline system in small dyads or triads.

Another way to engage Learning Lab members in the problem identification process is by having school data (e.g., suspension, expulsion) presented to them. We typically reach out to the school administrator (e.g., principal, or assistant principal to present the data). While educators might be familiar with school data, some parents might be unfamiliar with the data. Making the data visible through presentations may help both the educators and parents to understand the existing school data even better. In one elementary school in a suburban community, through data presentation, Learning Lab members discovered that the majority of school discipline referrals start with incidents in the school playgrounds. Members collectively pushed to understand the division of labor, rules, and expectations guiding recess times at the particular school.

After unpacking the breakdown of the school discipline system, Learning Lab members engage in a problem-solving process: modeling and examining. Following the creation of the new culturally responsive system, members plan for implementation. The research on Learning Labs showed that the implementation of the new system is a delicate process in and of itself. Members along with school and district leaders need to prepare infrastructure for implementation (e.g., personnel, curriculum). While initially we included planning for implementation as an integral part of the design phase, research shows a need to extend the process to a stand-alone stage (Fixsen et al., 2005).

In the next section, we present the stages in the design process in three main groups: formation of the team, problem identification, and problem-solving while also providing examples from one Learning Lab: Indigenous Learning Lab in Northwoods High School (NHS) as a case in point.

CASE STUDY: CONDUCTING LEARNING LAB AT A RURAL HIGH SCHOOL WITH AN AMERICAN INDIAN COMMUNITY

Indigenous Learning Lab was implemented at NHS, a rural high school serving American Indian students from the Anishinaabe Nation. The Northwoods school community struggled with addressing racial disparities in academic and behavioral outcomes and conspicuously racial disproportionality in school discipline. Even though American Indian students accounted for about 20% of the student population, they occupied 64.3% of in-school suspensions and 62.8% of out-of-school suspensions in the 2018–2019 academic year. Combined with settler-colonial histories of erasing Indigenous culture and language through forced assimilationist English-only education and tribal community's resistance and frustrations to reclaim lands and political sovereignty, racial disproportionality in behavioral outcomes aggravated the tribal community's distrust toward NHS (Ko et al., 2021).

Formation of the Learning Lab Team

The first step in launching a Learning Lab is *identifying* and *recruiting* members. To start the identification process, Learning Lab facilitators along with school leadership such as the principal and American Indian education mentor collectively identify initial members: parents, students, community members, and educators, who have firsthand experiences with racial disproportionality and are committed to systemic changes. School leadership may make initial reach out to the potential members identified. When the connection is made, facilitators may follow up with a more formal invitation along with paperwork (e.g., stipend) if applicable. These initial members meet, and they collectively identify if the team needs to invite more members. They ask themselves, "Whose voice is missing?" and "Who else should be included?" to ensure that Learning Lab has a strong representation and is not missing any critical voices.

Members should reflect the diversity of roles (e.g., parents, community members, students, teachers, administrators), racial/ethnic group, gender expressions, ability differences, and age. Particularly, we emphasie extending an invitation to BIPOC students, family members, and community members who have been exposed to systemic injustice in school, such as exclusionary discipline firsthand (Bal, 2011). The emphasis on bringing the voice of BIPOC students and family to Learning Lab indicates a paradigm and practical shift from having BIPOC students, family, and community members as objects of discussion to having them as the participants of the discussion. The critical feedback, epistemic knowledge, and experiences of BIPOC students and families are very important. There are no definitive numbers of individuals to recruit as Learning Lab members. However, our experience informs us that a formation of 10–15 people is the most manageable group size to provide ample room for every member to contribute.

To enable full participation, facilitators along with school leaderships provide accommodation such as child care, transportation, meals, and interpreters to minimize technical glitches that can hinder participation. For child care and interpreters' support, for example, Learning Lab facilitators may utilize local resources through local universities or community colleges. Many higher institutions provide their students with opportunities to engage in service-learning/community engagement activities. Learning Lab could be a potential venue for such kind of activity while also ensuring that Learning Lab members are accommodated.

In summary, forming a Learning Lab team could be accomplished through these steps:

1. Learning Lab facilitators and school leaders identify potential members, keeping in mind diversity in racial/ethnic, gender, class, and professional roles in school and community.
2. School leaders initially reach out to the potential member.
3. Learning Lab facilitators follow up with the school leadership to check if the initial contact has been made and if the potential member is on board or not.
4. Learning Lab facilitators follow up with members who agreed to join the Lab by sending institutional invitations and required paperwork.
5. The facilitators continue working on the team composition in the first couple meetings and always ask the team, "Whose voice are we missing?"

Problem Identification

This stage comprises *questioning* and *analyzing*. At the questioning stage, Learning Lab members collectively identify the most pressing disturbances or contradictions they experience daily pertaining to exclusionary school discipline or other behavioral incidences. CRP-BIS considers experiential knowledge(s) of school stakeholders as qualitative data and is as equally important as the quantitative data (e.g., school discipline data) collected by educators in the school. Experiential knowledge(s) within the school help(s) members be exposed to systemic contradictions (e.g., microaggressions, differential treatment; Bal, 2018). Artifacts such as the school's existing behavioral system, student handbook, and geographical map of the community are considered as the second stimulus through which members identify systemic challenges and develop new concepts, tools, or practices to break away from the existing systemic breakdowns (Bal, 2018). At the *questioning* stage, members are given ample room to question what might be perceived as a racially neutral referral process, decision making, rules, and assumptions about behaviors. For example, the principal of NHS presented academic and behavioral outcomes data in seemingly neutral ways, masking the achievement gaps between White and American Indian students. A community member pointed out the need to analyze disaggregated data as follows:

> "Because in this area we're like a raft on a lake. We're like an island in the ocean. We're a small part of this population, us natives here. So, I like to get a visual of what the bar chart is. Not to throw you under the bus, but I like to see so you have all [students], and all natives, and white students, and then IEP students."
> —a Native American parent, ILL #1

In this instance, the parent is challenging the race-neutral representation of school systems that assume a race-neutral academic and behavioral outcome. After the push from the parent, the principal disaggregated the data and by doing so the gap of academic (i.e., SAT scores) and behavioral outcomes between White and American Indian students became visible.

In Learning Labs, tension and contradictions in a school system are taken as sources of learning and democratic participation toward improving the school system instead of a barrier to avoid collaboration. To do so, facilitators need to set a safe space by collectively establishing Learning Lab rules so that all members feel comfortable to share ideas. The rules or collective agreements in NHS Learning Lab sprcified (1) keeping conversations and names in Northwoods Learning Lab confidential; (2) sharing floor time—keeping voices balanced; (3) avoiding jargon; (4) asking and receiving questions with openness; and (5) focusing conversations on problem solving. In addition to those rules or agreements, the Learning Lab at NHS also used Anishinaabe Nation's seven-grandfather teaching: respect; love, truth, bravery, wisdom, generosity, and humility as the guiding principles.

In every meeting, the facilitators recite and display the seven-grandfather teaching before delving into the core agenda of each meeting. In some instances, the facilitator asked members to recognize each other's presence through the seven-grandfather teaching.

In the *analyzing stage*, Members engage in unpacking the school's existing system to analyze "the crack" in the system. In this stage, members utilized historical data and day-to-day processes to understand how the existing school system operates in everyday interactions. Often, members work in small dyads or triads to enable more room for discussion and open tensions and contradictions. Some discussion prompts we used in the analyzing stage were "What is working/not working in the system?" and "Why/when/for whom are things working/not working?" We also encourage members to think about examples from their day-to-day experience in school to support their responses. After small group discussions, we ask the members to share their discussion in the large group and wrap up with a closing comment from members.

To illustrate a small group discussion at the analyzing stage, here is how a small group discussion may be able to unpack how a disciplinary procedure takes place. An American Indian student in her small group consisting of two other students and a facilitator shared her experience with the way administrators implement hallway policy:

> STUDENT: It's also happened to me before too with the hall monitor. There's a new girl [Staff], and I had a pass to go to the bathroom with my sister. She asked me for my pass, and I showed it to her. Then I went into the bathroom, and she followed me there. I was mad, like "Why are you following me into the bathroom?" Then I walk out, and I go back to class, and she follows me still. I'm telling her: "Why are you following me?" And of course, I got mad and said some things. And then she called Mr. Trojan, they called him on me, and I almost got suspended but I didn't.
>
> FACILITATOR: How did you stop that [suspension]?
>
> STUDENT: I just had to lower my voice.
>
> FACILITATOR: But otherwise, you would get suspended?
>
> STUDENT: Yeah, probably.
>
> (Learning Lab #3)

Andrea's experience highlights those circumstances under which a perceived behavioral problem occurs must be carefully examined. Understanding how policies are enacted helps the members to understand what works and what does not in their existing behavioral system.

At the analyzing stage, members also engage in what we call "mapping out the system." They visualize the existing system in place using the second stimuli (e.g., school existing behavioral system) and the first stimuli (e.g., everyday experience of the system) to understand how the system is implemented vis-à-vis what the system was intended to do.

Problem Solving

This stage includes *modeling* and *examining*. After discussing the root causes of the racial disproportionality, members move from problem identification to problem-solving. At the modeling stage, members model their ideal system without feeling constrained on "reality check." Their creative and imaginative senses are unleashed at this stage. Members reflect and ask themselves, "What can we do to make the existing system work?" or "How can we improve the existing system?" Various ideas are then combined into one initial system. The ideal system encapsulated the complexity and messiness of the system. While members are mapping out their ideal system, they also notice what is ideal yet is currently broken. The complexity of the system encourages members to move away from designing interventions for individual students to exposing the need for structural support.

The examining stage occurs simultaneously with the modeling stage as members reflect on "What is still missing in the new system?" and "What is practical?" In other words, members engage in reality and feasibility checks of the new culturally responsive system to grasp the dynamics, possibilities, and limitations of the new culturally responsive system. For example, at this stage, NHS's assistant principal noticed that the school does not have universal, buildingwide behavioral expectations. The school received students from different feeder schools all with their unique school cultures and behavioral expectations. Particularly, for American Indian students, their formal education before high school took place exclusively within the reservation, and the high school presented a whole new cultural challenge for them. By having a universal behavioral expectation, Learning Lab members were hoping to teach the students about their cultural expectations (i.e., norms and rules) before "punishing" students if they do not meet the expectations. Members then agreed to collectively create a behavioral expectation, which details are expanded in the implementation stage as the members prepare the infrastructure to support implementation.

Reflection and Implementation Plan

After designing a new support system, members reflected on their collective problem-solving process. The reflection stage helped members build institutional memory that may help the NHS community adopt and adapt the Learning Lab process to address future problems of practices. In the implementation planning, members generated multiple implementation strategies to institutionalize new solutions designed. Notably, they suggested creating the implementation team whose primary responsibility would be building enabling infrastructure for implementation (e.g., professional development for school personnel and realignment of resources and school policies). Learning Lab members also develop a social validity check strategy to gather school stakeholders' feedback on the new culturally responsive support system, which is essential to increase the buy-in among the school community. In the next academic year, we will be working with the NHS community on the sustainability of the new system and inclusive decision-making process.

CLOSING THOUGHTS AND REFLECTIONS

The social, political, economic, and ideological contexts of schools and school districts are ever-changing. School communities face multidimensional local and global crises such as budget cuts, teacher shortages, racism, ableism, income disparities, and the COVID pandemics that are not under any one entity's control and cut across multiple systems (Engeström, 2018). Manifestations and the impact of those challenges change from one location to another and one year to another year. There are no universal solutions (e.g., top-down policies, and checklists) to those issues that would work all the time and for all local communities. The Learning Lab methodology is a research-based process through which local schools and school districts can examine the complex and adaptive challenges they face and develop systemic solutions through a student–family–school–community–university partnership based on the resources, needs, interests, and goals of their community.

Our research showed that it is possible to form and sustain inclusive problem solving and systemic design teams at schools owned and led by local stakeholders, especially with the minoritized communities. Schools are often highly siloed and hierarchical. They are not designed for coordination, collaboration, and communication among practitioners. Learning Lab provides a process and a much-needed space of critical dialogue and future-making for educators, education leaders, community members, policymakers, researchers, and teacher educators to design inclusive, positive, and transformative learning developmental contexts for *all*.

We encourage educators who are interested in conducting Learning Lab to check the following resources:

- CRPBIS website: *http://crpbis.org*
- Bal. A., Schrader, E., Afacan, K., & Mawene, D. (2016). Using Learning Labs for culturally responsive positive behavioral supports and interventions. *Intervention in School and Clinic, 52*(2), 122–128. *https://doi.org/10.1177%2F1053451216636057*
- Bal, A. (2018). Culturally responsive positive behavioral interventions and supports: A process-oriented framework for systemic transformation. *Review of Education, Pedagogy, and Cultural Studies, 40*(2), 144–174. *https://doi.org/10.1080/10714413.2017.1417579*
- Bal, A., Afacan, K., Clardy, T., & Cakir, H. I. (2021). Inclusive future making: Building a culturally responsive behavioral support system at an urban middle school with local stakeholders. *Cognition and Instruction, 39*, 279–305. *https://doi.org/10.1080/07370008.2021.1891070*
- Ko, D., Bal, A., Cakir, H. I., & Kim, H. (2021). Expanding transformative agency: Learning Lab as a social change intervention for racial equity in school discipline. *Teachers College Records, 123*(2). *www.tcrecord.org*

CHAPTER 4

Assessment in Family–School Collaboration

This chapter provides a review, discussion, and practical suggestions for integrating assessment practices in family–school collaboration. The chapter begins with a review of two essential areas for data collection and assessment with families, including characteristics and practices that make up the family–school collaboration partnership and family-reported data on child performance and well-being outcomes. We review examples of tools and considerations for obtaining these data in practice, as well as considerations for collection and use of family–school collaboration data and assessments within MTSS systems and practices along with a case study to provide an example of these recommendations.

This chapter will provide the reader with:

- enhanced understanding of data to collect from families to inform services provided to students as well as to inform how partnerships are approached with families
- a review of tools and resources that would allow educators to collect data from families to inform student supports as well as family–school partnership efforts
- an exemplar of how one school, Maxwell Elementary, utilized data from families to inform both tiered interventions, provide supports for students, and make an effort to engage and partner with families

Family–school assessments and family–school data enable school teams to make sustainable improvements and promote proactive family–school collaboration, communication, and mutual trust. Access to high quality, efficient, and actionable data is essential to assist schools with continuous improvement efforts toward integrated and effective family–school collaboration within MTSS (Garbacz, Minch, Cook, McIntosh, et al., 2019; Minch et al., 2020). To advance this work in districts and schools, it is essential to have quality assessment tools and evaluation systems that allow schools to identify current status, strengths, and areas for improvement with respect to family–school collaboration efforts along with tools that position families as co-equal partners in the identification of student learning goals and needs.

THE FAMILY–SCHOOL PARTNERSHIP

Meta-analyses investigating educator and family collaboration activities and behaviors associated with improvements in student outcomes identify two-way communication, home-based involvement, behavioral support, parent–teacher collaboration, and the overall parent–family relationship as the essential home–school collaboration ingredients that demonstrate the strongest associations with improved student outcomes (Cox, 2005; Sheridan et al., 2019). Features of these ingredients include positive, trusting, and consistent communication and engagement between families and educators (Adams & Christenson, 2000; Sheridan et al., 2019; Smith et al., 2020). Comparisons of home-based forms of engagement (e.g., discussing school and educational aspirations at home, reading books together) and school-based forms of engagement (e.g., attending school meetings, conferences, participating in the school's PTA) reveal that home-based involvement, except for homework assistance, is consistently associated with a range of improvements in functioning across various demographic groups and age levels (Barger et al., 2019; Jeynes, 2007, 2010). Thus, schools should focus on measuring features of family–school collaboration that include activities of families and educators and discussions and activities of families and children at home as these family–school collaboration activities have a significant impact on student success in school.

Identifying outcomes schools intend to achieve through implementation of family–school collaboration practices within MTSS is an important first step and will inform what and how each school approaches family–school collaboration data collection and use. Family–school collaboration practices implemented in schools should be put in action to achieve important family–school collaboration outcomes, including high quality parent–teacher relationships, two-way communication and collaboration, and the high degree of these supportive interactions enabling families to support children's well-being and providing educationally supportive environments at home (Sheridan et al., 2019). Therefore, schools' data should allow measuring of these key features of family–school collaboration partnerships associated with student outcomes and allow schools to answer the questions like "Do families and educators have positive and trusting and relationships in our school?" Data measuring the quantity or quality of home–school communication and collaboration should include educators' and families' perceptions including their attitudes, beliefs, and perceived skills (e.g., efficacy) as well as more observable behaviors and practices. Measuring families' *and* educators' beliefs and perceptions about family–school collaboration is important for changing practices (Hoover-Dempsey et al., 2002). Collecting data on family perceptions is more challenging for schools as families are less accessible than educators for data collection. However, including family perceptions is critical for improvement given that family–school collaboration is a relationship that in order to improve requires efforts from both parties.

> "Parents should be asked to be part of the decision-making process at a school and be given access to schoolwide data. For me that's especially important because I have a Black daughter. I think some of the punishments I've seen at her school have been really punitive, especially to minority children."

Furthermore, family perceptions of the relationship quality are associated with family reciprocity to educator outreach and subsequent engagement and support in their child's education (Cox, 2005). The degree to which educators and families value collaboration to support students is associated with their practices and behaviors for collaboration (Drummond & Stipek, 2004; Hoover-Dempsey et al., 2005). When educators and families see communication with one another as central to their roles for supporting youth, they are more likely to collaborate (Seitsinger et al., 2008). The degree to which families and educators report feeling skilled and equipped to engage in home–school collaboration and communication efforts is associated with the degree to which they follow-through on family–school collaboration strategies and practices consistently and successfully (Hoover-Dempsey et al., 2005). These domains are important to assess because they can be targeted for professional development and coaching supports among educators and families alike. In addition to families' and educators' perceptions about the quality of the parent–teacher relationship, data collection should target the degree to which family–school collaboration behavior and practices were implemented as intended.

The strategies or practices implemented to achieve these outcomes are features to target for data collection and assessment. These kinds of data are often referred to as fidelity data and allow schools determine the degree to which they implemented family–school collaboration practices the way they intended to. These kinds of data allow schools to answer questions that often come up after reviewing outcome data such as these: "How often or to what degree do families receive updates and opportunities for discussion from teachers?" or "How often or to what degree to educators receive input or responses when they initiate communications with families?" Assessing educators' and families' reports of the frequency, quality of family–school collaboration practices, and strategies of family–school collaboration allows teams to determine if planned approaches are being received as intended by families and educators alike. Two broad family–school collaboration practices to target for fidelity assessment and monitoring include two-way communication and shared decision making (Cox, 2005; Sheridan et al., 2019). When assessing two-way communication, multiple check-ins with families and educators on preferences for quantity, methodology, and content/focus throughout the year can ensure adjustments are made as needed. The COVID-19 pandemic brought to light the importance of regular check-ins about home–school communication preferences and needs, and it's imperative that we maintain these lessons moving forward. When assessing shared decision making including prompts about how families are invited to engage in shared decision making with educators ranging from general services within the school to those specific to their child, we can enable improved practices at Tiers 1, 2, and 3.

Data indicating the status of the family–school relationship and the degree to which planned family–school collaboration practices were implemented as intended can enable schools' ongoing improvement efforts. For example, one school found educators reported more positive and trusting relationships compared to families. Fidelity data were reviewed to help identify the source(s) of differing perceptions about the quality of the relationship and to inform areas for improvement in family–school collaboration practices. Comparing families' and educators' perceptions about consistent communication between home and school showed that educators were reaching out to families consistently through email and social media, yet families were not reciprocating those outreach efforts because they didn't use email or Facebook as much as phone or text messages. Therefore, the school improved outreach efforts by reducing email and social media and increasing phone calls and text messages to families. Subsequent monitoring showed families reciprocated outreach more, and their perceptions about relationships with teachers improved. Using both outcome and fidelity data to monitor family–school collaboration enables schools to have good information to improve practices.

FAMILY REPORTS OF STUDENT PERFORMANCE AND WELL-BEING

In addition to assessing outcomes of the parent–teacher relationship and fidelity of practices implemented to achieve those outcomes, schools' data collection with families should include their perspectives about student learning goals, skills, and performance. Families' critical perspective about student well-being and learning provides a comprehensive picture of the child, enabling schools' prevention and early intervention supports. Collecting data from families about their children's strengths, goals, dreams, culture, and routine family experiences allows educators to develop learning experiences that ensure students and families feel connected to the curriculum and improve learning. Including measures of family strengths and needs can supplement the school's existing tiered support system and offer areas of priority and consideration for ensuring families and students are supported. Areas for family input and assessment linked with student outcomes include family perceptions of students' strengths and needs with academic, social–emotional, and behavioral skills (Garbacz, Beattie, et al., 2019; Garbacz et al., 2020); parents' aspirations, expectations, and beliefs about child performance (Hill & Tyson, 2009; Jodl et al., 2001; e.g. "How far would you like your child to go in school?"); effective parenting strategies such as limit setting (e.g., McEachern et al., 2012; Stormshak et al., 2020), parent warmth (Metzler et al., 1998), and positive reinforcement (Dumka et al., 2008); and knowledge and tracking of their child's behavior (i.e., parent monitoring; Stattin & Kerr, 2000).

Families can be identified as respondents to schoolwide screeners to single out students who would benefit from additional Tier 2 and 3 supports and co-monitors of student progress within Tier 1, 2, and 3 instruction and intervention to supplement educator assessments and support skill generalization or practice needs unknown to educators. As part of classroom/Tier 1 instruction and support, including family perspectives about strengths, challenges, culture, and experiences can improve the effectiveness of low-intensity interventions and strategies within the classroom and prevent minor challenges from escalating to intensive needs requiring Tier 2 or 3 supports. As co-developers of student learning goals, family input in student needs and strengths should be obtained and considered within teams developing supplemental and intensive intervention plans for students receiving Tier 2 and 3 teams supports. Below we review tools and resources for collecting and using data to monitor family–school collaboration efforts and for collecting family input on student outcomes.

TOOLS FOR COLLECTING DATA

Strategies for to collecting family–school collaboration data include quantitative data in the form of scores or ratings derived from surveys, assessments, and qualitative data such as themes from comments or discussions during interviews, focus groups, or open-ended comments. A common approach is to use quantitative data, such as surveys or fidelity ratings, that provide a global rating of family–school collaboration efforts that allows schools to identify broad family–school collaboration areas that need improvement. Then, further understanding of the strengths or areas of improvement for family–school collaboration can be obtained through qualitative data such as interviews, focus groups, or open-ended questions on surveys. These approaches provide rich, detailed information and can be focused on smaller groups of families if needed to inform *how* to implement strategies for improving family–school collaboration efforts. Tools to collect family–school collaboration data are summarized below, and most full versions of tools are available upon request.

Measuring the Family–School Partnership

Below are tools used to obtain measures of family–school collaboration fidelity and outcomes, and family reports of student well-being and learning needs. In practice, these data can be combined and collected from families in a single questionnaire or interview. Many of the surveys reviewed below combine questions about outcomes of family–school collaboration and fidelity into a single measure. Schools may consider including questions about student learning and well-being needs within family–respondent versions of these tools to efficiently obtain the information from families.

Outcomes of Family–School Collaboration

EDUCATOR RESPONDENTS

One measure designed to assess teachers' perceptions of the parent–teacher relationship includes the Parent–Teacher Relationship Scale II (PTRS II; Minke et al., 2014; Vickers & Minke, 1995), a 24-item measure that assesses teacher perceptions of parent–teacher joining and communication within the parent–teacher relationship. A brief measure to examine proactive outreach to families and to gauge the overall status of family–school collaboration within the school includes three items from the PTRS II: (1) Parents are contacted before child behavior problems get out of hand; (2) parents are regularly informed about their child's positive behaviors; and (3) this school clearly communicates with families about expected student behaviors at school (Garbacz et al., 2020).

The Classroom Family Engagement Rubric (Flamboyan Foundation, n.d.) is a self-assessment tool that allows teachers to rate their skills and practices for family–school collaboration with families in their classroom. This can be encouraged in the beginning of the year and regularly throughout the school year to identify and monitor areas of improvement that are targeted by the schools' professional development supports.

FAMILY RESPONDENTS

In addition to gathering educator perspectives, it is equally important to gather family perspectives about the quality and fidelity of family–school collaboration efforts. Depending on the resources available within the school, these tools can be administered to all families to inform schoolwide family–school collaboration systems and practices that are responsive to family input and can be administered to a smaller subset of families to inform focused areas of improvement. One measure intended to be administered to all families to inform family–school collaboration efforts within tiered systems of support is the Stakeholder Input and Satisfaction Survey—Family (SISS-F; Center on Positive Behavioral Interventions and Supports [PBIS], 2020b). The SISS-F is a 37-item survey administered to all families in the school and includes questions about (1) family perspectives on the implementation, quality, and frequency of the school's practices for family–school collaboration; (2) family preferences for collaborating and communicating with the school; and (3) open-ended questions about the school's overall strengths and areas of improvement. Although no studies to date have been published about the use of the tool in practice or psychometric properties of the tool, the items included within the tool demonstrate promise for improving responsive efforts to partner and collaborate with families. The SSIS-F is available upon request to the authors.

Additional measures designed to obtain family perspectives about important features of family–school collaboration may not be freely available or accessible for use in practice. For example, the Family Involvement Questionnaire (FIQ; Fantuzzo et al., 2000; Manz et al., 2004) asks families to rate their frequency of engaging in school-based, home-based, and home–school communication and includes early childhood (Fantuzzo et al., 2000) and school age (Manz et al., 2004) versions. Schools can administer this questionnaire to all families or a smaller, targeted group to assess the level of and ways families are engaged and supporting student learning. Schools can use this information to better align their outreach and collaboration efforts with family preferences for family–school collaboration.

Parallel measures allow schools to ask similar questions about family–school collaboration efforts to both families and educators to be able to compare and identify gaps for improvement. The Family Engagement in Problem-Solving/Response to Intervention Survey—Family (FERS-F; Minch, 2012, 2016; Castillo et al., 2016) and the Family Engagement in Problem-Solving/Response to Intervention Survey—Educators (FERS-E; Minch, 2012, 2016; Castillo et al., 2016) can be administered to both families and educators to compare areas of discrepancies to target for professional development, support, and improvement. The FERS-F is a 40-item survey that assesses families' (1) beliefs about the importance of family engagement, (2) perceptions of knowledge and skills for participating in family engagement activities, (3) perceptions of their own practices for supporting student learning, and (4) perceptions of educators' practices to reach out to and engage families in student learning. Families respond to items by rating their level of agreement (1 = Strongly Disagree to 5 = Strongly Agree) or frequency (i.e., communication with the school, 1 = Never to 4 = Always). As part of tiered prevention frameworks, the intensity of interventions and supports matches student need, and therefore, some of the items allow for a Not Applicable option as not all families may experience Tier 2 or Tier 3 interventions for their child. The FERS-E mirrors the family version. Both are freely available upon request for use and/or adaptation in practice.

Family–School Collaboration Fidelity Assessments

Educators responsible for leading improvements in tiered systems of support, such as leadership teams, can assess key features of family–school collaboration and work to develop identified areas needing improvement. The tools below include examples of schoolwide fidelity assessments completed by school leadership teams. These assessments can be used in a formative approach wherein school leadership teams assess current status of family–school collaboration in MTSS practices multiple times throughout the year to inform ongoing improvements.

The TFI-FSC (Garbacz, Minch, et al., 2019), a tool currently being piloted by schools, allows schools to supplement broader fidelity assessments such as the TFI (Algozinne et al., 2014) with a brief but detailed assessment of the fidelity and quality of family–school collaboration practices that guide action planning for improvement efforts. The TFI-FSC is a 14-item measure completed by school leadership teams to assess six domains of family–school collaboration:

1. positive relationships
2. two-way communication
3. shared decision making
4. family voice in equitable discipline
5. training and support for family–school collaboration
6. evaluation

Each of 14 items is rated on a 0 (Not Implemented) to 2 (Fully Implemented) paradigm. The TFI-FSC prompts teams to consider specific data sources (e.g., school plans and policies, meeting notes, survey or focus group data) when rating each item. The scoring criteria emphasize the process and quality of implementing key practices and proactive use of family input to design and continuously improve their practices. The emphasis on continuous improvement ensures that schools remain responsive to changing family needs and preferences. Ideally, a tool such as the SISS-F (Center on PBIS, 2020b) is used by schools to obtain family voice and input and considered when rating items about representative family perspectives. The TFI-FSC can be used to provide an initial and ongoing assessment to monitor progress and changes in family–school collaboration systems and practices. The TFI-FSC is currently being piloted, but most recent versions are freely available upon request from the authors.

Another family–school collaboration fidelity tool completed by school leadership teams is the Family–School Practices Survey—School Teams (FSPS-Teams; Garbacz, McIntosh, et al., 2019). The FSPS-Teams is designed to assess the level of implementation of family–school collaboration practices within PBIS across five domains:

1. communication
2. family–school activities
3. PBIS practices at home and school
4. decision making/shared ownership
5. resources

School teams rate the level of implementation of practices from 0 (Not in Place), 1 (Partial), to 2 (In Place) in addition to Yes/No questions about the school's practices for family–school collaboration as well as items that ask schools to rate frequency and perceptions of the quality of those efforts. Results from the FSPS-Teams can be used to help inform school team action planning as part of ongoing evaluation and improvement efforts related to family–school collaboration. State leaders have used the FSPS-Teams as part of their PBIS approach to supporting districts and schools with family–school collaboration utilizing the FSPS-Teams to identify areas of family–school collaboration for strategic planning and improvement (Feinberg et al., 2020).

Another measure completed by school leadership teams to assess the level and quality of implementation of family–school collaboration practices is the Family and Community Engagement—Innovation Configuration (FACE-IC; Minch et al., 2017). The FACE-IC is completed by school leadership teams and designed to help schools determine the quality and level of implementation of family–school collaboration efforts within their tiered systems of support across six domains and 21 practices, including:

1. leadership
2. data-based outcomes
3. positive relationships
4. multidimensional/multi-tiered approach
5. empowering families
6. collaborative problem solving

The measure is intended to serve as a reflection guide to help schools identify, monitor, plan, and refine areas of family–school collaboration for improvement. Schools rate their level of implementation on a scale from left (1 = Exemplary) to right (4 = Planning) with values ranging from the most exemplary level of implementation of the practice on the left (1 = Exemplary) with decreasing levels or variations of implementation along the right (3 = Implemented; 2 = Partially Implemented; 1 = Planning). Innovation configurations are designed for use within local contexts and allow for adaptation and refinement based on specific needs of local teams and communities (Learning Forward, 2013). This measure has not been used in research but has been adopted by various state MTSS centers to assist district and school teams with ongoing efforts to improve family–school collaboration within tiered systems of supports. The FACE-IC is freely available upon request to the authors.

Family Reports of Student Learning and Well-Being

The second purpose of family-reported data is to obtain family perspectives of student learning and well-being needs to inform supports for children. These data supplement existing assessments of student performance and help inform tiered services and supports for students. In addition to obtaining families' needs and concerns about students, including prompts to obtain student strengths creates a positive tone for collaboration, validates areas of student success, and opens opportunities for bi-directional forms of communication and collaboration (Moore et al., 2016).

One measure that is administered to all families as a parent–respondent schoolwide screener is the Positive Family Support—Strengths and Needs Assessment (PFS-SANA; Garbacz, Beattie, et al., 2019). The PFS-SANA is a parent-report screener to understand parents' perspectives about their children's academic and behavioral strengths and needs and is available at the elementary and middle school level. Items assess parents' perspectives about their child's social, emotional, and academic needs (e.g., sad, worried, irritable, willing to share with others) on a 4-point scale from 0 = No Concern to 3 = Serious Concern. The PFS-SANA can be embedded at Tier 1 within a school's MTSS framework and used to complement teacher ratings of the child's social, emotional, and academic needs and Tier 2 or Tier 3 interventions and supports. In addition, the PFS-SANA can be used as an avenue to reach out proactively to parents/caregivers as part of a larger schoolwide emphasis on family–school collaboration. Collecting information about families' strengths offers insight into areas of resiliency to leverage for prevention and intervention planning. Valuing family input about student needs and strengths communicates shared decision making and respect and helps ensure prevention and early intervention supports. When issues are identified as part of the screening approach, depending on the severity, a follow-up with families can range from a brief supplemental communication to intensive wrap-around supports.

Measures that obtain detailed information from families often require a greater time commitment for both educators and families to complete and are best suited for use with families of students identified as benefitting from Tier 2 and/or Tier 3 supports to inform intervention goals and plans. Generally, these tools gather more detailed information about family goals, concerns, and motivations for collaborating with the school to support children's success in school (Stormshak et al., 2011). Many of existing tools are a component of packaged curriculums requiring purchase for use (e.g., Family Check-up; Stormshak & Dishion, 2009), however, the domains assessed by these tools described in this chapter should be considered when obtaining information from families.

COLLECTION, MANAGEMENT, AND USE OF DATA

Across several frameworks for family–school collaboration, leadership and data are foundational to schools' ongoing family–school collaboration efforts within MTSS implementation (Minch et al., 2017; Minch, Garbacz, et al., 2020). Using high quality data can allow schools to sustain great partnerships with families over time. Below, we'll review how collected family–school collaboration data can be used to illustrate status/progress of family–school collaboration and family reports on student and family needs and strengths to inform instruction and intervention for students. Considerations including when and how frequently to collect data on the status/progress of family–school collaboration implementation efforts as well as obtaining and using input from families about student learning outcomes are described below.

Using Data to Improve Family–School Collaboration

At a schoolwide level, outcomes and fidelity of the family–school partnership can be assessed through surveys administered to both families and educators. Given the resources needed to collect, summarize, and use survey data from families and educators, this approach is likely best for less frequent formative assessment purposes such as once or twice a year. Within MTSS, teams can use the information for improving strategies and collaboration opportunities for families and educators. At the beginning of a school year, initial family perspectives are utilized to plan schoolwide family–school collaboration strategies and approaches and involve obtaining feedback from families throughout the year on their satisfaction with approaches and strategies employed by school to allow for improvements and adaptations as needed. Surveys can be individually administered to all teachers within the school to gather representative educator reports of the quality and fidelity of family–school collaboration practices in school and used to inform professional development and coaching opportunities for educators. Families' responses to surveys can be aggregated and compared to educator responses to identify areas wherein families and educators' relationship may be experienced differently across home and school contexts. Areas of discrepancy may suggest a mismatch in the ways families experience the approaches to the intention or objective practice employed by educators. For example, educators may report consistent two-way communication using text messaging with families, but if families are not receiving these messages, their experience with that approach will differ from the reports of educators. Relying solely on one member of the collaboration relationship in assessments of family–school collaboration limits the information available to inform improvements. Data from family and educator surveys assessing their perspectives about the value, importance, and success of family–school collaboration efforts can inform changes in strategic plans for home–school collaboration as well as opportunities for supporting skills and practices associated with partnership efforts. Data obtained from tools such as the TFI-FSC or FSPS-Teams help to provide teams with a schoolwide perspective on systems and practices prioritized for improvement. Data from tools assessing perspectives about family–school collaboration could be aggregated to inform schoolwide approaches and plans as well as analyzed and considered when collaborating with families around students' Tier 2 or 3 intervention development and implementation. The case study included at the end of this chapter provides examples of reports and action plans illustrating the use of data obtained from family–school collaboration tools to inform strategic improvements within MTSS.

Family Perspectives to Inform Supports for Students

Including family perspectives on student performance and well-being to inform tiered services and supports can enable comprehensive assessments of student learning and supplement educator reports. Data from families collected through the PFS-SANA can be used as part of schoolwide screeners to complement educator perspectives of student strengths and needs and inform needed interventions and supports for students. Families could be followed up with after completing the PFS-SANA to conduct interviews to gather in-depth information from families to inform student supports that leverage strengths and connect closely with students' families and cultural contexts. Creating prompts within meeting agendas and action plans for Tier 2 and Tier 3 teams can support the proactive collection and use of family–school collaboration data when developing intervention plans.

For concerns that are better suited for additional supports within the classroom or less intensive Tier 2 intervention, follow-up approaches to learn more about families' unique strengths, contexts, and needs can help to inform approaches for collaboration and supporting the student. Classroom teachers can utilize individualized outreach to identify more frequent correspondences with families about classroom behavior and learning needs (Fefer et al., 2020). Additional considerations at a classroom level include opportunities for families to share strengths and needs, enabling the teachers to create opportunities for bridging the home–school contexts and creating schools in which students feel at home and are able to "see themselves" in the learning environment. These might include learning about family structure and routines, family beliefs and values, and family support needs. Knowing about student family-life transitions or events can enable empathy and support for students when experiencing transitions or traumatic events. Having insight into the family's priorities and values can enable educators to connect students' contexts and make transitioning between home and school less challenging for students. Creating opportunities for families to share areas in which they would appreciate further information, skill-building, or advocacy support allows schools to plan family capacity-building opportunities in response to family needs. The Family Interview for Culturally Responsive Practices is a great example of a family interview (Wisconsin RtI Center, 2019).

For more intensive or severe concerns that are better served through Tier 2 or 3 interventions, educators are encouraged to follow the PFS-SANA with a thorough interview and assessment process that includes families as partners in determining student learning goals and designing supports aligned with students' needs. This might include detailed information from families, including a primary focus on family goals for children, family perceptions of student areas of concern, family motivations, and perceptions of their role for supporting student success in school. Additional considerations for collaborating with families at Tier 2 (Boone et al., 2018) and Tier 3 (Boone et al., 2018) can provide school teams with considerations for developing systems for communicating and ensuring authentic collaboration with families as part of Tier 2 and 3 interventions and supports. Including opportunities for family–school communication about student well-being and progress with intervention and skill-development integrates both fidelity monitoring and home–school communication efforts. Including opportunities for families to respond and ask questions allows for two-way communication and can provide insight into areas for consideration across Tier 2 systems. Missouri PBIS Center (2017) provides a nice example of a tool for family and educators to share updates about student progress and includes opportunities for parent signature and comments from each teacher of secondary student (see Appendix 4.A).

Data Management and Use Infrastructure

Teams should leverage existing resources and infrastructure for the collection and use of family–school collaboration data. Teams should also integrate their roles to ensure collection and use of family–school collaboration data within existing teaming roles, data systems, and practices, including strategic priorities, plans, and schoolwide policies to ensure family–school collaboration is not viewed as a separate initiative from MTSS implementation. Doing a comprehensive analysis of existing priorities, policies, and strategic plans that connect to family–school collaboration data will ensure teams do not duplicate efforts and leverage existing practices already being implemented.

Identifying a team member role whose job it is to collect, report/summarize, and share back family–school collaboration data within existing MTSS leadership teaming structures can facilitate effective use of family–school collaboration data for planning and improvements. This team member can develop graphical displays of family–school collaboration data for teams to action plan areas for improvement. When reviewing schoolwide family–school collaboration tools such as the TFI-FSC or FSPS-Teams, schools might display the level of implementation of the key domains within each measure and facilitate action planning for strategic improvements to low-scoring domains and items.

Leveraging existing data systems and policies for the collection and management of key pieces of information/data and strategic plans about family–school collaboration ensures that teams capitalize upon existing resources and reserve new/additional data collection for features and family–school collaboration characteristics that are unknown to school teams. Furthermore, this enables teams to review and rethink existing plans for identifying approaches to improve family–school collaboration. Areas of alignment or consideration for family–school collaboration for schools implementing MTSS might include Title 1 strategic plans, existing MTSS fidelity and action planning tools, and any local state or district requirements and expectations related to family–school collaboration (e.g., SEBA plans, literacy plans). Below is a case study of Maxwell Elementary (a pseudonym) to guide the reader through considerations for which measures to administer when and considerations for using the data to inform student supports and inform ongoing improvements.

CASE STUDY: FAMILY–SCHOOL COLLABORATION DATA COLLECTION AND USE AT MAXWELL ELEMENTARY

Maxwell Elementary wanted to determine how families and educators were experiencing their family–school collaboration and to identify areas of improvements and changes and considerations for integration within the school's larger MTSS implementation. The MTSS leadership team started by doing a self-assessment of the TFI-FSC in the summer to identify areas for improvement and strategic planning for the upcoming school year. Based on the team's scores and discussion about priorities, the team identified three domains to focus on development during the upcoming school year including:

1. two-way communication
2. shared decision making
3. training and support for families and educators.

Figure 4.1 displays Maxwell Elementary's TFI-FSC data. Table 4.1 includes action-planning activities and associated strategies.

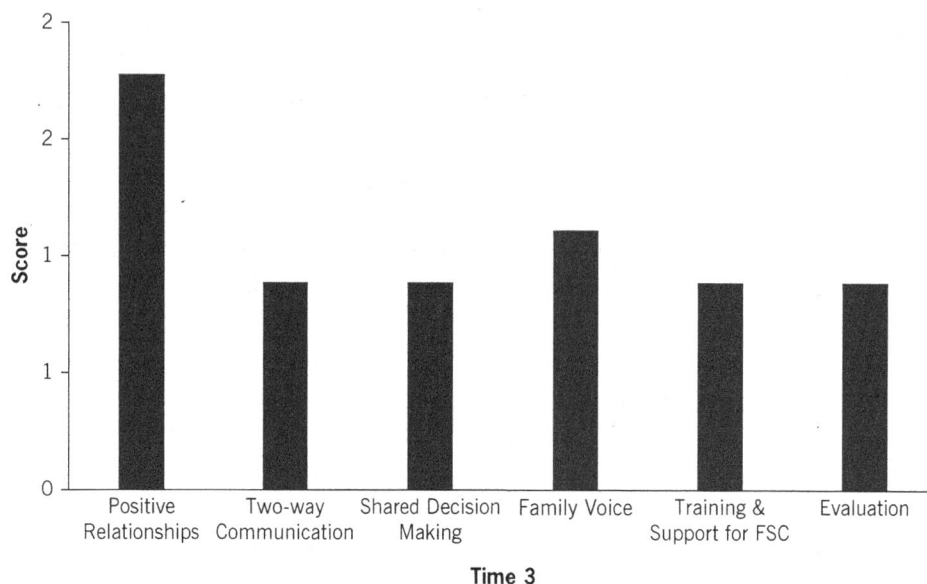

FIGURE 4.1. TFI-FSC scores at Time 3.

TABLE 4.1. Maxwell Elementary School Family–School Collaboration Action Plan and Strategies

Family–School Collaboration Action Planning	Strategy	Stakeholders/Who
Create a clear role for family–school collaboration in PBIS	Define family–school collaboration at Tier 1, Tier 2, and Tier 3	Tier 1, Tier 2, Tier 3 teams
Reach out to families proactively	Clarify role expectations, use data from families to inform actions, and make positive phone calls home	Tier 1 team, teachers, school counselors, school psychologists, administrators
Enhance the school atmosphere	Enhance school spaces, use warm greetings, use social media, make PBIS materials family friendly	Tier 1 team, all school staff and faculty
Emphasize two-way communication	Ask parents for feedback and use it. Hold "town hall" meetings or parent focus groups. Coordinate behavior support plans across home and school	Tier 1 team, administrators, teachers
Provide guidance and support for family collaboration in PBIS	Create a family subgroup of the Tier 1 team and use a tutorial about serving on school teams	Tier 1 team, State consultants

Note. Adapted from Minch, Garbacz, et al. (2019).

Based on the training and support focus, the school planned to review the Classroom Family Engagement Rubric (Flamboyan Foundation, n.d.) with staff asking they complete the self-assessment and return to the team. The team aggregated responses and planned professional development and coaching that was integrated into monthly staff meetings, reviewing best practices around the areas that needed the most support according to staff. This was shared with staff during the summer with opportunities to partner with the MTSS leadership if an identified area is a strength for opportunities to co-lead the professional development session to showcase their efforts with other staff and offer coaching to those that may be interested. The MTSS leadership team also used the FERS-E (Minch, 2012) to monitor changes in educators' beliefs, perceptions of skills, and practices for family–school collaboration as a result of training and support.

Maxwell Elementary included the questionnaire below within the school registration information packets, asking families to complete and return to the school with a chance to be entered into a raffle for a gift card. The questionnaire was adapted from existing features of family–school collaboration that staff wanted to assess in terms of prioritizing opportunities for two-way communication and shared decision making among families while maintaining a brief survey that could easily be completed by families.

The MTSS leadership team identified a member whose responsibility was family voice and input. This team member oversaw the collection and management of the survey data at the beginning of the year. They initially aggregated all responses in the school, identifying the top three communication methods preferred by families. These were targeted areas for supporting home–school communication within the school. These included email, website, and phone call. The MTSS leadership team also shared the school's plans for supporting home–school communication with families at a schoolwide level based on the information provided by families in the back-to-school questionnaire. Given the school's focus on PBIS during the upcoming year, they shared plans for communicating with families in their preferred methods around the school's Tier 1 PBIS plan during the first few months of school and previewed plans for expectations and supports for connecting with families as part of Tier 2 and 3 interventions during the upcoming year. As part of their efforts for communicating with families at Tier 1, the team planned the following:

1. Obtain family input through a short survey planned for October focused on key PBIS features (Tier 1 expectations, e-Cash, discipline responses).
2. Disseminate family tip sheets on Tier 1 expectations through the school's website.
3. Support teacher–family relationships through individual follow-up to Beginning-of-Year Questionnaire.

In addition to a schoolwide home–school communication plan, the MTSS team developed supports for classroom teachers to easily access and utilize scripts and templates for home–school communication around key events, times of year, and common reasons for communicating with families using those methods. These were shared as part of back-to-school meetings before students arrived during a staff meeting wherein the team reviewed the supports and plans with teachers, stating clear expectations that teachers should respond to each family in their classroom (homeroom) within the first 30 days of school to thank them for completing the survey and for reflecting on the families' responses, encouraging ongoing dialogue between the classroom teacher and the family. As part of the initial professional development/staff meeting, teachers received the data from families in their classroom and had time to practice developing follow-up with one to two families while the leadership team was there to provide support.

Based on classroom teachers' follow-up with families by October, the information was shared with the school's Tier 2 team to inform follow-up and family collaboration around Tier 2 and Tier 3 interventions for identified students. The team combined family input with data on student learning and teacher input to identify and organize students into appropriate interventions aligned with their needs. More information about how schools can approach using family–school collaboration data specific to students and families within Tier 2 and 3 interventions is reviewed in Chapters 6 and 7.

Following the initial staff meeting, the schoolwide MTSS leadership team used information from the Beginning-of-Year Questionnaire along with the PBIS expectations to develop tip sheets with links to additional resources and information aligned with the values, principles, and common behavioral challenges that families might experience to support families' use of positive behavioral supports and strategies at home. These were disseminated on the schools' website, and teachers were encouraged to link to them in their classroom-specific communications. The school partnered with a community family services organization to offer parenting classes and supports aligned with the top three identified concerns families indicated and offered those sessions once/week during the fall with options to attend virtually or in-person. Recordings of the sessions were saved and made available for families to access later. In October, the MTSS leadership team administered a survey about the school's PBIS plans including the Tier 1 expectations, plans for rewarding students using e-Cash, and the school's plans for responding to problem behavior and disciplinary strategies.

In November and December, the MTSS leadership team focused on positive communications with families, encouraging classroom teachers to reach out to and make positive phone calls celebrating student strengths, successes, and positive behavior to the top five families whose communication and engagement have been more challenging throughout the year. The MTSS leadership team recruited the school's itinerant and support staff to provide additional class coverage during these months to provide additional time to classroom teachers for this outreach and collaboration with families. Following the holiday break, the MTSS leadership administered a quick survey to families asking for input on communication and collaboration approaches developed during the year to allow time for adjustments before the end the year. The survey included three questions allowing families the opportunity to provide feedback and suggest improvements.

Between January and April, the MTSS leadership team shared the results of the winter check-in with staff, which indicated an overall rating of 6.5 out of 10 from families. Additionally, feedback from the survey was reviewed, and plans for addressing feedback were summarized and shared on the school's website. The MTSS leadership team continued with family workshops, sharing information and tip sheets on their website and connecting families to additional resources and supports as needs were identified. Additionally, the MTSS leadership team continued providing ongoing professional development to staff around

TABLE 4.2. Calendar of Events

June–August	• MTSS leadership team self-assessment using the TFI-FSC to identify areas for improvement and strategic planning for the upcoming school year. • Include family questionnaire in school registration packet
September	• All staff complete classroom self-assessment
October–March	• Monthly professional development around identified need areas based on TFI-FSC, staff self-assessment, and family survey data, as part of staff meetings; focused on supporting home-school communication and relationships • Teachers give family PBIS survey and share information with families about classroom PBIS expectations and values
December–January	• Brief check-in with staff and families on how efforts are going; adjust as needed
February–May	• Efforts to partner with families of students engaged in Tier 2 and 3 supports increase. • Professional development and supports to families and educators continues

family–school collaboration best practices within the monthly staff meeting and celebrated successes based on each teacher's individual classroom approach to maintaining communication with families. In the final month of school, the MTSS leadership team administered a survey to all families and educators asking about families' and educators' perspectives about family–school collaboration over the past year including feedback on how the current year was experienced and suggestions for improving plans the upcoming year.

See the proposed school calendar of activities for Maxwell Elementary (Table 4.2) and consider how your school might proactively plan collection and use of data to improve family–school partnerships.

SUMMARY

Key assessment data are essential to advance family–school collaboration. A better understanding of current practices and relationships will guide action planning. Then, those data can be reviewed yearly to determine progress and create new action plans. Data to promote family–school collaboration include relational and cross setting data that can track practices across and within settings. There are several tools and measures that school teams can use. Selection of such tools and measures is guided by the team's action plan.

Tier 2 Home–School Communication Example

Student Name _____   Date _____

3 = 0–1 reminder   **2** = 2 reminders   **1** = 3+ reminders

	Be Safe Keep hands & feet to self			**Be Respectful** Use polite language			**Be a Learner** Follow directions			**Teacher Initials**	**Success Notes**
Period 1	3	2	1	3	2	1	3	2	1		
Period 2	3	2	1	3	2	1	3	2	1		
Period 3	3	2	1	3	2	1	3	2	1		
Period 4	3	2	1	3	2	1	3	2	1		
Period 5	3	2	1	3	2	1	3	2	1		
Period 6	3	2	1	3	2	1	3	2	1		
Period 7	3	2	1	3	2	1	3	2	1		

Today's Goal: 50%   55%   60%   65%   70%   75%   80%

Today's Points _____   **Points Possible** _____   **Today's Percent** _____%

Parent/Guardian Signature _____

Congratulations for _____

CHAPTER 5

Building Family–School–Community Partnerships within Tier 1 of Schools' MTSS

As reviewed earlier, MTSS in schools represents a strategy for organizing programming across tiers involving schoolwide strategies (Tier 1), early intervention for students presenting early problems and or conditions of risk (Tier 2), and more intensive intervention for students with more serious challenges (see Shogren et al., 2017; Sugai & Horner, 2002a). The best way to articulate MTSS is probably through PBIS, a framework for organizing school practices across the three tiers emphasizing effective systems, data, and practices such as teams, data-based decision making, choosing, and implementing evidence-based programs, coaching and implementation support, and progress monitoring/outcome evaluation (Sugai & Horner, 2006).

Data documenting the effectiveness of PBIS are fairly comprehensive with studies documenting positive impacts in reducing school discipline (Bradshaw et al., 2010), improving perceptions of school safety (Horner et al., 2009), and in improving student academic performance (Lassen et al., 2006; Simonsen et al., 2012). However, implementing PBIS with fidelity presents a challenge for many schools (Bohanon et al., 2009; Scott et al. 2009), and there is also a need to tailor programming related to school demographics (e.g., rural, urban, suburban; elementary, middle, high school; race/ethnicity, socioeconomic status) and other factors (Putnam et al., 2009).

Notably, limited family engagement is common within PBIS and MTSS, and evidence indicates this factor limits the effectiveness of programming (Garbacz et al., 2016). For example, improvements in family engagement by schools are associated with greater consistency in behavioral expectations between home and school (Garbacz et al., 2016) which is a facilitator of positive student behavior (Feil et al., 2014) and school attendance (Allen & Tracy, 2004). There is also some evidence that when schools increase focus on family engagement and active involvement in the MTSS there is improved impact of interventions on students' social, emotional, behavioral, and academic outcomes (Feil et al., 2014; Pearce, 2009; Sénéchal & Young, 2008).

In 2015, the Center on PBIS, funded by the Office of Special Education Programs, recognized the critical need to enhance family engagement and leadership in schools' MTSS, convened a diverse workgroup to focus on this topic, and developed and widely disseminated an e-book in 2017: *Aligning and Integrating Family Engagement in Positive Behavioral Interventions and Supports (PBIS): Concepts and Strategies for Families and Schools in Key Contexts* (Weist et al., 2017). The e-book emphasized the need for a dramatic change in the construct of family engagement in schools:

> Increasingly, staff and leaders from all youth serving systems including education, mental health, child welfare, juvenile justice, disabilities, primary healthcare and others are recognizing the paradigm of professional "experts" telling children, youth and families what they should be doing is not effective. . . . This directive, hierarchical model suggests superiority of the professional over the student or family member, promotes distance in the relationship and negative reactions and feelings, and decreases the likelihood of positive change occurring. . . . Yet, these models perpetuate as in reality children, youth and families have little voice about what happens in the systems they participate in . . . However, a new paradigm is emerging and gaining strength, characterized by equal partnerships among children, youth, families, and youth-serving staff and leaders, and the research base is growing and documenting that when these partnerships are in place positive educational, health, mental health, social and occupational outcomes for youth are promoted. (p. 1)

Foundational to this work are schoolwide or Tier 1 strategies as reviewed in this chapter. Within e-book referenced above, Fix et al. (2017) recommended that at Tier 1, schools should use relevant resources to focus on the environment and consider whether it is engaging or stimulating for families. Schools should also focus on messaging that encourage families' active involvement in school programming. Fix et al. (2017) also recommended running workshops for school staff, students, and families focusing on mental health literacy, including review of mental health challenges commonly experienced by students, strategies for mental health promotion and wellness, and encouragement for families and students to play and active role in developing and leading these workshops. These recommendations are consistent with an increased emphasis on mental health literacy for children and youth around the world (Clauss-Ehlers et al., 2020; Kutcher et al., 2015) and its importance as a Tier 1 strategy, particularly in relation to significantly elevated mental health needs among families and youth related to the pandemic and other significant societal stressors experienced in the past two years (Dutch International Mental Health Hub, 2021; Hertz & Barrios, 2021). Fix et al. (2017) also urged families and youth to join school teams and plan for all actions within the MTSS—a critical theme within a broader effort focused on improving school team functioning, as a fundamental indicator of the quality of the school's MTSS (see Splett et al., 2017).

Increasingly, these strategies are being included in tools to measure family engagement in schools (see Minch et al., 2023). For example, the FSCA has led the development of the Tiered Fidelity Inventory—Family–School Collaboration (TFI-FSC; Garbacz, Minch, Cook, et al., 2019). This measure expands on a core fidelity assessment for PBIS—the Tiered Fidelity Inventory (TFI; Algozinne et al., 2014)—including 14 additional items completed by school teams to assess the quality of the school's family–school collaboration practices. The measure includes six domains, reflecting constructs reviewed in this chapter of (1) positive home–school relationships, (2) two-way communication, (3) shared decision making, (4) family voice for equitable discipline, (5) training and support for family–school collaboration, and (6) evaluation (Minch et al., 2023). Use of the TFI-FSC is consistent with schools prioritizing continuous quality improvement practices for their MTSS. Combining use of the measure with ongoing qualitative assessment and analyses (e.g., use of focus groups as in the Abshier–Scherder case study) will further engage families and youth as leaders of the MTSS along with the school environment, setting the stage for effective Tier 1, 2, and 3 programming.

Collier and Rizzardi (2020) reviewed studies on effective implementation of MTSS, and as above, found most literature related to PBIS, with five prominent themes: (1) implementing PBIS with fidelity, (2) assuring program buy-in, (3) providing effective training for staff, (4) scaling up effective strategies, and (5) increasing family engagement and leadership in programming, the focus of this chapter. As emphasized in earlier chapters, unfortunately, core MTSS practices in schools often do not include family voice/leadership (Garbacz et al., 2016), and this is true for Tier 1 practices.

Collier and Rizzardi (2020) conducted a focus group with 14 stakeholders including six family members, three teachers, two mental health providers, two researchers, and one student, with the emphasis on ways schools can strengthen schoolwide approaches within their MTSS. A number of themes were related to increasing family engagement and leadership, including participants feeling that (1) families were excluded and/or ignored during meetings with school staff; (2) students and their parents/caregivers were often feeling blamed for students' social–emotional behavior challenges; (3) there is a need for more purposeful efforts by schools to empower students and families to have a voice in MTSS programming; and (4) emphasis on mental health literacy is a particularly promising strategy for engaging students and families, reducing stigma about social–emotional behavior issues, and promoting appropriate help-seeking (as presented earlier).

The above research by Collier and Rizzardi (2020) was part of a broader project funded by Eugene Washington Engagement Patient-Centered Outcomes Research Institute (PCORI) Award. It focused on strengthening school behavioral health (involving clinicians from the mental health system working with schools' MTSS) and programming (*Developing the Southeastern School Behavioral Health Community*, EAIN-2874, 2015–2017). The project involved diverse stakeholders (including youth and families as in the Collier and Rizzardi study) to illuminate ways school behavioral health programming can be improved and to expand and strengthen the Southeastern School Behavioral Health Community (see *www.schoolbehavioralhealth.org*). In addition to the focus group conducted by Collier and Rizzardi, seven other focus groups focused on four other critical themes (quality improvement, cultural competence/humility, implementation support, family partnerships) and three priority populations (child welfare, juvenile justice, military families) for the advancement of school behavioral health. Project investigators, advisors, and stakeholders analyzed qualitative data from all eight focus groups (examined systematically with the Nvivo program) and identified 34 critical themes related to strengthening school behavioral health (Weist et al., 2020). While all 34 themes in some way relate to enhancing family engagement and leadership in schools' MTSS, 20 of them directly connect to this priority and reflect ways schools can build infrastructure for families to be more involved in the MTSS. These recommendations are grouped within theme areas included in Table 5.1. These theme areas are Enhancing Family Voice and Partnerships, Developing Resources, and Specific Programmatic Emphases.

To further illustrate how these strategies could be used to strengthen family and student voice in school planning/programming, we provide more detail here on recommendations 3, 8, and 9. Recommendation 3 is focused on effective school teams and family and student leadership and participation on teams. A randomized trial focused on the interconnected systems framework (ISF) for school mental health, and PBIS (see Eber et al., 2020) emphasized the importance of family leadership on school teams for participating elementary schools in two southern school districts. However, despite ongoing efforts by the research team and implementation coaches to increase such family leadership, with this theme also emphasized by an ISF fidelity measure (Splett, Perales, Al-Khatib, Raborn, & Weist, 2020), schools continued to exclude family members from teams. Discussion with school leaders revealed a concern that having families on teams would compromise confidentiality for students receiving Tier 3 intervention. To address this concern, project leaders emphasized that families should be involved in discussions of programming at all tiers, beginning at Tier 1, progressing to Tier 2, and then discussing systems, data, and practices at Tier 3, without discussing individual students. At the point in the meeting where individual students were to be discussed, family members would then be dismissed to avoid any confidentiality concerns. As a result of this clarification, more teams became receptive to family involvement, leading to a subsequent increase in such involvement. This example illustrates that at times barriers perceived to limit family leadership in schools can be openly discussed and overcome.

As presented above, recommendation 8 emphasizes user-friendly school and community resource directories. This work could be conducted through a District–Community Leadership Team (DCLT) charged with evaluating and continuously improving MTSS efforts in district schools (see Eber et al., 2020). Ideally, DCLTs meet at least quarterly, have strong meeting agendas and well-organized meetings (see the Team-Initiated Problem Solving process, Todd et al., 2011), and are inclusive of all relevant stakeholder groups (e.g., families, students, teachers, school administrators, mental health staff, leaders and staff from other youth-serving systems, faith community members, and business leaders). Through a resource mapping/analysis process, the DCLT would assess programming occurring in district schools across Tiers 1, 2, and 3, identifying programs that have intended positive impacts and organizing resources on each of them. In addition, team members would identify needed but missing resources through lens of specific programs for specific issues (e.g., to assist students contending with attention issues, to maximize positive impacts of virtual learning) as well as general resources for students and families (e.g., tutoring, after-school, recreational programs). This resource mapping team of the DCLT is co-led by a parent, teacher, and school counselor, seeks and obtains active student input, and keeps organized and evolving directory maintained on district and school building websites. The team regularly evaluates material included in the directory, adds new important resources once they are identified, and removes resources that are not being used or are deemed less helpful.

Recommendation 9 reflects collaborative school–community health fairs. Prior to the pandemic, an elementary-middle school in Baltimore held these fairs on an annual basis, usually in mid- to late spring, which was associated with better weather. A range of community organizations including health and social service agencies, after-school and recreational programs, health promotion initiatives associated with churches, and community colleges, along with private businesses (e.g., restaurants, gyms) participated including materials for students, families, and school staff and mechanisms to sign up for health promotion programs. These health fairs were planned primarily by families, with the assistance of school and community staff, and often included athletic events (e.g., kick-ball games between school faculty, parents, and students) and food trucks. Funding for the fairs was supported by local foundations (*Effective Mental Health Promotion in Two Baltimore Schools;* Abell, Blaustein, Krieger, and Straus Foundations, $420,000; 2006–2009; M. Weist, Principal Investigator) that placed emphasis on improving school environments by significantly increasing family and student leadership. These became signature events, greeted with much enthusiasm by local families, and school and community stakeholders.

To further illuminate strategies used to promote family engagement/leadership within schools' MTSS, we present the case study below, developed by school system leaders Dama Abshier and Erin Scherder, who helped to lead the implementation of the ISF for school mental health and PBIS as part of a 4-year randomized controlled trial funded by the National Institute of Justice (*Interconnecting PBIS and School Mental Health to Improve School Safety: A Randomized Trial.* #2015-CK-BX-0018, 2016–2020). The ISF builds from core practices for effective PBIS as above and adds a systematic partnership with the mental health system to strengthen evidence-based practices within schools' MTSS (e.g., greater Tier 2 and 3 programming, enhanced interventions for students with internalizing issues; see Eber et al., 2020; Weist et al., 2018). Within a randomized controlled trial comparing the ISF to PBIS-alone, or PBIS with mental health clinicians (with no strategy for interconnecting efforts) operating in two southern school districts, Abshier and Scherder played key roles in ISF implementation and shared their observations on the critical role of family engagement/leadership within it.

CASE STUDY: SHIFTING THE PARADIGM FROM FAMILY/STUDENT INVOLVEMENT TO PARTNERSHIP

Dama Abshier, University of South Florida, and Erin Scherder, University of South Carolina

Family and youth partnership and leadership in schoolwide systems and practices contribute to positive outcomes for students, staff, and schools, yet continue to receive insufficient emphasis (Garbacz et al., 2017). Traditional efforts focusing on involvement are briefly described below as the impetus for this case study, which will provide practical examples of effective strategies and implementation recommendations for encouraging authentic family and youth engagement, based on the work of two ISF coaches. The ISF is a more streamlined approach to addressing school mental health and wellness, while eliminating barriers inherent in systems that previously have operated separately. This is achieved by blending the strengths of PBIS and school mental health into a single system of delivery focused on prevention and intervention within a multi-tiered framework (Barrett et al., 2013; Eber et al., 2020). The examples below highlight how families and students played leadership roles within the ISF, as stakeholders and collaborative partners, in creating a positive school culture, through the development of important policies, procedures, expectations, and celebrations.

Traditional positive family involvement consists of opportunities for families to provide a service (e.g., chaperone), observe student performances (e.g., talent show), and receive information (e.g., newsletter) and/or resources (e.g., Title I funded books), with the assumption that families have the time, ability, comfort, and shared vision of the school. Traditional positive student involvement consists of opportunities to assist with daily operations (e.g., safety patrols), receive acknowledgement (e.g., awards), participate in extracurricular activities (e.g., sports, clubs, arts), and perform (e.g., chorus), with the assumption that students are interested in such activities and meet the criteria to participate. Traditional corrective family involvement consists of communicating student academic or behavioral performance (e.g., progress reports, discipline referrals), requesting a parent conference, or expressing dissatisfaction about an incident. Traditional corrective student involvement consists of students receiving corrective feedback regarding academic and/or behavioral performance in need of improvement. Diverse stakeholders (in all relevant dimensions, e.g., age, gender, race/ethnicity) and researchers agree that these realities of family partnership in schools fall far short of the vision of effective partnership and the associated wide range of positive impacts for students and schools (Weist et al., 2017).

> "She [the teacher] always approached me that perspective of 'What's going on with him?' rather than 'Let me tell you all the things your child is not doing well in school' . . . our conversations were so productive because of that."

Families and Youth as Collaborative Partners

Established schoolwide expectations are an important part of the work in our school districts and in the collaborative study. They are further defined to include how students and adults can demonstrate the expected behaviors in specific locations across campus. In an attempt to move away from family involvement and toward family and youth partnership, we invited families to work alongside the Tier 1 team to create a matrix of family expectations and rules that they could use across settings within their home environment. During the creation of the Family Matrix, parents expressed that they were unaware of recommended developmental bedtimes; therefore, a hyperlink to a developmental bedtimes chart was provided as a reference for families to establish healthy bedtime routines at home. This opened up dialogue where families felt comfortable asking questions and sharing needs. As a result, educators added more hyperlinks to resources of the Family Matrix, thereby creating a more useful tool for families.

> "She always started off the conversation with 'What do you think would be helpful?'"

This approach was educational, practical, and beneficial for our families, and it provided the opportunity to ask for input related to our expectations and rules outlined in the schoolwide matrix. Having families create their own Family Matrix provided them with the opportunity to understand the concept of creating shared expectations and apply it in their home environment so they can see the value. It also provided them with a hands-on experience, which could be later used when providing authentic input on the schoolwide expectations and rules outlined by the schools' matrix. Simply asking for their input would have resulted in surface-level input and maybe even a "stamp of approval" rather than genuine collaboration. Through the MTSS team, collaboration with families became embedded through the use of interest surveys where families shared ideas on resources and strategies for the school to be more family-welcoming, regularly held parent focus groups, and social media outreach (e.g., polls, comments, messaging) to ensure families could partner and provide leadership in the format that was most convenient for them.

We engaged students at Tier 1 in the form of testimonials, skits, and integration into teaming structures. Students created and performed a play, *What It Means to SOAR*, to teach parents the schoolwide expectations during a Parent—Teacher Organization (PTO) meeting. The play was recorded and posted to the school's website. Student grade-level representatives participated in MTSS meetings to provide input related to universal behavior concerns. When the team reviewed universal behavior data and found frequent inappropriate behaviors occurring on the playground, student representatives hypothesized it was happening because teachers lacked a full view of the playground from their assigned supervision location. When the MTSS team informed the teachers of the problem location that was identified by the students, teachers adjusted their supervision location, increasing proximity, and the inappropriate behaviors decreased. Students felt empowered as important members of the MTSS team and gained credibility from their teachers.

Providing families and students with leadership and collaboration opportunities at a foundational level resulted in better understanding the value of establishing and teaching expectations at the schoolwide and/or familywide level. In turn, they were more confident providing feedback on our schoolwide expectations and were more comfortable having leadership roles within our Tier 1 discussions. Collaborating with families and youth beginning at Tier 1, rather than only at the Tier 3 level, naturally established a level of consensus and buy-in for families and students to have more proactive roles.

> "A teacher came to the house and met her students and the parents before the school year started, and that was kind of nerve racking, but it was really cool and I will never forget that . . . it felt really special."

Strategic teaming was required to determine ways to foster family and youth collaboration consistently across tiers, beginning with inclusion of family and youth voice at Tier 1 meetings. Selection of a natural fit for family member representation began with parents who are already involved with creating the Family Matrix, leading initiatives within the school, parent volunteers with school knowledge, and/or parents who have worked or currently work in a school setting. With this foundational understanding of the schoolwide Tier 1 practices, families were better-equipped to engage in the selection, implementation, and review of interventions and discussions regarding the Tier 2 and Tier 3 systems of support for our students. Pamphlets were created in collaboration with families and youth to be sent home frequently to inform families about the continuum of interventions available at school along with a list of relevant school and community resources and the best ways to access them.

We will continue to engage families and youth by seeking their perspectives, understanding perceptions, encouraging active participation in MTSS teams, supporting bidirectional communication, and collaborating to ensure families and students are truly partners and leaders in decision making. As a result of families and students being part of the teams and even leading discussions and sharing their recommendations, programming across all tiers within the MTSS is strengthened, and awareness is raised on what is working and what needs improvement. Furthermore, we are moving the needle toward enhanced social, emotional, behavioral, and academic outcomes for students. Table 5.1 presents a summary of our ideas for strengthening family and youth partnerships in schools.

Our Successful Family and Youth Partnership and Leadership Practices

- Include family member representation on MTSS teams (Tier 1, 2, and 3 team discussions) to enhance dialogue and assure family and youth voice.
- Ensure family members and students are a part of intervention selection, implementation, progress monitoring, and fidelity to maximize program effectiveness.
- Emphasize bidirectional communication and collaboration and transparently share school- and MTSS-based progress reports as frequently as possible to empower families and youth as co-creators of the school environment.
- Ask families to participate in the creation of behavioral expectations for the PBIS Matrix to ensure relevance and understanding of schoolwide expectations. For example, leverage active caregiver groups such as the PTO, booster clubs, and school improvement councils.
- Develop and revise the PBIS Matrix with family and youth input emphasizing their co-ownership of the system and moving to language that is accessible to all, with communication occurring often and in diverse formats (e.g., email, newsletter, documents sent home, creative use of diverse social media platforms).
- Collaborate with families to develop a Family Matrix, replicating the structure of the school's PBIS Matrix but tailored for family-determined expectations and values, to be used at home and to promote consistency of expectations and learning across school and home environments.
- Create opportunities for student engagement beginning at Tier 1 through testimonials, skits, and integration into teaming. Facilitate leadership opportunities for students to share and teach behavioral expectations with peers and family members.
- Solicit student and family voice through interest surveys regularly held focus groups and social media (e.g., polls, comments, messaging).
- Share the continuum of supports and interventions available to families through brochures and other communication outlets to increase awareness of and active utilization of these resources by families and students.

TABLE 5.1. Theme Areas and Practices for Advancing Tier 1 Family–School Collaboration

Enhancing Family Voice and Partnerships

- Provide multiple and varied ways for families and diverse community members to drive the SBH agenda and build relationships among school and mental health staff, students, and families.
- Develop resources for guiding and expanding SBH programs with families and students.
- Expand teams to ensure they comprise all disciplines, including families and students, and ensure clarity of roles for all team members and effective team meetings.
- Create authentic roles for students and family members as decision makers in schools and support in roles to co-create the education environment with school staff and mental health system collaborators.
- Include caregivers with experience in juvenile justice and child welfare in developing and implementing district- and state-wide policies to improve programs and supports for students encountering these systems.
- Develop a statewide advisory group that includes older youth and families to coordinate cross-system collaboration between education, mental health, child welfare, and juvenile justice in developing SBH programs accessible to the range of students who are impacted by these additional systems.
- In communities including more military stakeholders, ensure that soldiers, officers, and other family members have a role in decision making at the district and school levels.

Developing Resources

- Maintain student- and family-friendly directories of school and community resources to help students, families and school staff connect to these resources and provide ongoing staff support to ensure they are up to date.
- Conduct community fairs planned by school staff, families, and students to involve other community agencies and resources to help build connections with them.
- Embrace technology to improve communication/collaboration among all professionals and stakeholder groups.
- Make data easier to use and involve diverse school staff, families, and students in reviewing and making data-driven recommendations for SBH interventions.
- Ensure all programs and services within the multi-tiered system of support (MTSS) including Tier 3 treatment services are available to all students/families regardless of health insurance status, and significantly involve private insurers more in funding SBH

Specific Programmatic Emphases

- Stigma is a significant issue limiting the use and impact of SBH, and there is a compelling need to train teachers and students together in mental health literacy, which reduces stigma and is associated with improved help seeking and functioning.
- Build wellness-focused training (e.g., coping, exercise, nutrition, stress management, mindfulness) programming for students, families, teachers, and school staff including SBH staff from community agencies.
- Train staff, families and students on trauma and trauma-sensitive approaches in schools.
- Increase compassionate and effective approaches for students receiving exclusionary discipline (e.g., suspension/expulsion) to move toward reducing blame and building supportive programs to help re-integrate them into their schools.
- Reduce use of alternative school programming for at-risk students, and when these programs are used, ensure appropriate and supportive transitions are made to the program and then back to their home school
- Develop strategies to be able to identify students involved in juvenile justice and/or child welfare systems and provide supportive services in school to them and their caregivers.
- Provide supportive liaison/case management services to families/caregivers with connections to juvenile justice and child welfare to assist them and their students to stay connected to the school, its curriculum, and supportive programs.

- Share resources and accessibility of interventions available across the tiered continuum through multiple modalities (e.g., in-person, virtually, written, infographics) in caregiver language to improve family and community knowledge of universal practices.
- Create a staff directory of all school-connected personnel, including staff from collaborating community agencies and representatives/leaders from family- and youth-led organizations. Ensure the directory evolves to maintain accuracy and is broadly and regularly shared with families, students, and all school stakeholders.

SUMMARY

The movement to increase family and student engagement and leadership in schools' MTSS is gaining significant momentum (Garbacz, Minch, et al., 2020). Many Tier 1 strategies can be used to enhance family and youth leadership. These strategies include empowering student and family voice and having students and families in leadership roles in the development and sharing of user-friendly resources; organizing school–community fairs; running training programs focused on mental health literacy, wellness, and trauma (to name a few themes); expanding and improving communication strategies; using data for decision making and reducing exclusionary discipline; and reaching out to underserved populations. Qualitative research, including 20 recommendations grouped into themes of enhancing voice and partnerships, building resources, and specific programmatic emphases were presented to escalate progress on this paradigm change, with elaboration on specific examples, including families and youth as leaders on school teams, developing user-friendly school–community resources, and holding collaborative school–community health fairs.

CHAPTER 6

Embedding Family–School Collaboration in Tier 2 Systems and Practices

Sarah Fefer, Zack Santana, and Kimberli Breen

We begin this chapter by defining Tier 2 and outlining the features of Tier 2 intervention within MTSS. We then outline the multiple dimensions that can be considered when designing and implementing a robust continuum of Tier 2 supports with a focus on family–school collaboration. Next, we provide examples of simple and adaptable intervention starting points focused on collaboration to address both student and family-focused concerns. We then outline considerations to intensify interventions for students or families and share examples of Tier 2 practices within a continuum of family–school collaboration.

What do you think of when you consider family–school collaboration at Tier 2? What does your school offer to students *or* families who demonstrate a need for more support? If you're reading this, then it is likely that you can list examples of specific practices in response to these questions. It is also likely that the majority of the supports on your list focus on student needs. Over time, we have learned more about when and how to support student strengths, opportunities, and challenges through supplemental or Tier 2 supports in schools. As reviewed in earlier chapters of this book, many schools are implementing comprehensive MTSS using data-based decision making to organize and deliver proactive supplemental supports to cover the "BASEs" (i.e., behavioral, academic, social, and emotional

---

Sarah Fefer, PhD, is Professor in the College of Education at the University of Massachusetts Amherst.

Zack Santana is a doctoral candidate in the Department of School Psychology at the University of Massachusetts Amherst.

Kimberly Breen, MS, is a national educational consultant based in Chicago, Illinois.

domains) in promoting positive outcomes for all students (alternatively presented as SEBA or social, emotional, behavioral, academic domains). However, despite repeated demonstrations of the importance of family engagement in education (e.g., Fan & Chen, 2001; Smith et al., 2020), many schools use a *one size fits all* approach to family–school collaboration. Even in schools with efficient and effective MTSS in place for students, we do not often apply this multi-tiered logic to deliver supports for families (Weist et al., 2017). Common family–school collaboration practices include family outreach and schoolwide communication, such as a principal's newsletter and parent information nights (Garbacz et al., 2018), and increased communication with caregivers[1] of children identified as needing individualized supports such as caregivers hired through formal systems such as 504 accommodations or special education (Weingarten et al., 2020). Proactive communication from school to home has been shown to be a common and powerful way to engage families and promote positive student outcomes (Smith et al., 2020). However, many engagement practices place demands on families without considering the motivations and specific needs of caregivers, or they are narrowly defined by times when families physically enter the school building. A significant gap exists in our understanding of how schools can proactively partner with families who may benefit from early identification and supports to bolster protective factors and decrease risk. The purpose of this chapter is to discuss systems and practices to embed family–school collaboration within Tier 2 of MTSS, with a focus on providing supplemental supports for students *and* caregivers.

WHAT IS TIER 2 WITHIN MTSS?

Proactive early intervention is a central component of MTSS implementation widely acknowledged for enabling us to address challenges more efficiently and effectively right when they begin to emerge, rather than waiting for a larger concern or a more pervasive problem to develop. This is what Tier 2 is all about—identifying and supporting individuals or groups who are not responding to Tier 1 efforts (e.g., not meeting schoolwide expectations) in order to add additional supports proactively, rather than reactively, to promote positive student outcomes. Tier 2 interventions are meant to be simple, efficient, and delivered similarly for all students receiving the support (Anderson et al., 2012). These supports are offered in addition to Tier 1 supports and aim to prevent the development and escalation of problem behaviors, along with mental health, academic, and social–emotional challenges, by reducing risk factors and enhancing protective factors in students' lives (Yong & Cheney, 2013). Establishing effective Tier 2 systems should be an essential priority within our schools given that supplemental supports are needed by approximately 20% (i.e., 15% who need Tier 2, and 5% who need Tier 2 + Tier 3) of students in schools implementing MTSS with fidelity, and these supports can delay or even prevent the need for more time

---

[1] Throughout this chapter, we use the terms "family" and "caregiver," rather than "parent," to ensure that our language is inclusive of all family arrangements.

and resource intensive service delivery (Hawken et al., 2009). Consideration of student and family resources and needs is a necessary, and often missing, focus to meet the core prevention goals of Tier 2 supports.

The critical features of Tier 2 include providing additional instructional time for skill development around schoolwide expectations, increasing structure and prompts, increasing opportunity for feedback, and having the intervention available to anyone at any time (Algozzine et al., 2014). Schools with established MTSS systems have a range of Tier 2 interventions to meet specific needs, train staff in Tier 2 procedures, and adapt their approaches to enhance fit for the school, student, or family (Hawken et al., 2009). Data from multiple sources should be used to identify those who are most likely to benefit from brief low-resource interventions, and there are procedures in place for students, teachers, and caregivers to request assistance as well (Algozzine et al., 2014). Screening and progress monitoring data are reviewed regularly to evaluate intervention effectiveness and to determine whether supports should be modified or faded. Some resources specifically include school–home communication (Anderson & Borgmeier, 2010; Anderson et al., 2012) or caregiver involvement at home (Yong & Cheney, 2013) as critical features of Tier 2. Given the evidence of more positive student outcomes associated with family–school partnership (e.g., Smith et al., 2019), we propose that family input and preferences should be integrated within each of the aforementioned Tier 2 components *and* that the needs of caregivers should also be considered within Tier 2. In this chapter, we define Tier 2 as a layered framework of service delivery that increases the duration, intensity, and/or frequency of instruction and/or support based on the response, strengths, and needs of students, families, and school staff. Appendix 6.A includes example language that could be used to introduce the concept of Tier 2 within MTSS to families.

MULTIDIMENSIONAL APPROACH TO FAMILY–SCHOOL COLLABORATION IN TIER 2

A focus on a multidimensional continuum of systems and practices within Tier 2 may be essential to address calls for more sustainable, equitable, and systematic approaches to family engagement (e.g., Weiss et al., 2010). However, it is unsurprising that the middle of the MTSS triangle remains a relatively uncharted territory for family–school collaboration given the complexities of extending our Tier 2 logic into the family domain (Hawken et al. 2021; Weist et al., 2017). It is well documented that educators request and require support to effectively collaborate with families, and that capacity-building for school staff is an essential component for building effective family–school partnerships (Mapp & Kuttner, 2013). Tier 2 data, systems, and practices that embed family–school collaboration are layered and multi-faceted. Next, we outline several challenges and complexities.

Tier 2 family–school collaboration requires us to consider data and requests indicating areas of challenge or struggle, alongside indicators of strengths, exceptionalities, interests, and leadership opportunities among educators, families, and students. This focus on strengths and challenges across multiple stakeholder groups may be difficult for school teams, as our current systems and practices may operate from a deficit perspective and/or may focus only on students. It is common for schools to place blame on families for student challenges, while also having high expectations for caregivers to engage in school-based involvement activities (e.g., parent–teacher association/organizations, volunteering, conferences). Embedding family–school collaboration within MTSS may help school staff minimize potential biases in their perceptions and practices through the development of data-based decision rules and clear application of expectations for all students and families (Leverson et al., 2021). Another challenge for schools is that a foundation of trust and communication between school and families may be a necessary prerequisite for effective collaboration at Tier 2; however, this can be fostered by Tier 1 family supports in MTSS such as proactive outreach about student behavior or a schoolwide caregiver assessment of strengths and needs (Garbacz et al., 2020, 2021).

To add an additional layer of complexity, educators may approach family–school collaboration within Tier 2 with supports provided to students, caregivers, or both simultaneously. Most commonly, we provide Tier 2 interventions because Tier 1 supports are not sufficient for a student's needs or goals, and therefore, we may partner with caregivers to plan and deliver Tier 2 interventions focused specifically on the child's success in school. When family–school collaboration is embedded within MTSS, schools can also partner with families because the caregivers themselves have not demonstrated a response to universal supports or responded to invitations for involvement from the school. We would then implement Tier 2 supports to enhance caregiver success or encourage increased caregiver participation in their child's education rather than starting with a child-focused intervention option. In other cases, student and family needs may overlap, and we provide Tier 2 interventions that bolster student and caregiver success simultaneously. To build this layered and multi-target Tier 2, schools must offer training and support for families *and* school staff to provide knowledge, skills, and resources needed to effectively partner across home and school contexts. This approach is aligned with a dual capacity-building framework (Mapp & Kuttner, 2013) that highlights a need to build the capabilities, connections, cognition, and confidence of both educators and families around family–school partnerships to promote student success. This approach to Tier 2 is anchored in the idea that culturally responsive practices are a prerequisite to effective family–school collaboration, and that family–school partnership is an essential element of culturally responsive education (Hammond, 2018). An MTSS framework cannot be fully implemented without direct consideration of family and school culture due to the focus on contextual fit to guide decisions about specific practices within and across each tier, and therefore, the specific elements of family–school collaboration in Tier 2 may vary across schools and communities (Leverson et al., 2021). The purpose of this chapter is to share systems and practices aligned with this layered, multi-target, asset focused, culturally responsive, and capacity-building perspective to ensure that students and families who could benefit from Tier 2 support are identified and matched with simple and effective interventions in a time and resource efficient manner.

STATUS OF COLLABORATION IN TIER 2

There are many opportunities for family–school collaboration within Tier 2 of MTSS. Caregivers may be actively involved in Tier 1 or Tier 2 teams, in the identification of students for Tier 2 supports (e.g., parent-rated screening forms), in designing or tailoring the specifics of the intervention (e.g., to specify intervention targets, to design a reinforcement systems), in implementing components of the intervention (e.g., to provide feedback about student behavior, delivering incentives), or in evaluating intervention success (e.g., to provide input about effectiveness or feasibility or about whether the intervention enhanced family quality of life). However, there is variability in terms of the extent to which family participation in Tier 2 interventions is documented and discussed. Although the most commonly used Tier 2 interventions include a component of caregiver participation, limited empirical research is available about the fidelity and potential added value of the caregiver components specifically (Hawken et al., 2009). A review of empirical support for Check-In, Check-Out (CICO) showed that 94% of studies included a caregiver signature on the points card as a component of the intervention (Wolf et al., 2016). It is promising that a review of Tier 2 social–behavioral interventions found that caregiver involvement, in the form of signing and providing feedback on daily progress reports or direct caregiver training, was present across 83% of the studies reviewed and is a common element of evidence-based Tier 2 supports such as CICO, First Step Next, and Fast Track (Yong & Cheney, 2013). However, another review of Tier 2 behavioral interventions within MTSS showed that only one of the 28 studies reviewed included caregiver input for identification of students in need of Tier 2 supports and did not include other information about caregiver components (Bruhn et al., 2014). Within the research on CICO specifically, a lack of school outreach to families and low caregiver participation has been documented along with some evidence that positive student outcomes can be achieved without caregiver participation (e.g., Hawken et al., 2007). Some studies have even eliminated the caregiver component of CICO in schools, reporting a history of caregiver unresponsiveness (McDaniel & Bruhn, 2016), while others have elaborated upon the caregiver component by providing training on CICO procedures directly to caregivers (Turtura et al., 2014). Current CICO guidelines (Hawken et al., 2021) suggest a more family-focused approach by providing families with choices about how we communicate and collaborate with them. Rather than requiring that the daily progress reports be signed and returned, families should be asked at the beginning of CICO about whether they want to see and sign the report card daily or weekly, or whether they would rather receive updates in another way. We have found that there is much more information available about caregiver involvement in student-focused interventions, compared to information about school-based preventive interventions for families or targeting family outcomes. More information is needed to understand the specific benefits and challenges of family–school collaboration in Tier 2 interventions, and about when, for whom, and for what concerns family–school collaboration is most essential or beneficial. Since the benefits of family–school collaboration are well documented and far reaching (e.g., Jeynes, 2003; Sheridan et al., 2019; Smith et al., 2020), it is logical and worthwhile to conclude that partnering with families in Tier 2 can enhance student and family outcomes.

IDENTIFYING STUDENTS IN NEED OF MORE SUPPORT

Effective Tier 2 systems rely on efficient methods to support a swift and data-based transition to Tier 2 supports, which should always be built upon and added to the existing universal instruction and strategies implemented at Tier 1. Within MTSS, the data-based decision making around Tier 2 supports for students often includes one or more of these three methods:

1. use of existing data (e.g., attendance, office discipline referrals) to determine cutpoints for access to more support
2. request for assistance forms or processes
3. universal screening (Algozzine et al., 2014).

Schools are often encouraged to start with data they are already collecting and determine how to review and use those data systematically. Although these processes do not explicitly include family–school collaboration, caregiver input may be welcome through either a request for assistance (i.e., caregivers share their concerns about their child's progress and request support for their child or for their family; see Form 6.1 for an example) or ratings on screening forms related to their child's academic, behavioral, or social–emotional strengths and challenges. Although a review of school-based behavioral screening processes showed that caregivers were rarely asked to serve as informants (Hendricker et al., 2017), recent findings indicate that to plan multi-tiered positive family supports, we need proactive caregiver-rated screeners and a brief, positively worded solution that could be used to identify student and family strengths and needs (Garbacz et al., 2021). There is certainly room for improvement in collaborating with families to identify students who may benefit from increased supports through Tier 2, and we know even less about how to identify caregivers who may benefit from more support than what is provided universally to all families.

A Sample Request for Assistance Form to Be Used by All Stakeholders

REQUEST FOR ASSISTANCE

Student Name: _____   Grade: _____

Date: _____   Student has an IEP/504 (circle one):   Yes   No   ?

1. I am a (circle one):   Teacher/team   Family Member   Student

Name: _____ Relationship to student: _____

2. Type of Support (check all that apply)

☐ Student   ☐ Classroom
☐ Family   ☐ School
☐ Other _____

3. Area of Support (check all that apply)

☐ Meeting basic needs   ☐ Social/Emotional
☐ Academics   ☐ Physical Health
☐ Behavior   ☐ Other _____

4. What led you to this request for assistance? *(provide available data or explanation)*

_____

_____

Submit to front office to be reviewed by a student support team member within 48 hours.

One primary challenge related to increasing collaboration with families in Tier 2 is the limited guidance on determining which families may benefit from support beyond what universal efforts provide. However, we can draw from our knowledge related to successful student identification methods for Tier 2 and extend them to the identification of caregivers who may benefit from increased supports to enhance collaboration between families and schools. Establishing processes to identify families who may benefit from additional outreach or support should be approached carefully, with consideration of potential biases, and should occur with a team that includes caregivers. Unfortunately, many schools continue to value school-based involvement efforts like volunteering for school activities or attending a parent–teacher conference over important aspects of home-based family involvement like providing space and materials for homework or supporting students in getting to school on time and ready to learn. Others may blame families for their lack of engagement rather than thinking about this as a proof that the universal partnership efforts were not effective (Mapp & Kuttner, 2013). It is important to consider the various ways that families may respond to Tier 1 supports and to invitations for collaboration, and to define engagement in a way that considers all of the ways that families support the school and their child's education. If more than 20% of families are "not engaged" based on the schools established criteria, then the responsibility is on the school to develop more effective Tier 1 practices rather than attribute this lack of engagement to family motivation or abilities. Determining what engagement looks like, and the criteria that needs to be demonstrated to initiate additional layers of family support, should be an iterative process open to adaptation given that limited guidance is available on how to identify families in need of more supports or how to conceptualize family–school partnership along the MTSS continuum. Defining what a response to Tier 1 partnership efforts look like will help schools to appropriately and proactively target their efforts to the families most in need of an additional layer of support.

School teams are encouraged to consider sources of existing data at their school before collecting new information from families and should develop and monitor decision rules to determine which caregivers may benefit from additional outreach or support. It can be challenging to think of existing data to identify caregiver strengths and needs given that schools often have much more information on students than they do their families. Schools may consider a two-pronged approach to identifying caregivers in need of more support:

1. Use data about the families themselves (e.g., any family who has not returned an emergency contact card by a certain date, repeated non-response to phone calls from the teacher, number of times the caregiver accesses electronic report card or homework systems like PowerSchool, etc).

2. Use student data that could to identify a challenge for caregivers (e.g., attendance or tardy records, caregiver-rated screeners showing behavior problems at home, repeated office discipline referrals, poor homework completion). Data about caregiver identification and response should be reviewed regularly to determine whether the selected data-based decision-making approach shows that the majority of family

needs are met through universal supports, and that families who need more are benefiting from increased support.

In terms of the request for assistance method for identification, this could be expanded to address potential caregiver supports more directly. Schools could make it very clear to families from the start of the school year that they can request supports for themselves in addition to for their child. Caregivers could directly request increased partnership or communication with their child's teacher or another school staff, request training or coaching related to supporting their child at home, or request support in connecting to available school and community resources or interventions tied to their specific family needs. The specific form or process for the request (i.e., to who and how?) should be readily available and understood by all families. While we have not yet observed a request for assistance process framed in this way for families, we have seen these requests occur informally in schools that have dedicated family coordinators who are accessible and whose roles are understood by caregivers. A request for assistance could also be expanded so that a teacher or other educator could nominate a family for extra assistance, or so that a student could request assistance for their families. For example, if a teacher if worried about their lack of communication with a family or about the way the family is responding to feedback sent home with the student, then they can request assistance from another school staff to support their outreach to caregivers. A student can request support from the school for their caregivers who are frustrated when helping them with their homework; when their family is struggling to meet their basic needs; or when other family members are struggling with social–emotional–behavioral concerns (see Form 6.1).

Although universal screeners for families are not yet commonplace, many schools have existing systems to collect information from all families at the beginning of the school year. It is common for kindergarten screening sessions to actively seek and weigh caregiver input along with other ratings and observations, and many schools ask families to update student emergency contact information yearly. Establishing a schoolwide process to survey families directly about their relationship with the school or their child's teacher, communication preferences, access to materials to support their child's learning, and/or perceived student and family needs is a recommended tool for universal family engagement (Garbacz, McIntosh, et al., 2018). Additionally, non-response or limited response on a schoolwide survey could serve as an indicator of families who may benefit from more support to enhance communication with the school. Screening of potential family needs could also occur through the teacher. Each teacher could be asked to consider the families in their classroom and respond to basic indicators such as these questions: Do you know this family? Do they respond to classroom communications? Do they seem to have what they need, in terms of basic needs and educational materials, to help their child be successful this year? It can be challenging to identify families in need of support, and school teams should collaborate with caregivers from their school while brainstorming potential identification methods in to increase the likelihood of success. We hope that the ideas included here can help school staff consider how to include caregiver perspectives on student needs and add methods to identify families in need of more support.

WHERE TO START?: SIMPLE AND ADAPTABLE TIER 2 PRACTICES

A primary goal of family–school collaboration within Tier 2 of MTSS is to develop standardized assessment and intervention methods to increase strengths across multiple domains for students and families who demonstrate risk. Here we propose new ideas for the implementation of family–focused supports through schools within Tier 2 of MTSS in addition to collaborating with families continuously and at various levels within student- and family-focused interventions. Past work related to Tier 2 of MTSS has demonstrated some benefits of a standard protocol approach, which involves beginning with a single standardized yet adaptable intervention approach that serves as a point of access to Tier 2 for all students (Hawken et al., 2021). We begin with this approach for enhanced feasibility in order to ensure that interventions can be accessed as soon as a need for more support is identified, and that the simplest/lowest resource intervention is attempted first before increasing intervention intensity. We introduce CICO (Hawken et al., 2021) and Positive Parent Contact (PPC; Fefer et al., 2020) as potential "first step" Tier 2 interventions for students and families, respectively. We then elaborate on potential additional layers of intervention to ensure the availability of a continuum of interventions within Tier 2 to support those who do not fully benefit from the first layer of simple proactive intervention strategies. We also include a framework to consider increasing the level of family–school collaboration in school-based interventions as a means to increase the intensity of intervention offerings at Tier 2 before moving to Tier 3 or formalizing supports through special education.

Check-In, Check-Out

The most common Tier 2 school-based intervention for students is CICO (Hawken et al., 2021; Park & Blair, 2020). The procedures to implement CICO include having a trusted adult facilitate multiple check-ins per day/per student, organized by using a Daily Progress Report (DPR). These check points are structured to facilitate consistent feedback on student behavior, increase opportunities for positive adult attention, and increase students' understanding of pre-established schoolwide behavioral expectations (Hawken et al., 2021). Family-oriented components of CICO include using data from families to inform CICO procedures, proactively contacting families to support a collaborative problem-solving process, and using the DPR at home and in school to support caregivers in understanding the purpose of the intervention and the ways to provide consistent reinforcement in the form of positive feedback. See Form 6.2 for a template of a DPR with caregiver signature and an area for teachers and caregivers to communicate about student performance. As mentioned earlier, school staff should collaborate with caregivers to determine how they would like to be involved in the intervention and their preferred frequency and method for sharing progress.

Daily Progress Report Template for Check-In, Check-Out, with Prompts for Communication between Teachers and Caregivers

Student Name: _____

Goal	8 A.M.–10 A.M.	10 A.M.–12 P.M.	Lunch/Recess	12 P.M.–2:30 P.M.
Schoolwide Expectation #1	0 1 2	0 1 2	0 1 2	0 1 2
Schoolwide Expectation #2	0 1 2	0 1 2	0 1 2	0 1 2
Schoolwide Expectation #3	0 1 2	0 1 2	0 1 2	0 1 2
Schoolwide Expectation #4	0 1 2	0 1 2	0 1 2	0 1 2

Teacher Signature: _____ Caregiver Signature: _____

Points Goal: _____ Points Earned: _____

Message from teacher: _____

_____

Message from caregiver: _____

_____

Key
0 = Not Quite (insert behavioral anchor)
1 = Good Job (insert behavioral anchor)
2 = Awesome! (insert behavioral anchor)

TABLE 6.1. Embedding Family-School Collaboration in Check-In, Check-Out

Implementation Step	Considerations for Caregiver Collaboration
Identifying student as a good candidate for CICO	Include caregiver input in determining need for Tier 2 intervention, including caregiver request for assistance. Communicate full continuum of MTSS support, framing Tier 2 as an additional layer of support to ensure that the school is meeting student needs.
Develop and finalize daily progress report procedures	Seek input about intervention procedures. (How frequently do they want to receive communication? What method do they want to use?)
	Determine if caregivers want to share information about home behavior with school.
	Help define expectations in ways that are most relevant to family context. Consider home-based feedback and reinforcement.
Implement CICO and ongoing data monitoring	Engage caregivers in teaching expectations and in the acknowledgement process.
	Obtain ongoing caregiver feedback ahead of and during implementation.
Progress monitoring and fading	Share outcome data
	Incorporate caregiver input regarding acceptability of CICO and useful supports that should stay in place or be added for fading.

CICO is the most common Tier 2 intervention implemented in schools and is often used as the "first step" intervention for students demonstrating a need for more support because it is simple to initiate and has demonstrated a host of positive effects for students (e.g., Park & Blair, 2020). CICO is aligned with the need for Tier 2 supports to be accessed quickly and can be put into place in less than 48 hours from identifying a student in need of more support (Hawken et al., 2021). This is a critical component of Tier 2 preventions at-large, as students at-risk for developing chronic challenging behaviors need to be met with swift and effective tiered behavioral supports. Another strength of CICO is that the intervention components require little training to implement and can be utilized by all school staff regardless of their training or behavioral expertise. As presented, one drawback of CICO implementation is that there is limited guidance about how to best integrate family–school collaboration into CICO. Asking for caregiver consent for student participation in the intervention and inclusion of a caregiver signature on the DPR are the two primary ways that caregivers have been involved in CICO. However, there are ways to expand caregiver collaboration in CICO beyond the daily signature request to enhance family–school collaboration and align with culturally responsive practices. A study by Goldman and colleagues (2019) lends support for more caregiver collaboration in CICO planning and implementation. It demonstrates that both caregivers and teachers viewed positively the use of daily behavior report cards and delivery of home-based reinforcers for students with autism spectrum disorder (ASD), and such approach led to improvements in school–family communication and partnership. See Table 6.1 for methods for engaging families throughout the CICO process.

Positive Parent Contact

Many schools also have an informal "first step" strategy that they implement when care-givers request additional support, or when a student demonstrates a need for increased connection and communication between home and school. Pause and ask yourself: "What does my school do when a caregiver asks for more support *or* when a family is considered by school staff as 'challenging to engage'?" The most common response that we have encountered in both research (e.g., Smith et al., 2021) and practice is *increased communication!* This response comes in many forms, including "We follow up with more calls or voicemails"; "We send materials home so that they understand the curriculum"; "We try multiple forms of outreach and document our communication efforts"; "If the parent doesn't respond to the teacher, then we ask the counselor to try calling too." Unfortunately, sometimes this question is met with an exasperated reply of "Eventually we give up and just focus on the things we can control in school." These responses underscore the fact that many educators expect, value, and implement school-to-home communication efforts, and realize the need to use multiple communication methods and attempts in order to reach all families. However, these varied responses also demonstrate that we have yet to formalize our systems and practices to proactively identify and support all families who may benefit from increased communication and collaboration with their child's school.

Existing research also supports this emphasis on communication. Two recent large-scale meta-analyses of multiple family–school partnering strategies showed school-to-home communication as the relational component of partnership interventions with the largest positive effect on student academic achievement and social–emotional outcomes (Sheridan et al., 2019; Smith et al., 2020). Recent research also suggests that middle schools that engage in more proactive outreach to families may be perceived as safer by teachers and have fewer student and teacher reports of behavior problems (Garbacz, Bolt, et al., 2020). Additionally, multidirectional communication was highlighted as one of four essential elements for family–school partnership within MTSS (Weingarten et al., 2020). Therefore, we propose a structured way to increase positive communication from teachers to caregivers as a potential "first step" or point of access intervention at Tier 2 for caregivers who have not fully responded to the school's universal family–school collaboration efforts. This novel family-focused Tier 2 intervention approach, referred to as Positive Parent Contact Plus (PPC+), combines two very simple and promising communication-focused interventions that have been recently described in the literature: PPC (Fefer et al., 2020) and Parent Wise Feedback (Houri et al., 2019). Both interventions focus on teacher communication to care-givers through brief, strength-based, and efficient protocols to maximize the potential benefits of teacher outreach efforts. The goal is to enhance communication between school and home, as a means to promote bidirectional or reciprocal communication between caregivers and teachers and build a foundation for successful family–school collaboration efforts in the future. This approach also provides students with additional opportunities for feedback about meeting schoolwide expectations and may therefore be a way to indirectly improve student behavior through a family-focused intervention approach (Fefer et al., 2020; Houri et al., 2019).

The PPC intervention is a teacher implemented communication approach that we developed after conducting focus groups with educators and caregivers to better understand their perceptions of one local school districts family–school partnering efforts. Caregivers told us loud and clear that they were quite satisfied with schoolwide communication efforts (e.g., principal newsletters, information about school events) but desired more direct communication from their child's teacher and communication relevant to their specific child. Additionally, we heard from both caregivers and educators that communication from school to home was most often centered around illnesses or discipline concerns and rarely focused on strengths or successes. This pattern of negative communication topics between teachers and parents has also been documented in the literature (e.g., Cherng, 2016). Lastly, we sought to apply the behavioral concept of response efficiency (Horner & Day, 1991) to this communication challenge and develop a strategy that would ensure that both teachers and caregivers were met with more reinforcement than demand, which has been shown to increase the likelihood of a behavior happening in the future. We also wanted to ensure that the intervention was feasible and included low demand for teachers despite being fully teacher implemented.

PPC is a very simple intervention that involves teachers adding two structured positive contacts a week for a small number of identified caregivers. First, teachers are asked to share their top three communication preferences (e.g., a specific app, email, phone) with caregivers identified as needing Tier 2 supports or with caregivers of students identified as needing Tier 2 supports. Caregivers are then asked to select their most preferred communication method from the list and share that with the teacher. This approach ensures that teacher and family preferences are both considered in designing the specific PPC approach in order to enhance contextual fit, acceptability, and feasibility. This initial communication can also serve as a time to share your goal of increased communication, to seek more information to tailor the communication for this specific student or family, and to allow caregivers the opportunity to opt out if desired (i.e., passive consent). Teachers receive given specific communication guidelines for PPC, as well as scripts to use as starter templates for the contacts (see Appendix 6.B and Fefer et al., 2020). Teachers are asked to look for specific examples of the student engaging in behaviors that align with the schoolwide expectations and communicate these specific examples to the caregiver at least twice a week using their preferred communication method. PPC states that the feedback must be genuine, specific, connected to one or more of the schoolwide PBIS expectations, and varied (i.e., avoid using the same script template or the same behavior multiple times). Additionally, teachers are asked not to include any questions or requests to reply in these communications so that there is no demand or expectations for communication placed on caregivers. Teachers are also asked to log all communications to or from that caregiver to determine if the intervention is effectively increasing the primary target variable of reciprocal communication between teachers and caregivers. Teachers may also use a DPR, similar to CICO, to monitor student behavior if this is also an important target for change. In our initial pilot study, we found that this intervention improved on-task classroom behavior for target students and showed increased reciprocal communication during the PPC phase of the intervention despite no requests for caregiver response (Fefer et al., 2020).

The Addition of Wise Feedback

The "plus" of the PPC+ model introduced in this chapter adds a "Wise Feedback" component to the intervention to align more closely with culturally responsive educational approaches (Hammond, 2018) as well as from social psychology related to overcoming mistrust associated with racial barriers (Yeager et al., 2014). We incorporate the specific "Parental Wise Feedback" intervention that showed promise in a recent study by Houri and colleagues (2019) as a means to enhance caregiver trust and engagement and to set the stage for reciprocal communication between teachers and caregivers. The wise feedback was delivered in the form of a one-time personalized letter to a caregiver of the target child, written by the teacher. The letter includes three components:

1. a positive greeting
2. specific description of the purpose and desired goal of the communication
3. a "wise statement" about the teachers' high expectations for their child, and a strong belief that their child will be able to meet these high academic and behavioral expectations

The personalized letters were sent by email and mail to ensure delivery, and caregivers who received the letters were more engaged in a school—home communication system and had higher ratings of the parent—teacher relationship than caregivers in the control condition (Houri et al., 2019). This wise feedback approach could certainly be implemented as a one-time contact at the beginning of CICO or PPC to enhance parental engagement in these student- or family-focused approaches. Alternatively, the wise feedback structure could be incorporated into PPC scripts along with the specific schoolwide expectations, and teachers could be instructed to start with scripts that align with Wise Feedback before branching to other varied PPC scripts or embedding more of their own language and structure (see Appendix 6.B for example scripts). Wise feedback may be a particularly important addition for families from minoritized backgrounds and those who have negative experiences or mistrust associated with school.

Another potential adaptation to PPC+ would be to consider expanding beyond text-based communication and introduce pictures (e.g., of their child engaging in positive behavior, emojis to express enthusiasm) or permanent products (e.g., written assignment, creative work) to align with either student or family communication preferences or to increase the specificity of the feedback. This could also help to overcome potential linguistic or learning barriers to communication and ensure that scripts are translated into caregivers' home language and communications are aligned with caregiver reading abilities. Consider sending brief audio or video recordings as additional options for caregivers who may prefer communication that does not require reading.

A Continuum of Collaboration within Tier 2 Interventions

Students who benefit from additional support after these "first step" interventions may find adaptations helpful. If adaptations are not effective, additional layers of Tier 2 interventions should be available for students and caregivers. Our first step upon seeing evidence that the desired effect of the intervention is not being achieved is to determine whether the intervention is being implemented as intended and to provide implementation supports to reach fidelity. If the intervention is implemented as intended and the desired response is still not achieved, we should consider adaptations to our "first step" interventions as the next step. These interventions are designed to be adaptable, and modifying your approach rather than starting again is much more time and resource efficient. If a student or caregiver is not responsive to CICO, or a caregiver is not responsive to PPC+, we begin to consider strategies to increase the duration, intensity, or frequency of our approaches. For students, we may modify CICO to be more individualized for the student (i.e., change reinforcers or make expectations more specific), include more frequent feedback or check-ins, provide group-based instruction related to specific areas in need of improvement (e.g., social skills groups), conduct a brief functional behavioral assessment (FBA) to select a function-based modification or addition, or add mentoring or tutoring on top of CICO. For caregivers, we may increase the frequency of communication, change the method or approach to communication, or change the person who is attempting to collaborate with the family. Increasing the level of collaboration with caregivers is another important consideration when increasing the intensity of Tier 2 interventions, as collaborating across contexts may serve to enhance intervention fit and effectiveness. We will introduce a continuum of collaboration with families within school-based Tier 2 interventions, drawing from existing classification systems related to caregiver involvement in child-focused interventions both within and outside of schools. We include examples of various levels of family–school collaboration within existing Tier 2 intervention approaches that are both student and caregiver-focused.

Though there is no universally agreed upon metric for categorizing the extent of family–school collaboration within MTSS or Tier 2 interventions specifically, several related examples can inform our thinking of a continuum of family–school collaboration within Tier 2. For instance, Reynolds and colleagues (2012) examined the role of caregiver involvement in mental health interventions and classified family involvement in interventions as follows:

1. Significant involvement: Caregivers are involved in all or almost all of the intervention components.
2. Some involvement: Caregivers are less involved in the intervention than their children.
3. Minimal involvement: Caregivers are involved in some intervention components (e.g., psychoeducation only) but largely uninvolved in the intervention.
4. No involvement: Caregivers have no engagement with any intervention components.

A separate, but equally useful, metric that may be more aligned to school-based practice is described by Rispoli and colleagues (2019) in their literature review examining the role of caregivers in school-based interventions for children with ASD. They suggest that family–school collaboration in interventions will fall into one of these three categories: family school partnership, parental involvement, or no involvement. They define family–school partnership, the highest level of collaboration, as a process where family members and

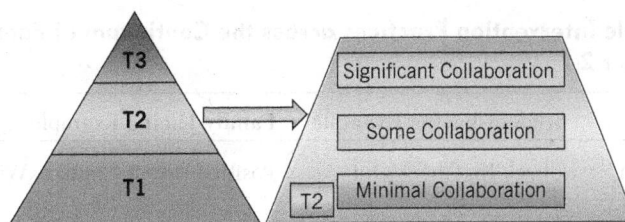

FIGURE 6.1. Zooming in on a continuum of family–school collaboration in school-based Tier-2 interventions.

school staff extensively collaborate throughout the stages of intervention implementation to support students' social, emotional, behavioral, and academic outcomes across contexts. Parental involvement, the middle level of collaboration, describes instances where caregivers engage in interventions at the direction of school staff but lack the collaboration components present within family–school partnerships. Their "no involvement" category means that caregivers are not involved in any components of the intervention.

Although these two classification systems are a helpful starting point, no existing framework can describe the continuum of Tier 2 supports in relation to increasing the level of collaboration with caregivers. As a result, we share Figure 6.1 to combine existing frameworks (Reynolds et al., 2012; Rispoli et al., 2019) and to organize our discussion of a continuum of increased intensity of family–school collaboration within Tier 2 supports, aimed at preventing problems, decreasing risk, and providing schools with multiple options to support students before jumping to Tier 3 or to special education. This continuum is based on the assumption that schools and caregivers should work together more closely when the specific challenges to be addressed are more significant, or when non-response to lower levels of intervention and collaboration is demonstrated.

> "We would just start brainstorming and her [classroom teacher] overall approach was let's try something and see how it goes, then she would come back to me, and we'd tweak it and then she'd come back to me again, so it wasn't a one and done thing. She really made it clear early on that she was going to stick with this . . . it was very clear to me that she recognized that only by working together could we solve this puzzle or crack this problem because she knew she couldn't do it by herself . . . and I couldn't do it by myself because I'm not in the classroom."

We purposefully exclude a "No Involvement" category because Tier 2 interventions for students in schools require a thorough description of the intervention and passive caregiver consent, as the bare minimum. We conceptualize this bare minimum practice as representing the lower end of "Minimal Collaboration" in our Tier 2 continuum. It is important to note that a school's decision for selecting the level of family–school collaboration within their continuum of Tier 2 interventions should be dependent on each student and families' unique strengths and needs. Tailoring the level of family–school collaboration using family input and preferences is an important method to support the culturally responsive implementation of Tier 2 practices.

TABLE 6.2. Example Intervention Practices across the Continuum of Family–School Collaboration at Tier 2

	Student-Facing Example	Family-Facing Example
Minimal collaboration	Check In, Check Out	Positive Parent Contact, Wise Feedback
Some collaboration	Coping Cat	Behavioral Parent Training (targets selected by school)
Significant collaboration	First Step Next	Modularized Behavior Parent Training (targets selected by family)

Note. Examples included in this table do not represent an exhaustive list, and the specific level of collaboration will vary depending on the implementation procedures and adaptations adopted

We define the levels of collaboration within Tier 2 as follows (see Table 6.2 for specific examples):

- *Significant collaboration* occurs when input from caregivers and school staff are equitably collected and used to inform the planning and implementation of a Tier 2 intervention. The desires, culture, and expectations of the school and home context are granted equal weight during the problem-solving process from initial identification of the problem to intervention implementation and evaluation. Because focus on Tier 2 specifically, it is important to keep in mind that this collaboration occurs in the context of an intervention approach for a group of students, not for one specific student, and therefore, caregiver input is valued for adapting existing Tier 2 supports to enhance effectiveness and fit.
- *Some collaboration* occurs when school staff meaningfully incorporate caregiver input in planning and implementing school-based interventions. School-based interventions delivered directly to caregivers, who expect their attendance and engagement, would most often fall within this level of collaboration. Tier 2 interventions in this range of collaboration are often driven by the established systems and culture within the school, yet include systematic ways to seek and include caregiver input in the delivery, implementation, and evaluation of student and caregiver-facing interventions.
- *Minimal collaboration* occurs when school staff share intervention information with caregivers but do not directly seek caregiver input. This level of collaboration could also include simple caregiver-facing interventions that do not require direct input or action from caregivers. Student- and caregiver-facing Tier 2 interventions in this range of collaboration often expect negligible levels of caregiver input and interaction.

Tier 2 Practices along the Continuum of Collaboration

Tier 2 interventions can have various target outcomes, and can be student-facing (e.g., small group academic interventions) or family-facing (e.g., behavioral parent training), or they can include both students and families in a comprehensive program. Next, we share examples of possible school-based Tier 2 interventions and discuss where these example interventions may fit within this continuum of family–school collaboration.

Student-Facing Practices

Many common Tier 2 approaches used in schools, such as Social Academic Instructional Groups (SAIG), CICO, Check and Connect, or brief FBAs to inform function-matched Tier 2 approaches, include *Minimal Collaboration* upon initial implementation. Schools often have a menu of available student-focused Tier 2 offerings and aim to quickly match students to interventions based on their needs. The most common type of caregiver involvement in these interventions is information sharing. It may be helpful to proactively provide information to all parents about the range of potential Tier 2 offerings and have prepared descriptions to share with families in multiple formats (e.g., brief written description of each support for email or text, a phone script, brief video descriptions) and languages. This can help to facilitate getting caregiver consent and input while ensuring access to the intervention within the recommended 2–3-day timeframe (Anderson et al., 2012; Hawken et al., 2021). Schools typically have specific procedures and approaches identified, and the overall process is unlikely to deviate based on specific caregivers' needs or preferences. Other common examples of caregiver collaboration practices within these common Tier 2 approaches include a collecting data via caregiver interview, gathering caregiver signatures when sharing information from school to home, partnering with caregivers to provide home-based reinforcement, and seeking caregiver input about intervention acceptability or response. Some schools use manualized group interventions that may directly plan for or provide resources to encourage caregiver participation, while other schools may use a broader behavioral skills training approach and may have to plan for ways to engage caregivers. It is common to start with minimal caregiver collaboration in Tier 2 and increase it if modifications are needed to intensify the intervention or if caregivers are actively seeking more information and input depending on the student or family response to the intervention in place.

One example of a Tier 2 small-group approach that could be classified as minimal collaboration with families is a positive psychology intervention called the Well-Being Promotion Program (WBPP; Suldo, 2016). The manualized student-focused curriculum aims to increase student well-being through direct instruction and practice with positive activities. WBPP includes two caregiver-facing components: a single caregiver information session before the 10-week program for students and distribution of a weekly information sheet for caregivers. These weekly handouts review the content of the students' session and provide suggestions for home-based discussion or practice opportunities to promote generalization of skills. However, the WBPP does not involve direct intervention with caregivers or provide avenues to collaborate with caregivers around implementation. We highlight this example because empirical evidence shows that the addition of this minimal collaboration with caregivers (i.e., one information session and weekly handouts) leads to greater improvements in the target outcome of students' positive and negative affect than previous version of the WBPP without the caregiver component (Roth et al., 2017). This example demonstrates that family—school collaboration, even at a minimal level, is likely to contribute to more positive outcomes from Tier 2 supports.

Other manualized intervention approaches plan for more collaboration by including student and caregiver-facing components or by seeking more collaboration with caregivers to carry out intervention procedures. One such example that has been used in schools is

Coping Cat (Kendall, 1994), a cognitive-behavioral intervention designed to reduce anxiety in children and adolescents. The intervention is predominantly child-facing, as it includes a mix of psychoeducation and exposure therapy across 16 weekly sessions. Coping Cat can be implemented individually or in small groups of students (around four or five students per group) as a Tier 2 mental health intervention in schools, where data indicate that anxiety symptoms are prominent within the school population. Coping Cat includes *some collaboration*, as there are two caregiver-facing sessions within the standard version of Coping Cat, and caregivers are also trained to support students in exposure tasks outside of session as needed. Caregivers have the opportunity to work with the clinician to tailor the exposure tasks to best meet the needs of their family, which can promote culturally responsive implementation. Coping Cat also includes supplemental caregiver-facing treatment components (i.e., sessions beyond the minimum of two sessions and engagement with exposure tasks) and a separate workbook for caregivers, which could be classified as *significant collaboration* due to the intensity of supports offered directly to caregivers.

First Step Next (FSN, previously called The First Step to Success; Walker et al., 2018) is a Tier 2 intervention that supports students with emerging social–emotional and behavioral needs. While the intervention is primarily student-facing and targets student skill development, FSN has many caregiver-facing components, including an orientation, ongoing team meetings to facilitate the caregiver's role in the intervention, daily notes or phone calls home, complementary rewards for caregivers to use at home, and a workbook to facilitate caregivers' use of FSN skills outside of the school setting. For this reason, the FSN intervention is a more intensive student-facing intervention within the Tier 2 continuum and could be classified as *Significant Collaboration* due to numerous opportunities to involve caregivers and to tailor the intervention depending on student needs and the unique context of each family.

Caregiver-Facing Practices

Interestingly, even a caregiver-facing Tier 2 intervention can require minimal family–school collaboration. As previously described, the basic implementation of PPC (Fefer et al., 2020) requires teachers to describe examples of positive student behavior to caregivers at least twice per week and deliberately places no demands on caregivers. Caregivers' input about their communication preferences is the only explicit family–school collaboration required for teachers to implement caregiver-facing PPC for a student in their classroom, and therefore, this approach can be classified as *minimal collaboration*. PPC targets aspects of family–school collaboration as the desired intervention outcomes and aims to establish an initial foundation of positive communication to build trust, relationships, and communication routines between teachers and caregivers. Therefore, PPC can quickly become an intervention with *some collaboration* or even *significant collaboration* depending on the outcomes of the initial teacher–caregiver communications. For instance, one probable outcome from successful implementation of PPC is increased reciprocal teacher–caregiver communication (Fefer et al., 2020). Teachers could capitalize on their newly increased communication to increase school–family collaboration, including consultative support in reinforcing target behaviors at home or eliciting caregiver perspective on effective and preferred school-based reinforcers. Examples like this help to illustrate the fluid nature of interventions across the continuum of family–school collaboration in Tier 2.

A review of school-based mental health interventions that included caregivers found that the majority of the Tier 2 interventions focused on the reduction of students' externalizing behaviors, and the most common method for including caregivers in Tier 2 was the delivery of group parent training (Raffaele Mendez et al., 2013). Behavioral Parent Training (BPT) is an example of an evidence-based caregiver-focused intervention to reinforce desired child behaviors and decrease their child's unwanted behavior through direct teaching of evidence-based behavior management strategies (McMahon & Forehand, 2005). Some multi-tier school-based programs, such as FSN (Walker et al., 2018) or Fast Track (e.g., Conduct Problems Prevention Research Group, 2007), include BPT within Tier 2 of their primarily student-facing interventions. Other examples of BPT are solely caregiver-focused and can be implemented at Tier 2 to prevent the escalation of behavior problems (e.g., Helping Our Toddlers, Developing Our Children's Skills [HOT DOCS]; Fefer et al., 2021). Despite many examples of manualized BPT, few have been implemented in schools (Raffaele Mendez et al., 2013), and those tended to be implemented universally at Tier 1 (e.g., Joussemet et al., 2018) or within Tier 3 of a comprehensive school-based family support program like Positive Family Support (Smolkowski et al., 2017). BPT could be classified as *some collaboration* if the program focus is driven by the school and there is minimal opportunity for caregiver input and experience to be incorporated to shape content or target outcomes. School-based BPT/family education that is classified as *significant collaboration* requires curricula and facilitators that can value and incorporate the input, perspectives, and expertise of caregivers to increase caregiver engagement and reduce barriers to service access. This level of collaboration can help to ensure that we are operating from the lens of asset-based practice and cultural humility when implementing caregiver-facing preventive interventions in schools. More research is needed to understand the potential of BPT as a Tier 2 support in schools. Emerging support for the potential effectiveness and efficiency of modularized approaches to partnering with families in schools currently focuses on students with specific mental health diagnoses (Weist et al., 2019); however, this could be an exciting step in considering how to feasibly integrate parent training within Tier 2 of MTSS to enhance student and family outcomes more proactively.

Taken together, there are many approaches within a continuum of Tier 2 intervention that include minimal, some, or significant levels of family–school collaboration. The majority of current Tier 2 approaches collaborate with caregivers within student-facing interventions, although there is promise for caregiver-focused interventions delivered through schools as well. The extent of family–school collaboration is one feature to consider in determining methods to intensify and expand Tier 2 interventions.

CASE EXAMPLES

Next, we share examples from our school-based work to exemplify challenges and to demonstrate intensifying the extent of family–school collaboration as a way to increase intervention effectiveness within the continuum of Tier 2. A student-focused example is shared first, followed by a family-focused example.

Our first example highlights a common challenge of caregiver dissatisfaction with a common school-based practice and a school team that uses their cultural humility to incorporate family preferences to adjust the intervention, which leads to sustained changes to their CICO system as a whole. An elementary school counselor we were working with reached out to the family of a second-grade student whose behavior was not improving after one month of CICO. Caregivers had previously received information about CICO and agreed that their child may benefit. However, they returned about 50% of the DPRs during the 4 weeks of implementation. The counselor reached out to caregivers to discuss the lack of student response to CICO and to problem-solve together. During this conversation, the caregivers specifically requested that student behavior data not be sent home daily and expressed frustration with the counselor's request to review and sign the DPR daily. The reason for their request was they did not want "bad day" data shared or sent home because they reported having a hard time staying positive in light of sub-optimal student behavior. As a result, the school team listened to the caregiver's input and waived the daily caregiver-facing portions of CICO in favor of sharing student progress weekly. Additionally, the school staff decided to add home phone calls on particularly good days so that those could be celebrated at home and at school, and as a method to model the use of specific positive praise for caregivers. In this example, the school staff meaningfully collaborated with caregivers and incorporated their thoughts and desires into the intervention implementation after initial non-response to CICO. They also provided a learning opportunity to caregivers (e.g., modeling positive feedback) to support their use of this skill in the home environment—layering a caregiver-facing component onto the student-focused CICO intervention. Additionally, the school team was open to learning from their experience with this family to better understand their family culture and decided to proactively ask caregivers about their desired frequency of data sharing before beginning CICO. This collaboration continuum, from minimal to some collaboration with caregivers, led to improved student outcomes but decreased the frequency of communication with caregivers. This demonstrates that the extent of collaboration may vary over time within the same approach, and that intensifying collaboration is about partnering with families to enhance the contextual fit of the intervention rather than adding more time or resources or trying out different intervention options.

Our family-focused example highlights the common challenges of historical events that leave families feeling unsupported by the school, and a school team proposing an intervention to change communication patterns with an aim to enhance trust between home and school. This example also highlights challenges associated with mismatched expectations or perceptions of student skills between home and school. We recently had the opportunity to support a second-grade teacher who identified one family that she felt she was struggling to engage. At the beginning of the school year, the teacher sent a class-wide survey to all caregivers to ask for information about their child, indicate anything that they were particularly excited or concerned about this year, and to ask them about their preferred methods and desired frequency for school-to-home communication. All but two families completed the survey within the requested one-week timeframe. The teacher sent individualized requests to these two families, through a follow-up email and left a voice message on a phone requesting them to reach out for a conversation and/or complete the survey. Only one of the two families responded, which prompted the teacher to submit a request for assistance form seeking support or input about how to reach the one family in her class that she had not yet had any contact with. This teacher's request for assistance with this family was reviewed by the student support team, who told the teacher that this family had requested a psychoeducational evaluation for their student back in kindergarten due to concerns about developing reading skills. The student was not found to have any concerns related to learning at that time and was meeting reading expectations in their current second-grade class. The team hypothesized that this evaluation experience may not have left this family feeling supported by the school, and the student's first grade teacher confirmed that she never felt like she had open communication or a positive relationship with this family. The team decided to initiate PPC for this family to change this negative communication trajectory, initiating two weekly positive contacts about their child's successes in the classroom from the teacher to the caregiver. After two weeks of PPC communications, the caregiver replied to an email about positive behaviors during the reading block with questions about their child's progress related to letter sounds and blending. The teacher was thrilled to receive a response from this caregiver and shared information about the skills they were working on, taking care to mention that the student was meeting all reading-related expectations. This initiated more reciprocal communication with caregivers sharing concerns about their child's reading and led the teacher to shift the weekly PPC communications to focus on academic successes specifically. Despite having no concerns about the student's reading at school, the teacher collaborated with the reading specialist to include brief video clips related to developmentally appropriate expectations and activities for reading at home within her weekly communications for this family. This experience showed us the importance of proactive and continued outreach to families and served as an example of the complexity of considering both student and family needs within MTSS. Although their child did not demonstrate a need for student-facing Tier 2 supports, this is an example of family-facing Tier 2 supports and of increasing the extent of family—school collaboration within PPC to intensify and individualize the approach and establish bidirectional communication around academics as an area of shared value across home and school.

SUMMARY

Family—school collaboration can be embedded throughout all aspects of Tier 2, from identification of student and family needs through outcome evaluation. Tier 2 should include simple, efficient, and adaptable "first step" practices that include family—school collaboration and address student and family needs, with the goal of proactively building connections across home and school contexts to decrease risk, enhance protective factors, and provide a foundation for intensifying interventions. Building and expanding Tier 2 to identify and serve students and their caregivers through multiple layers of intervention options may be the pinnacle of proactive and prevention focused school-based service delivery. If we can identify and address challenges early on, by identifying a broad group of students or their caregivers who do not respond to universal supports, we can save extensive time and resources related to resolving significant academic, behavioral, and mental health concerns. We may also be able to proactively enhance teacher–caregiver communication as a means to increase the likelihood of future family–school collaboration needed to address an array of possible academic, social–emotional, or behavioral concerns. We have historically focused our attention on collaboration with families at the schoolwide level (e.g., parent–teacher associations) or individual student level (e.g., IEP meetings) while simultaneously worrying about the students who may "fall through the cracks" in our schools. Tier 2 is the gap that needs to be filled to ensure that all students *and* families have the opportunity to understand and achieve schoolwide expectations through access to a continuum of proactive intervention options, as soon as there is an indication that they are not fully benefiting from universal supports. Building culturally responsive, effective, and efficient Tier 2 systems are a prerequisite for high quality Tier 3 supports in order to maximize the resources available for a small percentage of individual students or families who do not respond to a continuum of Tier 2 supports layered on top of universal supports. Conceptualizing Tier 2 as layered and on a continuum and as a framework for proactively responding to the needs of students *and* their families may begin to blur the lines between these tiers so that all students have access to additional supports when they need it, and fewer students require individualized special education to access the supports they need to be successful in school.

ACKNOWLEDGMENT

We would like to acknowledge the contributions of our friend, mentor, and colleague Dr. Meme Hieneman, who lost her courageous battle with cancer in August 2021. She championed the use of PBIS with families, and her ideas inspired much of our work that contributed to the content within this chapter.

Sample Language to Proactively Explain Tier 2
Interventions to Families

MTSS OVERVIEW/INTRODUCTION TO TIER 2

"Welcome, families, to our back-to-school night! We are so happy to have you here. As you know, we have been working hard to create the best school environment for all students, staff, and families. We use practices like response to intervention, positive behavior support, social emotional learning, and trauma informed practices to create what we call a multi-tiered system of support. All of these help us to do our very best in serving you and your children. At Tier 1, we provide universal supports for all children; then at Tier 2, we can provide additional supports for some children; and at Tier 3 we consider more intensive supports for the few students who show us that they need them.

[Label and define specific Tier 1 programming at your school, and specific ways that families can support these efforts at home.]

"We know that as hard as we are working to support all of our students, these universal or Tier 1 efforts may not be enough for some students or families. We know that as life ebbs and flows, there may be times when students need additional academic, behavioral, and social emotional supports. And sometimes, families need additional help from the school to meet student needs. We know from schools across the country that we should expect some students to need more support to be successful in school, and this doesn't mean that there is anything wrong with them or that they have a disability. We always plan ahead to proactively identify and address the needs of our students and families with what we call Tier 2 supports. These are not special education supports, 504 plans, or other more formalized ways to support students. Instead, we start with simple and low intensity Tier 2 supports, layered on top of and aligned with our strong Tier 1 practices, and follow their progress to ensure that we can successfully meet student or family needs."

Sample Description of a Potential Tier 2 Identification and Intervention Process

"At our school, we use data to determine which children might need more support to reach their full potential. This could be based on attendance, office referrals, academic grades, or a request for assistance from you, your child, or your child's teacher. When we have identified a student as needing more support from us to be successful, we start with an intervention called Check-In, Check-Out, or CICO. Research shows that this simple and brief program works for many students by providing them with a positive adult connection and reminders about expectations each day. Students receive daily feedback from their teachers, and we monitor progress to see if CICO is meeting their needs. Our goal is to provide the extra support to students quickly, to share information about progress through a daily progress report, and to have students graduate from the intervention when they no longer need any additional support.

"If we determine that we have not fully met your child's needs related to learning, emotions, or behavior, we will contact you immediately to provide details and let you know that we would like to

(continued)

offer your child additional opportunities to be successful through the CICO intervention. We strive to start this intervention within a day or two of our initial conversation unless you request otherwise. We will ask you for input about your child's strengths and preferences and about your own communication preferences too. We are really excited to have invested training and support into CICO, and we now have 10 school staff trained as facilitators in our school. Each adult will support 5–10 students.

"If a child does not fully respond to CICO, then we would be back in touch base with their family to suggest adding another layer of support in school to help them be as successful as possible. We may add a skills group with other students, mentoring, or tutoring. If we add more layers to CICO and a child is not fully responding, then we will schedule a meeting where we can look deeper and consider individualized supports to help them be successful.

"We want our families to understand this full system of support for our students, which you can think of as steps within a staircase. We will fully implement the lower-step interventions and supports as early as we can and increase supports for any students with a demonstrated need."

SAMPLE LANGUAGE TO INITIATE TIER 2 SUPPORTS

CICO for Attendance Example Phone Script

"Hello, Caregiver! Thanks for taking my call. I wanted to let you know that we'd like to offer your child additional supports because we've realized that what we've been doing is not helping him to have the best attendance. If it's OK with you, we will enroll your child into what we call Check-In, Check-Out or CICO. This will give him another positive adult at school so he knows we care about him. They will help remind him of the school expectations each day and make sure he has a positive contact for coming to school on time every day. His teachers will also help keep an extra eye on him and give more positive feedback each day as well. Over the course of about six weeks, we will monitor attendance improvements. If his attendance improves, he can exit CICO. If his attendance does not improve, then we will discuss adding another layer of support. Let us know if you have any comments or questions. More information on this is available in the student handbook that we discussed during orientation."

Introduction to PPC Example Note/Email

[This could be sent to one family to initiate PPC as a Tier 2 support, or to all families at the beginning of the year to gauge communication preferences and/or to see which families respond.]

"Hello, Caregiver! I am really enjoying having a STUDENT in class and would like to be able to share "positive shout outs" about things I see in my classroom as an extra way to let the STUDENT know they are doing a great job. I like to communicate with families through notes in students' take-home folders, by email, or though the Remind application. Which would you prefer? I look forward to sharing more updates about the STUDENT with you soon!"

Sample Scripts for PPC and PPC + Wise Feedback

The following examples are aligned with these sample schoolwide PBIS expectations: *B.A.R.K:*

1. Be Responsible; 2. Achieve Excellence; 3. Respect Self, Others, and Property; and 4. Keep Safe.

TWO PPC SAMPLE SCRIPTS

1. "I just wanted to reach out and let you know how **respectful** the STUDENT has been in the classroom this week! The STUDENT has been wonderful at following through with directions and was highly receptive to feedback regarding their assignments and behavior. This is something the STUDENT has been working really hard on, and I wanted to share their progress!"
2. "I hope you have had a wonderful week! I wanted to let you know that the STUDENT has done an exceptional job showing their classmates how to **keep safe** on the playground during recess _____ (today/this week)! They have been consistently following outdoor rules and kindly reminding other students to do the same. This behavior has had a positive impact on our entire classroom environment! This is something the STUDENT has been working really hard on, and I wanted to share their leadership!"

TWO PPC + WISE FEEDBACK SAMPLE SCRIPTS

Student-Focused

"I hope all is well! I am writing with the purpose of telling you how impressed I have been with STUDENT in the classroom _____ (today/this week). The STUDENT has been a stellar example of **being responsible** with organizing their desk and having their materials out and ready before the start of each lesson! I know it can be tough to keep all of the items organized for each day, and I expect a high level of responsibility from each of my students. I am sure that the STUDENT can continue to meet these expectations because they have shown responsible behavior by consistently bringing their math notebook with them after lunch. I appreciate your continued support of the STUDENT."

Family-Focused

"I hope all is well! I am writing to share a positive shout out about the STUDENT. I wanted to reach out to you given that we have not yet connected this fall and to determine if this may be your preferred method of communication. I appreciate that you are doing your part to help the STUDENT to be successful by getting them to school on time and making sure they have all of the materials needed for classroom activities. Our school has high expectations regarding open dialogue with families about student successes and challenges. I am committed to **achieving excellence** for all students by proactively communicating with their families, and I look forward to sharing my next update about STUDENT's performance in our classroom. Please do not hesitate to reach out to me at any point with any questions or concerns."

CHAPTER 7

Family–School Partnerships at Tier 3

DEVELOPMENT OF SOCIAL, EMOTIONAL, AND BEHAVIORAL CONCERNS

The development of social, emotional, and behavioral concerns in children and youth is contextual. Children may develop social, emotional, and behavioral concerns in early childhood or in early school years through interactions with parents and teachers who unintentionally reinforce social or behavior problems through positive or negative attention (Stormshak & Garbacz, 2018). Discontinuities across home and school can contribute to the development of social, emotional, and behavioral concerns. Discontinuities in expectations, safety and security, or reinforcement can be challenging for children to navigate (Christenson & Sheridan, 2001). Children who develop social, emotional, and behavioral concerns in their early school years are at increased risk for more intensive social, emotional, and behavioral concerns and mental health problems in adolescence and adulthood (Masten & Ciicchetti, 2010).

Some children may not have social, emotional, and behavioral concerns during their early school years but may develop them during middle school. Adolescence and the changing expectations of middle school increase the risk for children to develop social, emotional, and behavioral concerns, such as interaction with peers who are engaging in rule-breaking behavior or experiencing insufficient parenting support at home (Dishion & Patterson, 2016). Regardless of when children develop social, emotional, and behavioral concerns, the context surrounding the development and maintenance of social, emotional, and behavioral concerns positions family–school partnership interventions as essential (Garbacz et al., 2017). The purpose of this chapter is to describe the core features of family–school partnership interventions at Tier 3 to support students with social, emotional, and behavioral concerns.

RESEARCH SUPPORTING FAMILY–SCHOOL PARTNERSHIPS

Family–school partnership interventions join caregivers, school personnel, and children to coordinate support across home and school (Garbacz et al., 2017). The underlying logic suggests that improvements in parenting and teaching practices along with strengthened home–school connections will lead to improvements in outcomes for students. Research examining suggests family–school partnership interventions improve the parent–teacher relationship (Sheridan et al., 2017), parent competence in problem solving, and family–school engagement (Garbacz et al., 2019). In addition, research suggests family–school partnership interventions improve student adaptive behavior (effect size: $d = 0.39$) and social skills (Sheridan et al., 2012); decrease problem behavior (Dishion et al., 2002) and emotional and behavior problems (Garbacz et al., 2018a); and improve GPA and school attendance (Stormshak et al., 2009). Finally, evidence suggests that improvements in the family–school relationship and parenting and teaching practices are responsible for gains in child social behavior (Sheridan et al., 2017; Stormshak et al., 2021).

A meta-analysis by Sheridan and colleagues (2019) identified relational and structural elements of family–school interventions responsible for children's social–behavioral competence and mental health outcomes. Relational elements included communication, collaboration (mutual problem solving), and the parent–teacher relationship (e.g., creating joint perspectives). Structural elements included home-based involvement (e.g., talking about school), school-based involvement (e.g., working with teachers), and behavioral supports (e.g., praise, limit setting).

CHAPTER ORIENTATION

In this chapter, we review the core components of family–school partnerships at Tier 3. Research suggests that active ingredients of family–school partnerships at Tier 3 include partnership-centered components and problem-solving components. We review partnership-centered components first as they serve as a foundation for the problem-solving components (Dishion & Stormshak, 2007; Sheridan & Kratochwill, 2008). After describing the partnership-centered and problem-solving components, we describe how these Tier 3 family–school partnership practices can be aligned with and integrated into schoolwide systems and practices to improve family engagement in Tier 3 services and how they can promote coordinated implementation.

PARTNERSHIP-CENTERED COMPONENTS

Partnership-centered components within Tier 3 interventions apply to approaches that a school professional (e.g., school psychologist, social worker) can use to facilitate a problem-solving intervention with a parent and a teacher to support an individual student.

Partnership-centered components are implemented during meetings with parents and teachers wherein they discussion strengths, plan interventions, and evaluate the effectiveness of interventions. Partnership-centered components are also implemented between these structured meetings, such as during a phone call with a parent to discuss questions they may have about intervention planning at home. Use of partnership-centered strategies is just as important during informal interactions as it is during formal meetings.

Several partnership-centered components are relevant for Tier 3 interventions (see Table 7.1): Parent–teacher relationship building; focus on strengths; teaming and collaboration; encouragement; and sensitive, responsive, and effective communication promote skill development and resourceful sharing of information (Garbacz et al., 2008; Sheridan et al., 2019). Next, we review each of these components and describe their central features with examples. The case example, "Alex's Attendance Story," exemplifies several of these partnership components.

TABLE 7.1. Partnership-Centered Components of Family–School Interventions at Tier 3

Component	Description
Parent–teacher relationship building	Build connections across caregivers and teachers. Point out similarities and differences across home and school. Use collaborative language to promote partnerships.
Focusing on strengths	Identify strengths of caregivers, teachers, and students. Identify strengths of the home and school setting. Use those strengths to promote goal-directed change.
Teaming and collaboration	Promote a sense of caregivers and teachers as united to support student success. Focus on caregiver and teacher ideas and use those ideas in assessment and intervention planning.
Encouraging	Provide encouragement to caregivers and teachers in building new skills. Praise caregivers and teachers for their efforts. Validate experiences. Build caregiver and teacher agency in creating change.
Being sensitive and responsive	Ask about caregiver and teacher experiences and preferences and integrate them into the process. Seek out support based on arising needs.
Effective communication	Create and use multidirectional communication pathways so that caregivers and teachers can communicate back-and-forth about plans.
Promoting skill development	Use modeling, role playing, coaching, and other strategies to promote caregiver and teacher skill building. Make the process explicit so that plans, decisions, and procedures are transparent.
Being resourceful and sharing information	When suggestions or questions arise, respond by sharing relevant information, such as community referral options.

The parent–teacher relationship is a pivotal mechanism for promoting positive outcomes for students. Indeed, research suggests that improvements in the parent–teacher relationship within Tier 3 intervention is partially responsible for positive student social behavior outcomes. A school professional can strengthen a positive parent–teacher relationship by facilitating a discussion about shared goals, developing a common understanding for strengths and areas of concern, and building consistency across school and home.

> "Just listening to me, it doesn't even matter if you get it right sometimes, just trying . . . I think sometimes parents just want people to try, especially in special education."

When students experience improvements in outcomes, a school professional points to changes that parents and teachers had made to achieve those improved outcomes: "You both are interested in supporting Johnny and are committed to his success"; or "You made changes at home and school and collaborated to apply those changes consistently. And now Johnny is paying attention more often in class and completing work at home more independently. He is also sharing his successes with you and celebrating improvements." These shared positive experiences and explicit changes made across home and school highlight for parents and teachers the impact of their collaboration on student success. As a result of these interactions, it may be more likely for parents and teachers to seek out each other in the future when similar issues arise or when they have questions about other children or students.

A key element of a partnership-centered approach is a focus on strengths. At Tier 3, family–school interventions by design address concerns that require more intensive support than are available at Tier 1 or Tier 2. Thus, the primary concerns will always arise. A focus on strengths is paramount, allowing a consultant to facilitate the identification of student, family, and teacher strengths, which can then be used as a primary pathway to promote goal-directed change. Identifying family and teacher strengths will allow caregivers and teachers the opportunity to reflect on their capacities, which a consultant can use to promote motivation toward change. For example, caregivers may identify as a strength their agreement on family values, which can be used to create specific expectations to provide positive attention to a student when they engage in behaviors or make efforts to engage in behaviors that are aligned with those expectations.

The concept of teaming and collaboration refers to a process whereby a consultant works jointly with a family and teacher to (1) identify strengths, needs, and goals; (2) develop a shared understanding for data collection and plan development; and (3) promote shared responsibility for student success (Garbacz et al., 2008). A focus on teaming places all parties on the same side, united in supporting student success. Caregivers and teachers may see past areas of disagreement and come together to support the student. A focus on collaboration places shared responsibility on all for student success. Thus, one individual cannot move forward (e.g., with data collection or plan development) without the support and feedback from all.

Providing encouragement is an important skill for consultants to integrate. Caregivers and teachers are likely entering a collaborative Tier 3 process having already tried several strategies that did not effectively support student success. Thus, they may feel discouraged or even hopeless. Providing encouragement can help caregivers and teachers feel like they have a coach who is in their corner to support them, providing critical praise and words of encouragement to help them make decisions in the Tier 3 assessment and intervention process (Garbacz et al., 2008). Thus, a consultant can be a guide and source of social support for caregivers and teachers who need help with navigating their agency in the Tier 3 process.

> **"I'm really grateful for someone being willing to listen and work with us."**

Such agency can promote caregiver and teacher knowledge and skill building so that they have the confidence and competence to apply new skills in other situations (e.g., with other children or students).

At Tier 3, it is important for consultants who facilitate an assessment and intervention process that shows awareness for caregiver and teacher needs and responds appropriately when needs arise (Garbacz et al., 2008). This may involve reflecting on feelings that caregivers convey or providing an empathetic response when a teacher is expressing frustration. Additionally, consultants can also check in with caregivers and teachers to learn how they are experiencing the process. Caregiver and teacher responses to these questions may serve as helpful feedback for a consultant. For example, a caregiver may convey that they are feeling confused due to jargon or unfamiliar words a consultant and teacher are using. In response, caregivers and teachers can use words and phrases that are known to all and check in routinely about terminology.

> **"[As a parent] If you're made to feel like you don't understand the school environment, then you're not going to feel comfortable and you're not going to be able to communicate well . . . there's a way they [teachers] can make you feel like an insider versus an outsider . . . if they use a lot of jargon or school-based language that someone outside of the building isn't comfortable with, whether it's intentional or not, it can signal 'You're an outsider, you don't belong here,' or 'You don't know what you're talking about.'"**

Being sensitive and responsive also includes being honest and genuine in meetings, providing candid yet caring responses to questions (e.g., about other services a student may benefit from in the community or disagreements in co-parenting).

Communication underlies all human interactions. When effective, communication is often viewed as a facilitator to positive change. When ineffective, communication is often viewed as a barrier. Within Tier 3 services communication is used to guide the process and provide a clear understanding of operating procedures. Effective communication can include approaches such as using open-ended questions, paraphrasing a caregiver's response, and clarifying a teacher's perspective. It may also include pointing out areas of disagreement and developing a joint plan to move forward. A consultant who is facilitating a Tier 3 assessment and intervention process needs to use open and closed questions strategically to make efficient use of time. Starting with open-ended questions early in the process (e.g., "Tell me about some things your family does well"), and quickly moving to closed questions (e.g., "Do you think a focus on following directions during homework time or monitoring work completion is the more appropriate target for us?") allows a consultant to effectively guide an efficient Tier 3 process.

Promoting skill development is a key component of Tier 3 assessment and intervention. Caregivers and teachers arrange the environment to support students in reaching their goals (e.g., setting behavioral expectations, providing encouragement to students when following expectations). Thus, improvements in caregiver and teacher skills is expected to facilitate improvements in positive student outcomes. Consultants can promote skill development in caregivers and teachers through explaining or modeling assessment or intervention steps. Consultants can also provide encouragement to caregivers and teachers for correctly implementing steps in the process. Outcome studies of research on family–school interventions at Tier 3 and frequent findings report improved competence in problem-solving strategies as a result of their participation (Sheridan et al., 2017). This improved competence can support the student who is focused on this specific Tier 3 process while also facilitating improvements for other students or children's teachers or caregivers with whom they may work in the future.

The final partnership-centered component is being resourceful and sharing information. Consultants implementing a Tier 3 process help identify resources or supports for caregivers and teachers. For example, a family may benefit from community support through family therapy. A consultant can facilitate access to family therapy and coordinate with the therapist to promote consistency across services. In addition, consultants can share information when needed. This information is commonly germane to the specific issues discussed during the Tier 3 process, such as access to data collection forms or intervention materials. As consultants consider how to share resources or information with caregivers and teachers, they often provide choices to support their agency in the process and encourage their decision making as a team.

PROBLEM-SOLVING COMPONENTS

Problem-solving components of Tier 3 interventions refer to the content or objectives that are addressed during the Tier 3 process (see Table 7.2). Program developers and researchers have identified several core features of Tier 3 family–school interventions (Dishion & Stormshak, 2007; Fox & Swett, 2017; Sheridan & Kratochwill, 2008). Core features include (1) structured meetings, (2) co-creation of strategies, (3) multidirectional communication, (4) motivational interviewing, (5) implementation planning and support, (6) cross-setting support and coordination, and (7) sustainability planning.

Each family–school intervention at Tier 3 includes structured meetings that follow the problem-solving model (see Dishion & Stormshak, 2007, and Sheridan, 2014, for guides and workbooks to support implementation within these structured meetings). The process begins with an initial meeting to establish a collaborative and shared understanding for strengths and areas of need and to decide on an approach to collect data to better understand strengths and areas of need. The second stage includes ecological data collection to determine the nature of the areas of need as well as environmental factors that may be

TABLE 7.2. Problem-Solving Components of Family-School Interventions at Tier 3

Component	Description
Structured meetings	Structured meetings follow the problem-solving process (identification, analysis, implementation, evaluation); Meetings are conducted jointly as a caregiver–teacher–consultant team
Co-creation of strategies	Assessment and intervention plans are developed and evaluated collaboratively
Multidirectional communication	Communications are multidirectional, allowing caregivers, teachers, and consultants to communicate with each other back-and-forth
Motivational interviewing	Motivational interviewing is used as a method of communication; Consultants promote change talk by caregivers and teachers to move in the direction of addressing their goals
Implementation planning and support	Implementation planning includes discussing how to promote implementation of strategies as designed, such as by addressing perceived barriers and leveraging facilitators; Consultants provide support through modeling, role playing, and providing performance feedback
Cross-setting support and coordination	Assessment, intervention, and evaluation plans include home, school, and other relevant settings; Plans across these settings are coordinated
Sustainability planning	Plans for sustaining strategies and plans are initiated at the beginning of the process and discussed routinely to improve the likelihood that procedures will be maintained by the settings after the intervention concludes

contributing to the behaviors of concern. Data are collected on the presenting need (e.g., following directions at home, active academic engagement at school), what may be triggering the needs (e.g., nonpreferred activity leading to off-task behavior), and what follows the need (e.g., adult and student attention following off-task behavior). During a second meeting, a consultant facilitates a review of the data, and the team develops a shared understanding for the contributing factors. For example, a nonpreferred activity leads to off-task behavior, which is followed by adult and student attention. In this scenario, the team may hypothesize that off-task behavior occurs in the presence of a nonpreferred activity, and when the student engages in off-task behavior the teacher and other students provide attention, which may be maintaining the off-task behavior. Once the team develops a shared understanding for these conditions, they develop a plan of action. This plan is aligned with the family's ecological goals. Thus, the plan may include support for caregivers (e.g., family therapy in co-parenting) and students (e.g., a support plan to promote academic engagement in the classroom). The second meeting commonly also includes implementation planning and support so that caregivers and teachers are equipped to implement interventions in their classrooms. After the second meeting, interventions/plans are implemented, and data collection continues so that responsiveness to the intervention can be determined. During a third meeting, caregivers, teachers, and consultants review implementation data and decide whether to continue the intervention, modify the intervention, or begin fading the intervention. If data suggest goals have been met, it may be appropriate to end the intervention. Alternatively, if goals have not been met, the team will need to decide whether to continue the intervention the way it is (i.e., if there are signs of success) or modify it (i.e., if progress is not sufficient).

Problem-solving components are supported by the partnership-centered components and a few specific strategies. The first strategy is co-creation of plans. Within Tier 3, family–school intervention, caregivers, teachers, and a consultant work together to develop a shared understanding for strengths and areas of need, goals for improvement, the kinds of assessment/data collection procedures to use, the type of intervention plan to include, and ways to determine the progress toward goals. Thus, a consultant is present to support facilitation, not make decisions on behalf of the team. A second strategy is multidirectional communication. Effective communication was mentioned in the partnership-centered component section and is used strategically in a multidirectional manner. During the first meeting, the consultant facilitates a discussion about how the team will communicate, ensuring that communication avenues are in place for each team member to initiate and respond to communication. For example, the school sending a passive note home is insufficient, but it must include an opportunity for the caregiver to provide feedback and communicate back to the teacher.

Motivational interviewing can be used within Tier 3 family–school interventions as another strategy to facilitate progress. Motivational interviewing is often used in interventions as a method of communication to support client goal-directed change. A therapist, consultant, or provider supports client use of change talk, suggesting movement toward change, rather than sustain talk, suggesting a desire to stick with present circumstances. Within Tier 3 family–school interventions, a teacher may use sustain talk to comment on a classroom as too disruptive to really change or reflect on their inadequacy to create a more productive or engaging learning environment. Alternatively, a teacher who uses change talk may comment on a disruptive classroom but note their agency in creating change and hope in the procedures the team discussed. "I have been dealing with these class disruptions for a long time but based on what we talked about today I can really see a path forward. I think I can use these strategies to support students in being more active in their learning." The consultant's goal in using motivational interviewing can be to facilitate change talk between caregivers and teachers. For a comprehensive review of motivational interviewing as applied to schools, see Herman et al. (2020).

Implementation planning and support are used primarily during the second meeting and the third stage. During the second meeting, plans are made to support implementation, and it is useful to consider caregiver and teacher acceptability of the interventions, as well as their feasibility. Cognitive walk-throughs (Lyon et al., 2021) can be useful during this meeting as they allow individuals to walk through the steps of implementation, envisioning themselves in the natural setting. During this process, barriers may be identified that the team can problem solve to address. For example, a caregiver may identify that the interventions steps are too complicated to implement during a certain time period (e.g., homework time). Steps can then be removed to improve feasibility. In addition, implementation planning can support development and modification of plans to improve caregiver and teacher adherence to intervention plan steps (Sanetti et al., 2014). These approaches are used during the second meeting and during subsequent interactions as consultants, teachers, and caregivers check in about their progress. While caregivers and teachers implement plans, consultants serve as their coach, supporting their implementation through modeling, role playing, in vivo coaching, and praise or encouragement.

Cross-setting coordination is an important strategy within Tier 3 family–school interventions. The team works together to build continuity across home, school, and community settings. This is relevant for data collection, intervention planning, and implementation. The team focuses on supporting student success within home, school, and community settings. To effectively promote success across those settings, the team works together to strengthen their communication and create similar systems and supports across settings. These approaches ease transitions the student makes across home and school and provide access to similar supports across those settings.

Sustainability planning is a final strategy that consultants can use with caregivers and teachers to promote long term change. Sustainability planning starts from the first meeting and is reviewed routinely over the course of the process. Sustainability planning includes issues such as ensuring that plans and procedures are aligned with family and teacher culture and goals. In addition, the team aligns the assessment and intervention process with the home and school setting while planning for the natural contingencies in the environment to ultimately support the student's behavior. By aligning plans with classroom behavior expectations or those expectations with slight modifications, the team might find it easier to support long term change.

SCHOOLWIDE SYSTEMS TO SUPPORT IMPLEMENTATION OF TIER 3 FAMILY–SCHOOL PRACTICES

Family–school interventions at Tier 3 can be supported through schoolwide systems. When there are systems at Tier 1 to support family–school collaboration, families and teachers may be more interested in participating in Tier 3 services together. For example, families may have greater trust in the school when Tier 1 supports focus on family–school collaboration. In addition, teachers may experience family–school collaboration as a core function of their job rather than a novel approach only at Tier 3. Checklists can be helpful for school professionals to use and integrate problem-solving components and partnership-centered components in their work (see Forms 7.1 and 7.2).

Checklist for Integrating Partnership-Centered Components at Tier 3

PARTNERSHIP-CENTERED COMPONENTS

☐ Identify strengths of caregivers, teachers, and students.

☐ Support caregivers in creating goals that are consistent with their values.

☐ Use caregiver strengths to promote goal-directed change toward caregiver-created goals.

☐ Build connections between caregivers and teachers (e.g., point out similarities, use collaborative language).

☐ Validate caregivers in enhancing their skills and leveraging their strengths.

☐ Use multi-directional communication methods that allow caregivers and teachers multiple and varied ways to interact.

☐ Share relevant information with caregivers when requested.

☐ Use collaborative (e.g., we) language to promote partnerships across caregivers and teachers.

Checklist for Integrating Problem-Solving Components at Tier 3

PROBLEM-SOLVING COMPONENTS

☐ Follow the problem-solving modeling within four stages (identification, analysis, implementation, and evaluation).

☐ Develop and implement systems that allow caregivers and teacher to communicate back-and-forth outside meetings.

☐ Discuss possible barriers to participation and agree on strategies to address or cope with barriers.

☐ Tailor implementation support based on caregiver and teacher desires (e.g., modeling, role playing, and performance feedback).

☐ Collect data and implemented plans across and within home and school settings.

☐ Engage relevant community members to support problem solving (e.g., physicians, mental health professionals, and family advocates).

☐ Make plans early to sustain progress.

☐ Create authentic roles for student collaboration.

Garbacz et al. (2016) identified Tier 1 systems and practices to promote family–school collaboration that can leverage facilitators and overcome barriers that are commonly experienced by families and teachers (Garbacz, Hirano, et al., 2018; Garbacz, McIntosh, et al., 2018; Strickland-Cohen & Kyzar, 2019). Four approaches that are particularly relevant to family–school collaboration at Tier 1 and can promote implementation at Tier 3 are schoolwide teaming, administrator support, coordination across home and school, and family–school communication.

Schoolwide teaming involves a Tier 1 team identifying family–school data systems, family–school collaboration goals, and procedures to evaluate family–school data to determine progress towards goals, making modifications where necessary. Central to schoolwide teaming is inclusion of family and student voice in the process and outcome of the team's work. Families and students have a say in their experiences and are actively engaged in key decisions. For example, when determining school and classroom expectations, families and students provide input, and that input is integrated. Schoolwide teaming also involves understanding family and student culture and integrating their culture into school systems and practices. When families and school staff work together to create school systems, their collaboration is experienced as a shared space that reflects the values of all its members.

Administrator support is frequently noted as a key facilitator in adopting, implementing, and sustaining school systems and practices (McIntosh et al., 2014). Administrators can dedicate funding, align family collaboration with role descriptions, and provide leadership for advancing family–school practice integration within existing systems. What leadership administrators provide is visionary, concrete, and practical. Administrative presence at Tier 1 team meetings is important because it enables teams to move forward efficiently with key decisions and/or next steps. With administrative support for family–school practices in place, Tier 1 systems can better promote collaboration with families and set up Tier 3 systems for success.

Coordination across home and school can help promote consistency and continuity across settings. At Tier 1, after-school approaches such as school and classroom expectations are determined in coordination with families, those expectations can be made available to families for their use at home. For example, schools can hold a family night or an open house that provides families with support to adapt expectations in their homes. Then, caregivers can use praise and positive attention to acknowledge their child in a way that is similar to how the process unfolds at school. When implementing Tier 3 family–school interventions, the caregiver-teacher-consultant team can leverage these coordinated systems to support the development and implementation of support plans.

Communication across home and school at Tier 1 can support engagement in Tier 3 services and foster communication across home and school. We have previously mentioned the importance of family–school communication as a critical component of family–school collaboration. Establishing family–school communication systems at Tier 1 can provide a foundation for Tier 3 teams to begin setting up their communication practices. Sometimes, the Tier 1 communication systems can simply be adopted at Tier 3. Other times, the Tier 1 systems may help caregivers or teachers identify what is and is not working about communication systems and facilitate the identification of an adapted approach to communication that may better fit their preferences. In either case, having a starting foundation is helpful.

CASE EXAMPLE: ALEX'S ATTENDANCE STORY

This was a good week. All of Ms. Daniel's students were in class every day. This was especially significant considering it was the first time in several weeks Ms. Daniel has seen Alex consistently since the start of the school year. Ms. Daniel was pleased that the support plan put in place by the Tier 3 team was showing signs of success. Let's take a look at what steps were taken to meet Alex's needs.

Although the culture and practices at La Paz Elementary School encourage good school attendance for all students, at times, the Tier 1 attendance strategies, including attendance campaigns, monthly attendance assemblies, and awards, are not enough to ensure good attendance for all students. When the La Paz Attendance Team's review of weekly attendance reports reveal that the students are not meeting attendance goals, the team works to provide an increase in the level of support to those students. At Tier 2, the Attendance Team will communicate with students and families to identify and address any barriers that may be preventing the student from coming to school. Typically, Tier 1 and Tier 2 supports are successful for a majority of students, but at times, the team must respond to the attendance data and provide additional supports to the students who need them. Alex was one of those students.

Alex was a bright and well-behaved fifth grader. Although he did not appear to have any problem connecting with his friend groups, his academic performance was lower than expected, and he was not meeting benchmarks. The Attendance Team and Ms. Daniel suspected that because he was missing so much school, his grades and assessment scores were suffering. Despite a Tier 2 intervention that involved Alex attending regular Clock Club sessions, the campus support group for students who are struggling with regular school attendance, Alex continued to miss school. Ms. Daniel and the Attendance Team felt it was necessary to request a meeting with the Student Success Team (SST) to increase Alex's attendance supports. The SST is a multi-disciplinary team of a school-based staff (e.g., assistant principal, school psychologist, resource teacher, school nurse, school counselor, school social worker, and classroom teacher) who work together to develop a strength-based plan designed to provide appropriately intense support and interventions. In addition to the school-based staff, parents/guardians' attendance at the meeting is vital to the success of the SST. This would require the SST to extend an invitation to Alex's parents. In the past, Ms. Daniel has made several attempts to reach Alex's parents, Ms. and Mr. Chilton, via phone and email but was not always successful. After several failed attempts, Ms. Daniel waited in the student drop-off zone in the mornings when her students had music and was often able to connect with Alex's mother during drop off. Ms. Daniel relayed this information to Mr. Cooper, the SST coordinator when she submitted the meeting request. Once she completed the paperwork, the next step was to schedule the Tier 3 meeting with the team.

In preparation for the SST meeting, the team takes the following steps to promote a common understanding of the expectations and goals:

- The team holds an SST Pre-Meeting to review and discuss the referral, roles of team members, and family needs. They work to determine:
  - time of the meeting based on the family's schedule
  - confirm translator services if needed
  - facilitator
  - notetaker
  - timekeeper
  - family point of contact
- They review meeting norms:
  - Meeting will be conducted with compassion, empathy, and respect with careful attention to family input.
  - Glows and Grows format will be used:- Meeting starts with student's strengths (glows) from parent/guardian and teachers before discussing challenges (growth)
  - All suggested interventions are a team decision based and data informed.

Once the SST had held their pre-meeting, the next step was for Mr. Cooper to contact Ms. and Mr. Chilton to schedule the meeting and provide them with the meeting format and questions that would be asked. Using Ms. Daniel's advice, Mr. Cooper connected with Ms. Chilton at drop-off to invite her to an SST meeting. Mr. Cooper briefly shared information about the meeting and followed-up with a phone call to provide details and answer her questions. Mr. Cooper's goal was to ensure the family felt prepared, included, and welcome.

At the SST meeting, Alex's attendance and academic data were shared with Ms. Chilton. She expressed her embarrassment that she had not paid attention to the number of school days Alex had missed. She also explained that she works early Friday mornings and overnight on Sunday, and his father works out of town Monday through Friday. This overlap in their work schedules prevents Alex's parents from being able to drive him to school on Monday and Friday mornings. The original plan was for Alex to ride with a neighbor, but the family moved away, leaving Alex without consistent transportation. Upon learning of Alex's schedule, the team, including Ms. Chilton, devised a plan to support Alex. He was placed in the before-school program so that his parents could bring him to school prior to going to work. To address his learning loss, Alex was placed in intensive reading and math intervention after school two days per week and participated in structured after-school activities three days per week. Over the next six weeks, Ms. Daniel and the intervention teachers monitored Alex's progress at school, and Ms. Chilton monitored Alex's attendance at home. They then provided an update when the SST, including Ms. Chilton, reconvened in six weeks.

Their plan was working! Alex had only missed two days of school since he started the before-school program—a major improvement. Alex was still below benchmark on reading and math, but his scores were improving, and he was on track to meet benchmarks by the end of the semester. Ms. Chilton was proud of Alex's improved attendance and reported feeling much more confident in her ability to interpret his academic grades and interventions. She was relieved to know Alex was receiving high-quality before-school care.

CHAPTER 8

Overcoming Challenges to Family Engagement and Leadership in Schools' MTSS

As emphasized throughout this book, family–school collaboration in schools' MTSS (best articulated through the PBIS framework) is associated with many positive impacts for schools, educators, other school staff, and most importantly for students and families (see Garbacz et al., 2016, for a review). However, many factors mitigate against effective family–school collaboration. For example, reviewing the conceptual model of family–school collaboration conditions, variables, mechanisms, and outcomes presented in Chapter 1 (Figure 1.1) reveals challenges at every level. Conditions imply optimal state and local emphasis on family–school collaboration, but unfortunately, this priority is varies greatly across states and school districts. This is related to the combination of federalism (states' rights, local control) and site-based management, often giving school leaders significant autonomy over programming in their school building (see Weist & Paternite, 2006).

Further, each of the context variables, such as district and school investment in family–school collaboration, effective data systems to track and promote family–school collaboration, and bi-directional communication systems between schools and families, will be on a continuum, with clear strength in these context variables in some schools and complete absence in others. The condition and context variables in turn influence core variables (e.g., family–school collaboration treated as foundational to school systems and practices), which influence proximal (e.g., truly collaborative educator–family relationships) and distal (e.g., enhanced relationships among students) mechanisms, all of which implicate the achievement of valued student outcomes, such as their improved attendance and social, emotional, behavioral, and academic functioning. Processes can go awry at any given point in this conceptual model and contribute to the status quo of very limited family–school collaboration in schools (Weist et al., 2017).

Emerging literature points at factors that reduce the likelihood of genuine family–school collaboration in schools. For example, Huffman et al. (2021) reviewed literature about family engagement in schools and identified six categories of constraining influences:

1. poor buy-in on the importance of family–school collaboration by school administrators/leaders
2. ineffective MTSS implementation and tailoring of the MTSS to promote family–school collaboration
3. patterns of problematic communication and relationships with families that are at times even adversarial
4. limited priority by schools on cultural competence/humility in outreach efforts to families
5. excessive focus on negative behavior and stigma about student/family mental health issues
6. limited data and measurement systems to track and promote family–school collaboration

Similarly, Garbacz and Weist (2019) documented factors that limit family–school collaboration, including limited resources for PBIS team members focused on this theme, perceived lack of mutual interest in collaborating among both families and school staff, and poor systems for communication/collaboration (as above; also see Garbacz, Rose, Weist, & McIntosh, 2018). A significant problem is a general lack of protocols/guidance for family involvement in MTSS meetings (for example, how to be involved in the meeting and how to participate in Tier 1, Tier 2, and Tier 3 discussions; see Splett et al., 2017). A related problem is erroneous views that families should not participate in Tier 3 discussions as this could be associated with confidentiality violations (see Eber et al., 2020). Further, there may have been past problems between families and their child's school, associated with trust issues, resulting in families' hesitation to respond to invitations to participate in school events (see Carlson et al., 2020; Santiago et al., 2016).

A "COUNTERFACTUAL" OR NONEXAMPLE OF FAMILY–SCHOOL COLLABORATION PARTNERSHIP

In philosophy and other fields like economics, a "counterfactual" is a way to highlight a vision–reality gap, or "what isn't true but should be done," as a way to build discourse and support for a particular policy avenue (Starr, 2021). As shown in the reviews by Huffman et al. (2021) and Garbacz and Weist (2019), an unfortunate or counterfactual reality is that most schools are engaged in limited efforts to form genuine partnerships with families (McDaniel et al., 2014; Weist et al., 2017). Mapping on to the conceptual framework in Chapter 1, Figure 1.1, the scenario would involve limited school, district, state support for family–school collaboration; school-owned and unidirectional communication to families, conveying a relative lack of importance on their ideas/recommendations; limited collaboration with families in any aspect of the MTSS; limited relationships; the absence of partnerships between families and school staff; and missed opportunities for genuine family–school collaboration to enhance student social, emotional, behavioral, and academic outcomes.

MOVING AWAY FROM THE COUNTERFACTUAL TOWARD GENUINE FAMILY–SCHOOL COLLABORATION PARTNERSHIPS

To advance genuine family–school collaboration (and again consistent with Figure 1.1, Chapter 1), we need to focus at multiple levels, including the school building, the district, and the state context. This chapter focuses on effective two-way vertical communication/ collaboration and on collaboration from building to district to state and simultaneously in the other direction or state to district to building. Relatedly, at each of these levels there should be emphasis on effective horizontal collaboration, including effective interdisciplinary collaboration with students and families viewed as leaders as in other disciplines such as educators, school leaders, support staff and mental health staff (McCutcheon et al., 2014; McDaniel et al., 2014; Weist et al., 2012). For both vertical and horizontal collaboration, staff should make sure the views of families and students are highly valued, and their role as co-creators/developers of MTSS programming is highly appreciated. In this work it is also important for all to self-reflect on and try to reduce their own stereotypes and biases, and to reduce the use of language and practices that stigmatize or marginalize students and families, such as assuming the role of expert, telling families what to do, and emphasizing diagnoses involving pejorative labeling (e.g., "psychopathology," "severe emotional disturbance," see Weist et al., 2019). The next sections present strategies to promote genuine family–school collaboration at school building, district, and state levels.

Enhancing Family–School Collaboration at the School Building Level

We have developed an e-book on family–school collaboration supported by the Center on PBIS, (Weist et al., 2017) and have made a number of presentations at the Center's Leadership Forum (see *www.pbis.org/conference-and-presentations/pbis-leadership-forum*). In 2019, a presentation at the forum included more than 30 diverse stakeholders who problem-solved on ways to move toward genuine family–school collaboration within individual schools (Garbacz & Weist, 2019), with five primary recommendations presented below:

1. *Create a clear role for family–school collaboration within schools' MTSS.* This step involves defining what family–school collaboration in the MTSS looks like, and how families and school staff will work together in analyzing and improving programs across tiers. Ideally, there are at least a few family members that participate in school MTSS meetings, analyzing and providing recommendations for programming across all tiers. For example, at Tier 1, efforts can focus on general strategies to involve families in systems, data, and practices of the MTSS, to promote positive school climate, and to significantly enhance family leadership at schoolwide programs and events. At Tier 2, families can provide guidance on mentoring programs such as CICO (Crone et al., 2010), augmented with focused training in social–emotional learning. At Tier 3, families can problem solve issues pertaining on effective outreach to other families requiring more intensive services, and can identify and help them make connections to helpful school and community resources, as well as developing school to home and home to school communication systems to improve student behavior.

2. *Reach out to families proactively.* Although schools/districts should avoid unidirectional communication, it is important to develop proactive plans to communicate regularly with families (Reschly & Christenson, 2012). For example, a brief form could be sent to all families requesting their views on dimensions of their child's social, emotional, behavioral, and academic functioning and their thoughts on preferred ways to communicate to coordinate support for the student across home and school. This form could be expanded to describe schoolwide activities/events, and to invite family participation/leadership in them. This communication with families could be coordinated by a Family Outreach Team (FOT) of the MTSS team, including family members on the team. As presented in Chapter 6, ongoing positive communication to families about individual student behavior has broad positive impacts, and this team can help to coordinate this communication; for example. assuring that there are least four positive phone calls to families for each student in the school each year (Garbacz & Weist, 2019).

3. *Enhance the school atmosphere.* An important focus of the FOT is to help foster a welcoming school atmosphere (Christenson & Sheridan, 2001). This includes having team members scan all aspects of the school's physical environment, as well as having signage, artwork, and posted expectations to determine conditions that are welcoming and those that are off-putting. Similarly, routines of staff should be analyzed such as how families are welcomed into the building and if there is guidance/signage for them on finding offices and other resources within the school. Notably, school's atmosphere also includes its online presence, such as its website and various social media. Ideally, all online resources should be easy to navigate, relatively simple and straightforward, and exciting and can include active use of humor. Finally, bulletin boards, take one tables and other locations for the school's PBIS materials should be well organized, visually appealing, and they should encourage family interactions with school staff. Families and students should be involved in scanning these atmosphere factors, with clear mechanisms to make recommendations on their improvement (Garbacz & Weist, 2019).

4. *Emphasize two-way communication.* As underscored throughout this book, it is important for schools to move beyond the common pattern of one-way communication (school to home), often falling in one of two categories: (a) to inform families of school procedures and/or an event (e.g., fieldtrip) or (b) to convey a concern about student behavior or performance (e.g., noncompliant behavior with a teacher; see Christenson, 2004). In contrast to this common approach, conveying and demonstrating the expectation of two-way communication emphasizes to families the expectation by school staff of active collaboration with them in improving the school environment (Garbacz, Witte, & Houck, 2017). Examples of this two-way communication include having families contribute to the school materials such as newsletters and its PBIS matrix of expectations across settings, involving them in coordination og forums or "town halls" where families, students, and school staff discuss important issues/events happening in the school and/or in the community (Garbacz & Weist, 2019).

5. *Provide guidance and support for family–school collaboration in the school.* Unfortunately, many schools develop their PBIS systems with limited or no family guidance (Garbacz et al., 2017). While involving families this way will usually take more time, creating the opportunity for them to guide all aspects of PBIS programming will increase family buy-in

and help to increase their active involvement in all aspects of school functioning (Weist et al., 2017). Designated school staff should create lead liaisons with families and coordinate active planning with them in developing and enhancing PBIS procedures. Ideally, this would reflect all aspects of the MTSS including active involvement on the MTSS team and planning being involved at programming across tiers. A relevant and helpful resource is the Guidebook to Serving on Groups (see *https://servingongroups.org*), which provides step-by-step guidance to families on being involved in school teams (Garbacz & Weist, 2019).

Enhancing Family–School Collaboration at the District Level

In his second e-book on the interconnected systems framework (ISF) for school mental health and PBIS, Eber et al. (2020) emphasize the critical role of the school district in advancing effective MTSS that includes emphasis on family–school collaboration and family leadership. In this work, a District-Community Leadership Team (DCLT) meets regularly to guide ISF exploration and implementation, while also serving as a liaison between school buildings and providing resources at other levels, such as through state policy initiatives and regional and national centers, reflecting the vertical collaboration strategy reviewed above. Ideally, the DCLT should be inclusive of stakeholders with a vested interest in successful MTSS in schools. Given the connection between succesful MTSS and positive system change and social, emotional, behavioral, and academic outcomes in students (see Eagle et al., 2015; McIntosh & Goodman, 2016; Sugai & Horner, 2002b), one could argue that vested stakeholders reflect a broad group, including staff and leaders from education, mental health, child welfare, juvenile justice, and primary care, along with strong family and youth leadership, and involvement of faith and business communities (see Lever et al., 2003).

These DCLTs should meet at least quarterly, with inclusive representation and elevation of family/youth voice, and use a systematic strategy to guide meetings such as the Team-Initiated Problem Solving (TIPS) program (Todd et al., 2011). An initial step would be to gauge PBIS implementation in all schools using the District System Fidelity Inventory (DSFI; see *www.pbis.org/resource/pbis-district-systems-fidelity-inventory-dsfi-pilot-version-v0-1*). Use of the DSFI will highlight district strengths and challenges at Tiers 1, 2, and 3 of the MTSS, and such approach can help to strengthen all tiers in schools, identifying exemplary and struggling schools and developing individualized technical assistance and coaching plans for individual schools (Eber et al., 2021). Family and youth voice and leadership are essential, and DCLT leaders need to ensure such engagement is taking place (ideally at least one family member would serve in a leadership role).

A national workgroup provides resources and guidance to ISF implementation for many communities in the United States. Unfortunately, family involvement in school-level teams and in DCLTs is often very limited, consistent with growing literature in this area (Garbacz et al., 2017; Weist et al., 2017). For example, the third editor of this book (MW) led a randomized controlled trial comparing PBIS alone, co-located PBIS and school mental health, and the used ISF in two southern school districts. Over a 2-year period involving intervention and comparison of the three conditions in the study and using the Interconnected Systems Framework Implementation Inventory (ISF-II, Splett et al., 2020), we found consistent improvements in almost all areas of functioning for ISF schools. However, we did not find any consistent improvement in family engagement/leadership. In interacting with leaders and DCLTs from the two study sites, there was no clear consensus on this lack of family leadership, other than two factors of schools being very busy with other demands and not having a consistent ethic or set of actions associated with systematic outreach to families. This finding provides additional evidence for an overall theme of this book; that is, family–school collaboration in schools' MTSS may be valued but is often under-prioritized in most schools, emphasizing the critical work and opportunities ahead.

Enhancing Family–School Collaboration at the State Level

We were fortunate to include in this chapter a case study from Jane Walker and Susan Tager, two very experienced family advocates/leaders (each with over 30 years) with lived experience raising children struggling with emotional/behavioral challenges. Walker and Tager emphasized the importance of state level approaches in improving collaboration between family-run organizations and schools. Examples from five states, New Jersey, Pennsylvania, Maryland, Mississippi, and Arizona, include several relevant themes, such as family members partnering to improve schools' MTSS, creating awareness of mental health challenges and promoting mental health, connecting schools to community resources, providing training and coaching, and improving programming for students with disabilities.

CASE STUDY: FAMILY-RUN ORGANIZATIONS—PARTNERS IN SCHOOLS' MTSS

Jane Walker, Family-Run Executive Director Leadership Association, and Susan Tager, University of Maryland School of Medicine

Family-run organizations are uniquely suited to be effective partners with schools, school districts, and school systems in planning and sustaining MTSS for children and their families. Family-run organizations were started in the 1980s by family members caring for children with emotional or behavioral health needs as a way to support other families struggling to find help for their children. They are mainly staffed by parents and caregivers with lived experience in navigating the child-serving systems, and most report that the majority of their work involves families struggling with the complexities of the educational system. Across the nation, family-run organizations have become strong partners with schools in all tiers of the MTSS by promoting mental health awareness in schools, providing training and/or support groups for families and staff, and partnering on interventions for individual students and their families. Below are just a few of many examples from the field.

ROADSHOW in New Jersey

The Family-Based Services Association (FBSA) is the family-run organization in Monmouth County, New Jersey, and a member of the Children's Interagency Coordination Council

(CIACC). ROADSHOW is a collaboration between FBSA, the state's mental health care management organization and crisis services. The organization capitalizes on each school district's existing opportunities, such as in-service days or child study team meetings, to provide key information to schools regarding the services offered by FBSA, including crisis services and the care management organization. This method of outreach permits the FBSA to build relationships with teachers, school counselors, and other support staff in schools. Well-informed school staff can then more appropriately refer families to these resources, preventing reliance on police and other interventions that do not fit the needs of the child and family and could potentially escalate or traumatize them. Through FBSA, children, youth and their families receive assistance with developing individualized education programs (IEPs) and identifying additional supports necessary for student success. Linking families with additional resources helps them be successful in understanding options available in meeting their child's educational needs. ROADSHOW is supported as a community outreach function through existing state mental health contracts.

Student Assistance Program in Steel Valley School District, Pittsburgh, Pennsylvania

Allegheny Family Network (AFN) in Pittsburgh, Pennsylvania, is a partner of the Student Assistance Program (SAP) team in the Steel Valley School District. When a child is referred to the SAP, a trained family support partner from AFN provides information and education to the family, connects them to community resources, and provides emotional support for the family so that the SAP team member can focus on the needs of the student. The family support partner works both in and out of the school setting while the SAP team member is mainly school-based. AFN also holds parent support groups based on referrals from both the school and the SAP team. The school district is providing funding for this program using a mixture of grant funds and county funds.

Maryland Coalition of Families: The Family Leadership Initiative and Project AWARE

Since 2002, the Maryland State Department of Education has funded a Family Leadership Initiative (FLI) through the Maryland Coalition of Families (MCF). Provided across six consecutive weekends, this training informs families/caregivers about children's mental health in schools, especially as it relates to education and special education. Other youth-serving agencies, such as the Governor's Office for Children, the Behavioral Health Administration, and the Department of Juvenile Services and Child Welfare, also participate in the training. These agencies bring their expertise to the sessions to enhance the knowledge of the family members who participate in navigating those systems. At the end of the six weeks, families gain the knowledge needed to not only help their own child but also to help other families. Graduates of FLI move on to family support jobs, key volunteer leadership positions, and board membership in their counties.

The MCF was a critical partner in Maryland's Project AWARE, funded by the Substance Abuse and Mental Health Administration. MCF's role was to connect students with potential behavioral health needs and their families to community services. Two counties contracted with MCF to use trained family members with experience caring for a child with mental health needs to provide family navigation services in their schools. The navigators worked within the school system, supporting individual families by encouraging family engagement in the school and in their children's mental health services. The navigators also served on the student support team in each school. The value of family support in school can be illustrated by the way the navigators made a difference for a child and their family. A young student was struggling in class, acting out, and having trouble focusing. It was discovered that the child's parent often forgot to give the boy his medication in the morning. In a meeting with the parent, the navigator and the school all agreed it would be helpful if the school administered the student's medications during the week. The school nurse began administering the student's medication daily, and as a result, the child's attendance improved and grades increased. The child's mother reengaged with the school and began attending school meetings more regularly. The navigator was also able to support the mother in getting mental health treatment for herself. The outcomes were positive for the child, parent, and school.

Mississippi Families as Allies: Making a Plan Team in Jackson, Mississippi

With support from the Kellogg Foundation and the Mississippi Department of Mental Health, Families as Allies developed a two-pronged partnership with the Jackson Public School District. First, Families as Allies began facilitating the Making a Plan (MAP) Team to keep children in their homes and communities rather than having them placed in institutions. This multi-agency team partners with families and includes the Jackson Public School District (JPSD). Secondly, with the approval of the JPSD, Families as Allies developed a series of webinars on procedural safeguards to help families to understand their education rights. Families as Allies has also had the opportunity to partner with the Division of Medicaid to examine policies for school mental health (SMH) services that would lead to better academic outcomes and improve coordination between special education and SMH.

Family Involvement Center in Arizona

The Family Involvement Center (FIC), located in Maricopa County, Arizona, and operating statewide, provides parent peer support to individual families through both school and parent referral and employs a school liaison who conducts outreach and builds collaborations with schools. These programs are funded through Medicaid for eligible children/youth and families. With state funding, however, FIC is able to provide support to families whose children are uninsured or underinsured (non-Medicaid eligible) when behavioral health services are referred through the school and provided on or off school premises. FIC also operates a parent assistance line for families to access support, information, and connection to services. They have found that the majority of calls are from parents struggling with their child's school issues. Parents may need support to understand the process for receiving appropriate services for their child in school and to learn what to expect of the school, also what their own responsibilities are. In the process, they learn to be partners with the school staff for the benefit of their child. A parent peer support provider with FIC worked with a parent whose child had been in an out-of-home placement for two years due to behavioral health needs. When the child returned home, he struggled with issues brought on by not being at home with his family. The parent peer support provider supported the parent in reaching out to the school district to review the IEP that was in place from the school placement from the group home. The school district put in appropriate services in place throughout the day, and with these services, the student attained Honor Roll Status and outbursts in school gradually diminished. FIC is then a bridge for the family to engage with the school and facilitates open communication. FIC's Executive Director shared that parents appreciated the family-run organization, and that schools acknowledge that in order to help children, we first need to help parents.

Common Themes across These Examples

While each of these examples is different in its approach and the nature of the partnership, there are several common threads. Successful partnerships happen when leadership within the school, district, and state value collaboration with families. These partnerships should be embraced from the top down, and, just as in any culture shift, there must also be a commitment of resources, including funding and staff time to foster and sustain the partnerships. School budgets are tight, but schools have been creative in accessing local or state mental health funding, Medicaid, or private foundations for implementing innovative programs supporting student mental health. Lastly, successful partnerships are a shared responsibility and not the responsibility of one person in the school or one department in a district. Family-run organizations are independent nonprofit organizations found in almost every state. They have rich histories of supporting family engagement in education and partnering with schools to support student mental health. Building a collaboration with a family-run organization is an effective strategy in developing, implementing, and maintaining comprehensive SMH programming. Importantly, partnering with family-run organizations can help overcome many of the challenges that constrain family and youth leadership within schools' MTSS.

SUMMARY

In this chapter, we revisit a conceptual framework guiding strong family–school collaboration (Chapter 1, Figure 1.1), discuss the unfortunate reality of a significant gap between the vision of this framework and reality in most schools and districts, and present ideas to move toward genuine family–school collaboration at school building, district, and state levels. We emphasize the need for vertical collaboration between these levels and interdisciplinary, horizontal collaboration at each level, ideally with similar leaders and stakeholder groups being involved, particularly family leaders, through their work in family-run organizations. The chapter also emphasizes meta-themes such as building this work from a *shared agenda* involving all relevant stakeholder groups (led by families) with a vested interest in well-done

MTSS in schools (see Andis et al., 2002), and the value of building communities of practice, wherein diverse stakeholders work together across systems to build relationships, which are the foundation for the systematic work of enhanced family–school collaboration (see Cashman et al., 2014; Perales et al., 2017; Wenger et al., 2002). Moving beyond tokenism in family–school collaboration (see Weist et al., 2019), a fundamental theme is building genuine, mutually supportive relationships between schools and families, which enhance trust (see Murray & McCrone, 2014), and student and family connectedness to school, a powerful resilience factor (Serpell & Mashburn, 2011). As the work advances, students themselves become empowered for greater positions of genuine leadership (see Byrom, 2018; Gopalan et al., 2017), and ideally all of the factors reviewed earlier in this book and in this chapter coalesce toward real forward momentum to overcome challenges of the status quo of limited family–school collaboration and limited family and student leadership in schools' MTSS.

Funded by a Eugene Washington Engagement Award from the Patient-Centered Outcomes Research Institute (*Developing the Southeastern School Behavioral Health Community,* PCORI, EAIN-2874, 2015–2017, M. Weist, Principal Investigator), a team led by Mark D. Weist at the University of South Carolina conducted a series of eight focus groups in South Carolina on themes relevant to advancing effective school behavioral health programming (reflecting the ISF; see Eber et al., 2020; Perales et al., 2017). Focus groups included diverse themes relevant to effective school behavioral health, including quality of programming, cultural competence/humility, family partnerships, schoolwide approaches, and working with priority populations (i.e., connecting to juvenile justice, child welfare, and military systems). There were more than 100 themes represented across these focus groups, which were distilled into 34 recommendations for improving school behavioral health based on these themes and a comprehensive literature review (Weist et al., 2020). Notably, 18 of these 34 recommendations directly relate to enhancing family and youth voice/leadership toward effective and impactful programming. These 18 recommendations are presented in Table 8.1, covering a range of relevant dimensions towards families and youth as co-creators of schools' MTSS. These include enhancing family/student voice; moving toward genuine family–school–community partnerships; developing user-friendly resource directories for families; providing training and support to school staff, families and students on wellness, mental health literacy, and trauma sensitive approaches; improving communication and embracing technology; making data easier to use/analyze for families; and involving families in statewide advisory functions. The fact that more than half of these 34 recommendations related to empowering families and youth as key stakeholders/leaders in school behavioral health underscores the significant paradigm (see Garbacz, Minch, Jordan, Young, & Weist, 2020), and also highlights the timeliness and importance of this book.

As with any set of recommendations, this list is intended to be used by a school team as they action plan based on findings from a fidelity tool such as the TFI-FSC (Garbacz et al., 2020). This list can then support a school team in determining ways to leverage their strengths and address challenges they are experiencing as a school community. The list can also be considered by a school team as a reference guide that can then be augmented with content from other chapters. For example, a review of this list may prompt Tier 1, Tier 2, or Tier 3 teams to consider community resources for families that may support their school-wide, targeted, or intensive support efforts.

TABLE 8.1. Modified Recommendations to Enhance Family and Student Engagement/ Leadership in School Behavioral Health Programming

1. Expand the voices of family and diverse community members in driving the school behavioral health agenda and build relationships among school and mental health staff, students and families.
2. Attend to "siloing" among systems and groups of people and pursue cross-system collaboration.
3. Partner with families and community members to develop resources for guiding and expanding school behavioral health programs.
4. Maintain user-friendly directories of school and community resources to help students, families, and school staff connect to these resources and provide ongoing staff support to assure they are up to date.
5. Conduct community fairs planned by school staff, families, and students to involve other community agencies and resources to help build connections with them.
6. Stigma is a significant issue limiting the use and impact of school behavioral health, and there is a compelling need to train teachers, families, and students together in mental health literacy, which reduces stigma and is associated with improved help seeking and functioning.
7. Build wellness-focused training (e.g., coping, exercise, nutrition, stress management, and mindfulness) programming for students, families, teachers, and school staff, including school behavioral health staff from community agencies.
8. Train staff, families, and students on trauma and trauma-sensitive approaches in schools.
9. Expand teams to ensure they are inclusive of all disciplines, include families and students and assure clarity of roles for all team members and effective team meetings.
10. Empower students and families as decision makers in schools and support them in roles to co-create the education environment with school staff and mental health system collaborators.
11. Embrace technology to improve communication among all professionals and stakeholder groups.
12. Make data easier to use and involve diverse school staff, families, and students in reviewing and making data-driven recommendations for SBH interventions.
13. Assure all programs and services within the multi-tiered system of support (MTSS), including Tier 3 treatment services, are available to all students/families regardless of health insurance status and significantly involve private insurers in funding SBH.
14. Provide supportive liaison/case management services to families/caregivers with connections to juvenile justice and child welfare to assist them and their students with staying connected to the school, its curriculum, and supportive programs.
15. Include caregivers with experience in juvenile justice and child welfare in developing and implementing district- and state-wide policies to improve programs and supports for students encountering these systems.
16. Develop a state-wide advisory group that includes older youth and families to coordinate cross-system collaboration between education, mental health, child welfare, and juvenile justice in developing SBH programs accessible to the range of students who are impacted by these additional systems.
17. In communities that have higher percentages of military families, provide supports within the MTSS for the unique stressors these families and students encounter (e.g., frequent moves, changes in school systems, family member deployments, and reintegration).
18. In communities including more military stakeholders, assure that soldiers, officers, and other family members have a role in decision making at the district and school levels.

Note. Reduced from 34 overall recommendations from Weist, Collins, Martinez, and Greenlaw (2020). Furthering the advancement of school behavioral health in your community. In M. D. Weist, K. Franke, & R. Stevens (Eds.), *School behavioral health: Interconnecting comprehensive school mental health and positive behavior support* (pp. 123–128). Copyright © 2020 Springer Nature. Reprinted with permission.

CHAPTER 9

District Considerations for Building Capacity to Increase Family–School Collaboration

Lindsay M. Fallon, Adam B. Feinberg, Katherine Meyer, and Phylitia Jamerson

This chapter discusses the importance of district coordination of family–school collaboration in an MTSS framework. PBIS is used as the MTSS framework to guide a discussion about family–school collaboration, but similar principles and practices can be applied to other MTSS frameworks. First, we describe the rationale for district considerations for building capacity to increase family–school collaboration. Then, we outline how school districts function as complex systems with inputs and outputs. This precedes recommendations for action pertaining to a district's *executive functions* (inputs) as well as *implementation functions* (outputs). Finally, we provide a descriptive case example with a school district in the northeast United States to illustrate how district administrators and personnel have linked the theory described within this chapter to action in the district.

Lindsay M. Fallon, PhD, is Associate Professor of School Psychology at the University of Massachusetts Boston.

Adam B. Feinberg, PhD, is Professor at the Neag School of Education, University of Connecticut.

Katherine Mayer, PhD, is Research Associate at the Center for Behavioral Education and Research, University of Connecticut.

Phylitia Jamerson is Executive Director of Early College at the Massachusetts Department of Education.

IMPORTANCE OF DISTRICT COORDINATION OF FAMILY–SCHOOL COLLABORATION

Leaders within school districts play a critical role in schools adopting and sustaining MTSS such as PBIS. This is because district leaders are in positions to coordinate systems-level service delivery and build the capacity of school staff to support all students efficiently and effectively. District leaders do this by designating the resources (e.g., staffing, funds) and support (e.g., training, technical assistance) needed to promote stakeholder buy-in and consistent implementation of MTSS practices (George et al., 2018). Strong district leadership is critical for subsequently sustaining implementation of MTSS over time (McIntosh et al., 2013).

In developing and sustaining systems of support that are maximally effective and relevant, district leadership should prioritize family–school collaboration. This book describes decades-long research that examines the benefits of family–school collaboration (e.g., Raffaele & Knoff, 1999). Family–school collaboration can benefit students' social, emotional, and academic needs and improve parent–teacher relationships, communication, and trust (Smith et al., 2020). Promoting trust may be critically important for family members from minoritized backgrounds and underserved communities in particular who may not have always felt welcome in school, have had negative or challenging interactions with school staff, and/or experienced oppression while in school as children themselves (Baker et al., 2016; Yull et al., 2014). Trust is built when staff resist deficit thinking of caregivers and/or families and focus on developing and sustaining positive relationships and on connecting their home–school collaboration work to equity (Flores & Kyere, 2020). Trust may also be critically important to families who recently immigrated to the United States. Outreach efforts can proactively address challenges immigrant and refugee families face by removing barriers to educational access (e.g., with support of school liaisons, community organization involvement) and communication (e.g., translation of school materials, availability of translators at school meetings and events) (Georgis et al., 2014).

Cultural responsivity is critical for district leaders to consider when building capacity to increase family–school collaboration (Garbacz, 2019). Engaging in culturally responsive practice might include (1) attending to identity and identity development of school and community stakeholders; (2) valuing family and community voice in the design and implementation of MTSS systems; (3) creating an inclusive and supportive school climate; (4) acknowledging that behavioral expectations may differ across home, school, and community settings; and (5) analyzing available data critically to discern evidence of inequity in order to generate action steps toward appropriate change (Leverson et al., 2021).

Considering these general principles, district leaders can develop and coordinate systems where frequent and bidirectional communication takes place between home and school. They might also participate in shared goal setting, decision making, and accountability among stakeholders (Garbacz et al., 2018). These coordinated systems may be designed to support engagement to promote a variety of goals. For instance, the Oakland Unified School District (OUSD) proposed a hierarchical model for family–school engagement including four levels (Kehrer, 2019). Level one proposes activities to help family members gain information to support their child's success in school. Level two involves activities in which families can be involved to promote school improvement. Level three includes activities to support family involvement in school governance and decision making. Finally, level four proposes activities to support family involvement in district-level engagement. Family member involvement at level four offers an opportunity to gain diverse, local perspectives from the community which is not always included when district leaders plan and implement systems change efforts.

To promote family–school collaboration in an MTSS context, we urge school and district personnel to consider the many ways in which families might be involved in MTSS implementation. Figure 9.1 adapts the model presented by OUSD to propose considerations for maximizing family–school collaboration to achieve various aims related to the implementation of MTSS, specifically to support students' behavior (i.e., PBIS). At the most foundational level (Level 1), efforts to promote home–school collaboration are focused on how PBIS supports the student (i.e., family's child). Activities could include surveying families about students' social–emotional well-being and welcoming families to school for events, trainings, conferences, and celebrations. School and district personnel might also promote home–school collaboration focused on PBIS to improve school climate (Level 2). This may involve soliciting and incorporating feedback about PBIS practices and having family representation on the school PBIS team.

In addition, home–school collaboration could focus on PBIS to promote effective school policy (Level 3). Families might partner with school personnel to engage in analysis and evaluation, review aggregate student data, and work together to revise school policy to promote equity. For instance, families might work with staff to devise restorative and instructional procedures to respond to challenging behavior to replace discipline policies that emphasize exclusion from the classroom or school community (e.g., office discipline referrals, in-school suspension). Family members can also be part of fiscal and hiring committees to represent the school community in budget and personnel decisions. This might increase the chances of the local community members being hired for school-based positions. Such representation has been found to be promotive to youth development (La Salle et al., 2020). Finally, promoting family–school collaboration may improve district engagement (Level 4). By including family members on the district PBIS leadership team, educational leaders can provide space for family voice in district-level governance. This can have implications for how strategic priorities are developed and set, resources are allocated, and districtwide implementation is executed. Although our focus in this chapter is primarily related to district-level engagement, district leadership should also promote and support family–school collaboration across Levels 1, 2, and 3. Form 9.1 presents a worksheet to collaboratively generate action steps for each of the four levels outlined in the OUSD model.

Family–School Collaboration Focused on Improving District Engagement

Include family members on budget and hire committees for district-level positions pertaining to PBIS (e.g., district climate coach).

Partner with family and community organization to support outreach and bridge PBIS across settings.

Solicit family member input on district training activities.

Include family representation on District PBIS Leadership Team.

Include family members on district evaluation teams and partner with families to identify district improvement goals and strategies.

Family–School Collaboration Focused on PBIS to Promote Effective School Policy

Include family members on evaluation teams for students' social, emotional, and academic outcomes.

Partner with family members to revise school policy based on evaluation data.

Include family members on budget and hire committees for school-level positions pertaining to PBIS (e.g., climate coach, family-school liaison).

Partner with family members to identify school improvement goals and strategies.

Family–School Collaboration Focused on PBIS to Improve School Climate

Provide trainings to families to implement PBIS practices in the home setting.

Solicit and incorporate feedback from families about schoolwide PBIS practices.

Partner with family–school organizations (e.g., Parent–Teacher Organization [PTO]).

Include family representation on school PBIS team.

Family–School Collaboration Focused on PBIS to Support the Family's Child

Listen and learn about families' culture and community values.

Survey families about school climate, student well-being, and training needs.

Regularly share data relevant to PBIS with family members (e.g., school climate data, attendance data).

Welcome and support families to participate in school orientation, parent–teacher conferences, and PBIS trainings, as well as schoolwide events and celebrations.

Welcoming and Supporting Family–School Collaboration

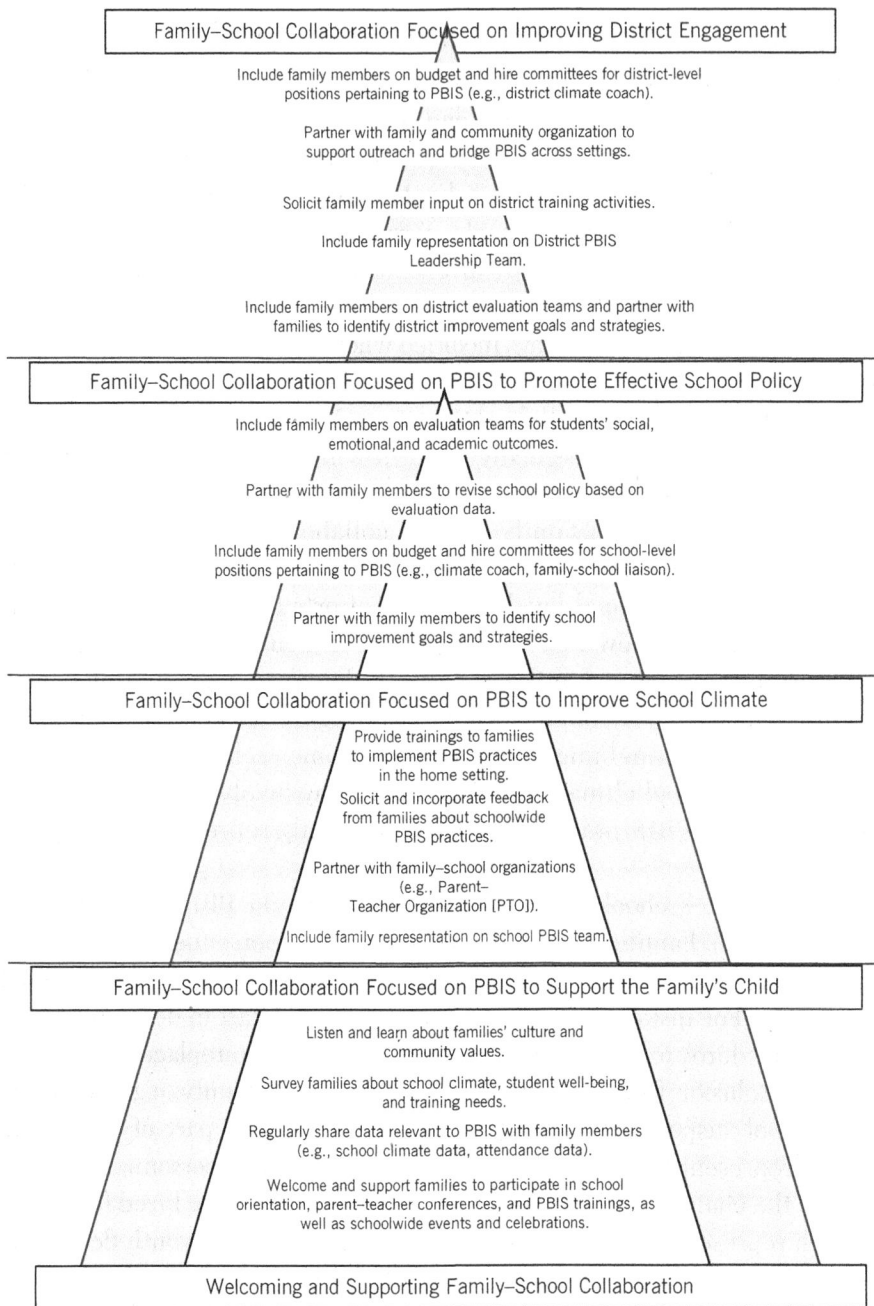

FIGURE 9.1. Suggested practices to promote school- and districtwide family engagement.

Worksheet to Plan Promotion of District- and Schoolwide Family Engagement

In what ways will the PBIS District Leadership Team promote family–school collaboration?

- _____
- _____
- _____
- _____
- _____
- _____

In what ways will the PBIS School Leadership Team support family–school collaboration to promote effective school policy?

- _____
- _____
- _____
- _____
- _____

In what ways will the PBIS School Leadership Team support family–school collaboration to promote school climate?

- _____
- _____
- _____
- _____
- _____

In what ways will the PBIS School Leadership Team support family–school collaboration to support the family's child?

- _____
- _____
- _____
- _____
- _____

Welcoming and Supporting Family–School Collaboration

SCHOOL DISTRICTS AS SYSTEMS

To build capacity to increase family–school collaboration districtwide, it is first important to understand that school districts are complex systems. A system is a set of interconnected components with individuals fulfilling specific roles, operating with a common set of norms, and regulating inputs and outputs (Forman & Selman, 2011). Inputs refer to what is invested in the system (e.g., resources, time, personnel) to support outputs (e.g., routines, interventions) enacted to ultimately promote successful outcomes (Sugai & Horner, 2020). For school systems adopting and implementing PBIS, the district leadership team coordinates *executive functions* (inputs) to support *implementation functions* (outputs). These functions are based on implementation drivers or elements that support comprehensive and sustained delivery of systems-level change initiatives (Fixsen et al., 2013). All functions are critical to promoting successful practice and outcomes for youth in school (Center on Positive Behavioral Interventions and Supports, 2017) but require time, resources, and personnel to develop.

Research in implementation science proposes several stages for adopting and scaling up change in a system. These stages include (1) *exploration/adoption* (in which a change or initiative is considered), (2) *installation* (in which infrastructure for the initiative is established), (3) *initial implementation* (in which the initiative is piloted so that stakeholders can learn how to implement effectively before expanding), (4) *full implementation* (in which the initiative is used more expansively), and (5) *continuous regeneration* (in which results from regularly scheduled evaluations guide changes necessary to maximize the efficiency and effectiveness of systems implemented; Fixsen et al., 2005). The questions a team might ask throughout the systems–change process is "Should we do this?" (exploration/adoption); then "Can we do this right?" (installation, initial implementation) before asking, "How can we make this better?" (full implementation, continuous regeneration; Kincaid & Horner, 2017). When asking these questions, family voice and perspective are critical for efforts to be successful.

Below, we use this systems–change model in the context of coordinating PBIS implementation to provide guidance about how to build capacity to increase family–school collaboration across school districts. First, we focus on the composition and activities of the district leadership team. Then we target the district team's *executive functions* (inputs) including (1) stakeholder engagement, (2) funding and alignment, (3) policy, and (4) workforce capacity. Subsequently, we offer considerations pertaining to the team's *implementation functions* (outputs) including (5) training, (6) coaching, (7) evaluation, as well as the value of identifying local implementation demonstrations. We align our description of the district leadership team, executive and implementation functions, and demonstration site selection with the categories and items on the PBIS District Systems Fidelity Inventory (DSFI; Center on Positive Behavioral Interventions and Supports, 2020a), a tool to guide districtwide implementation of PBIS. These categories and items are similar to those described in the PBIS Implementation Blueprint (Center on Positive Behavioral Interventions and Supports, 2017). We use items from the DSFI to provide targeted recommendations for how the district leadership team might maximize family–school collaboration both in the sections to follow as well as in Appendix 9.A. Finally, we synthesize recommendations with an illustrative case example from a public school district in the northeastern United States.

LEADERSHIP TEAMING

Research on effective teaming suggests the importance of team membership. Specifically, teams should be coordinated by a leader representative of the broader community of interest, have a member (or multiple members) with the authority to make policy and/or fiscal decisions, and contain members with relevant expertise (Horner et al., 2014). District leaders can build capacity to promote family–school collaboration by including family members on district leadership teams. This might include an individual to represent the voice of the community and district families on an executive leadership team. Alternatively, the district might have advisory groups comprised of caregivers from various schools or representing certain student groups (e.g., youth with disabilities) to solicit feedback and incorporate family members' voice and preferences into key decisions. Another option is that families can provide input on policies and practices that the team will consider in decision making. The emphasis is on providing multiple and varied ways for families to help drive school decisions. School team members can invite families to participate and incorporate their feedback into school policies and practices. Family members have a unique perspective on local family concerns and values and may be able to connect the team to other community organizations to support the team's functioning.

Best practices in teaming also suggest a team has systems in place to ensure the group meets regularly and with efficiency (Bruhn & Hirsch, 2017). To promote attendance during meetings, district leadership teams can remove barriers to active family participation. This might include offering the option for family members to participate in meetings remotely (via video conferencing), selecting to meet in the evening or on weekends (i.e., not during daytime working hours), offering childcare, serving meals, and/or providing a translator during meetings, if needed (Baker et al., 2016).

During meetings, the team can prioritize understanding the needs of families and the community. By creating opportunities for community members' voices to be heard (e.g., holding listening sessions, engaging in community outreach; Leverson et al., 2021), district teams can support family member(s) on the team in communicating their needs. This will allow the team to better understand the values of family groups in the community to ensure district team conversations are aligned with that of the local community. The team's communication should be bidirectional. That is, the team listens deeply to understand the concerns of the community, and in return, the team communicates how that information will be used to support youth and families in the school community through implementation of PBIS.

EXECUTIVE FUNCTIONS

The *executive functions* (inputs) of the district leadership team include stakeholder engagement (collaborating with those who are involved with the district and schools), funding and alignment (allocating sufficient resources strategically), policy (creating and sustaining supportive policy to ensure successful implementation) and workforce capacity (having a sufficient number of well-trained personnel to facilitate comprehensive implementation).

These functions are described and linked to considerations for building capacity promoting home–school collaboration within the district.

Stakeholder Engagement

Stakeholders are people interested in the success of a school or district (Center on Positive Behavioral Interventions and Supports, 2020a), and they include a variety of individuals: educators, support personnel, administrators, community members, providers from outside agencies, representatives from community-based organization, etc. Since this book describes family–school collaboration (e.g., active or passive parent involvement in educational decisions and planning with school staff), we encourage districts to engage families and school professionals in an active and dynamic coordination and collaboration that removes power differentials by eliminating barriers to full participation in systems planning and implementation (Garbacz et al., 2016). We acknowledge that district and school PBIS leadership teams might partner with different stakeholders in the design and implementation of PBIS to promote its relevance and effectiveness. Families should be involved in all relevant activities including goal setting, policy development, training, and evaluation. The team should open multiple pathways for communication with families based on input about preferences (e.g., use of email/text messaging, newsletters, video briefings, social media posting) and preferred language (e.g., translation of all materials). Family engagement might also be bolstered by leaders and team members being visible at family and community events. This can signal support and investment in authentic collaboration.

Funding and Alignment

Funding and alignment refer to the intentional and strategic allocation of budgets (and other resources) to support activities that will promote desired outcomes (Center on Positive Behavioral Interventions and Supports, 2020a). Research related to systems change and implementation science reveals that educational leadership might support and sustain PBIS by (1) defining a funding source that can be maintained for at least 3 years; (2) prioritizing the visibility of the work through active and consistent messaging to staff, families, and other stakeholders; and (3) garnishing support from staff and key decision-makers prior to initiating training (Horner et al., 2014). To maximize family–school collaboration, district and school leaders might (1) include in designated funding the resources needed to engage in outreach to families (e.g., hiring or reallocating funding to support a parent liaison or outreach coordinator); (2) welcome families to events that increase the visibility of PBIS (e.g., school events, workshop, trainings); and (3) gain support and input from families by offering the opportunity to co-design PBIS systems and/or offer feedback on specific practices or policies (e.g., school leadership team involvement, family focus groups). School team members can help advocate for funding and additional support through sharing the benefits from family–school collaboration for their teaching, classrooms, and students.

To further increase alignment with family and community values, the PBIS leadership team might seek to collaborate with community agencies, which might include pediatric healthcare practices for medical and mental health care as well as community organizations (e.g., Boys and Girls Club, YMCA). Staff from community agencies may have greater awareness of family needs and larger community efforts as well as more established trust with families based on past engagement or support. Collaboration could also provide opportunity for wraparound supports in home and community contexts (Fallon & Mueller, 2017). This insight might inform the development of strategic district improvement goals and encourage explicit mapping of the goals according to needs of school communities, families, and neighborhood groups. District leaders might also gather input from stakeholders (e.g., public comment periods, open listening sessions during school committee or board meetings) with an effort to systematically integrate feedback provided into system practices and policy and share input with school communities for subsequent design, planning, and implementation. For example, the district leadership team might solicit feedback about universal and intensive interventions offered to youth in schools to ensure the interventions are perceived as culturally and contextually relevant by families (Sugai et al., 2012).

Policy

Policy refers to laws (e.g., federal, state) or local (e.g., state, district, school) guidelines supporting implementation of MTSS such as PBIS. To build sustainable systems, policy should emphasize the importance of support for social behavior for students (Horner et al., 2014). Frequently, the initial development of PBIS systems begins by crafting a mission, vision, or outcome statement (Eber et al., 2002). District and school PBIS leadership teams should partner with families to co-develop this mission or vision statement so that it is consistent with family and community values. This statement could drive not only the practices developed as part of the coordinated tiered service delivery models (e.g., teaching expectations, acknowledgment procedures) but also policy related to discipline. Instead of a reactive approach to discipline, families can work with educators to co-develop discipline policy that is proactive, strength-based, and culturally affirming. The goal might be to create policy which promotes socially supportive, predictable educational spaces where there is an emphasis on positive relationships between staff, families, and students (Allen et al., 2013). Policy should also dictate that when challenging behavior occurs, responses are instructional and involve collaboration with families rather than being punitive or exclusionary (Hambacher, 2018). If families are not involved in the co-development of policies, district and school PBIS leaders can solicit feedback from family and community member to ensure policies are clear, reasonable, and in line with educational equity.

Workforce Capacity

Finally, workforce capacity pertains to district leadership that hiring staff designated to support PBIS implementation and to evaluate implementation efforts regularly (e.g., annually). District leadership should consider including in position detailed descriptions of responsibilities associated with family–school collaboration. In addition, family members might be actively involved in selecting criteria for hiring or evaluating district personnel supporting PBIS and/or family outreach efforts and in both evaluating and promoting such positions in the community. It is important that district key district personnel are selected with expertise in family outreach as well as understanding local community needs. Hence, it is advisable to include family members in the identification and selection processes (e.g., hiring committees) for these roles.

IMPLEMENTATION FUNCTIONS

The *implementation functions* (outputs) of the district leadership team include (1) training (providing initial instruction), (2) coaching (offering ongoing support), and (3) evaluation (assessing progress and making changes to improve outcomes). In addition, local implementation demonstration is also critical to model effective supports for other sites. These functions and critical elements are described below and linked to considerations for building capacity to promote home–school collaboration within the district.

Training

District leadership coordinates high-quality training with opportunities for didactic instruction, modeling, practice, and feedback (Fallon et al., 2018). This occurs in the context of initial training as well as technical assistance (e.g., coaching) to promote sustained fidelity over time (Kittelman et al., 2019). School district personnel might partner with regional or state technical assistance centers as well as university partners to support training efforts (Garbacz, 2019). District leaders and training partners can collaborate with family and community stakeholders to generate and execute a professional development plan based on the district's strategic goals. Collaboration can help ensure that the outcomes associated with professional development are aligned with family support efforts and that they benefit the needs of the community. These training efforts might emphasize effective family–school collaboration practices as well as offer spaces for both families and educators to collaborate and learn. Topics of training should be relevant for all parties. For example, a district might offer training in de-escalation strategies to school staff, parents, and members of the community (e.g., law enforcement agents, mental health providers). Families can help to ensure that the program or approach selected is culturally and contextually relevant, and that such a training can benefit youth and stakeholders across a variety of settings (Whitcomb et al., 2021).

In addition, families might provide input when evaluating the outcomes of training and professional development effort (e.g., via family survey). Feedback might be collected after trainings about (1) what supports are available to their child across tiers (i.e., Tiers 1, 2, and 3); (2) how families can request assistance for supports if they have concerns about their child; and (3) how intervention efforts might be designed to maximize family–school collaboration, ensuring a more comprehensive approach to student support.

Coaching

Coaching expands professional development by providing more targeted support to promote implementation of new skills and practices, frequently including modeling, observation, and/

or offering feedback (Freeman et al., 2017). External coaching is often provided by an outside consultant (e.g., a provider from a local behavioral health agency or university research partner) with expertise in behavior, systems, and positive supports. An internal coach typically has the same expertise as an external coach but is employed by the district or school (Lewis et al., 2016). District leadership can provide both opportunities and support for internal and/or external coaches to partner with families to ensure they have the knowledge and awareness of local family concerns and community efforts. This will help coaches support the needs common to school stakeholders and family groups, as well as integrate family engagement strategies within a district- and schoolwide PBIS practices. Examples include promoting shared ownership of behavioral expectations and collaboratively teaching expectations across settings (Leverson et al., 2016). Coaches can then communicate directly with families about successes and challenges of school-based implementation, leveraging communication and relationships with families to address implementation barriers. Coaches can also support school teams or individual educators in proactively reaching out to families to create a partnership-centered relationship. In response, family, and school staff members can generate effective solutions (e.g., redesigning how expectations are taught, developing new acknowledgment procedures).

Evaluation

Generally, evaluation refers to the methodic review of systems to understand areas of strength and opportunity for improvement. District leadership teams might include family and community representation in the development and decision making of the district evaluation plan. In addition, leadership might solicit family input through community surveys and/or focus groups as part of the evaluation process. Data collection might target not only family perceptions across all targeted community groups but also mechanisms and success of family engagement efforts. It may be particularly important to ensure that data are collected on family knowledge of supports provided across tiers. Furthermore, district-level evaluation reports should include all stakeholder, process, and outcome data relative to family–school partnerships. This information could then be shared and reviewed by family and community stakeholder groups with the opportunity to provide feedback on report findings. A key emphasis when collecting data from families is to have a plan for incorporating family feedback into policy and practice changes at the school and then transparently communicating with families about how their feedback led to schoolwide change.

Local Implementation Demonstration

Local implementation demonstration typically refers to schools implementing PBIS practices with high levels of fidelity. These practices are designated as learning or observation sites for other schools (Kincaid & Horner, 2017). This approach supports scaling up within the district. Considerations for engaging in family–school collaboration include family members or community groups providing input as to which schools are selected as demonstration sites. Ideally, these schools have successful family–school partnership efforts, and these efforts are then highlighted and shared with other sites in the school district.

An example of a local demonstration of family–school collaboration is included by Bal and colleagues (2016) and is also described in Chapter 3 of this book. In the article, the authors describe how the PBIS team at a high school in a midwestern state engaged with families to redesign the school discipline process to include more opportunities for (1) conflict resolution, (2) restorative practices, and (3) data collection, involving families throughout each stage of the redesign process. This redesign was then shared with other schools via districtwide professional development and planning workshops to support staff in other buildings to adopt a similar process (Bal et al., 2016).

In the section to follow, we provide a comprehensive case study with a school district. The example highlights areas of strength and opportunity, considering district teaming and leadership, the team's *executive functions* (stakeholder engagement, funding and alignment, policy, and workforce capacity) and *implementation functions* (training, coaching, and evaluation), as well as local implementation demonstration.

CASE STUDY

Lynn Public Schools is a large, suburban school district outside of Boston, Massachusetts, educating approximately 16,000 students. The city of Lynn has historically been a manufacturing town and today is home to a large immigrant population; over one-third of Lynn residents were born outside of the United States (U.S. Census Bureau, 2020). Within the schools, 79.5% of enrolled students are considered high needs (economically disadvantaged, English learners, and/or a student with disabilities), and most youth come from minoritized backgrounds (67.6% Hispanic, 8.2% Black, 7.6% Asian, 3.2% multiple races; Massachusetts Department of Elementary and Secondary Education, 2021). For parents of children in the Lynn Public Schools, the median household income is $58,406 (National Center for Education Statistics, 2020), falling below the national average of $68,703 in 2019 (U.S. Census, 2019). Most parents are employed (85.1%) and have at least a high school degree (73.1%); approximately 90% of staff are White (Massachusetts Department of Elementary and Secondary Education, 2021). Teacher demographics in the district align with national teaching trends (Hussar et al., 2020) yet do not reflect the cultural and linguistic backgrounds of most families within the district. This misalignment has presented challenges to facilitating effective communication (La Salle et al., 2020). Challenges include families whose first language is Spanish initiating communication with predominately English-speaking school staff. District practices that communicate clearly and accessibly with families, often times through translated materials in Spanish, ensure family members are receiving critical information from school partners. Considering these and other challenges, we present details below pertaining to the executive and implementation functions implemented by the district leadership team within the Lynn Public Schools. We begin by supplying information about initial PBIS training and coaching to provide context before describing the team and its functions.

Training and Coaching

Staff within Lynn Schools were first trained to implement PBIS in the 2009–2010 academic year by an external PBIS consultant (Adam B. Feinberg). The first two schools trained in the district were alternative education schools, one supporting elementary-aged students and the other supporting students in secondary grades. There were two primary reasons district leadership decided to focus training efforts initially on these two demonstration sites. First, students within the schools had intensive behavioral needs and seemed to present the most immediate need for comprehensive positive behavioral supports involving active family participation. Second, an internal PBIS coach supported both schools on site a few days each week (i.e., workforce capacity) and was able to support implementation more intensively than the external coach alone. Supports were scaled to include advanced tiers (Tier 2 and 3 interventions) in addition to universal prevention over subsequent years, and the sites served as examples in the district.

In the 2015–2016 academic year, two additional elementary schools received training to implement PBIS by an external coach (Katherine Meyer) who continued to coach the schools until 2019. Each year, two to three additional schools within the district were trained and technical assistance was provided to teams to promote and sustain PBIS implementation. In 2019, three additional schools as well as schools not fully implementing Tier 1 (per scores on the Tiered Fidelity Inventory; Algozzine et al., 2014) enrolled in the Massachusetts PBIS Training Academy, a comprehensive cohort-style multi-year training effort coordinated by the Northeast Positive Behavior Intervention and Supports Network.

Leadership Team and Evaluation

In the Lynn Public Schools, the district leadership team includes district-level staff from the superintendent's office; the Curriculum, English Learner, and Social Emotional Learning Departments (e.g., social worker); and school-based staff including PBIS coaches, a principal, social worker, and behavior specialist. The team is currently lead by the Director of Special Education for the district; however, there is a strategic plan to expand the representation of the team to include family member representation as well as clearly defined roles to create a sense of shared responsibility. Roles will include an individual to coordinate regular meetings, annual evaluation, and data sharing. Currently, this does not happen consistently but is recognized as an area to promote future growth. In addition, the current team sees the need for an individual to coordinate communication with family and community stakeholders. Specifically, this individual would be responsible for coordinating outreach to families and the community in support of designing and implementing PBIS systems.

Stakeholder Engagement

Prior to the COVID-19 pandemic, leaders within the school district made several efforts to engage families within the school community. Strategic planning for district improvement included creating a vision for where the district wanted to be in five years. To do this, the superintendent hired an external educational consultant who met with district leaders, school principals, school-based staff, parents, and representatives from community agencies (e.g., Girls, Inc. of Lynn, Lynn YMCA) to run focus groups. The consultant shared information gathered from focus groups back to the superintendent and district leadership to guide the creation of strategic goals. The consultant then sought feedback for these strategic goals from educators, families, and community members by attending school-level strategic planning meetings (which included family representation) as well as parent advisory committee (PAC) meetings for various groups (i.e., elected parent representatives for English Learner and students with disabilities). This feedback supported school improvement planning and included efforts to promote students' social and emotional wellness (e.g., implementation of PBIS).

Once school closures were enacted in response to the spread of COVID-19, school staff engaged in more outreach to families. In response, district leadership sought to strengthen the coordination of family engagement. Specifically, district leadership recognized an opportunity to confront previously identified barriers to family engagement (e.g., communicate with families who primarily speak a language other than English, accessing families with caregivers who work outside of the home). Confronting these barriers required planning and strategic resource allocation, but also offered greater and more sustained access to families. One example of these efforts was to utilize text messaging to communicate important messages to families. This expanded the ways in which important communications (e.g., school meetings, behavioral expectations) could be sent to families. The district also coordinated the distribution of laptops to all students and staff within three months of COVID-19-related school closings. Providing a device to each school community member was part of the strategic plan for the district and was set to occur over three years. However, in the context of COVID-19, the distribution happened much faster. Devices were distributed to not only support students' access to continued instruction, but also allow for families to be in communication with school and district leaders electronically amidst the pandemic. District leadership are resolute in their efforts to continue these new methods of outreach (e.g., electronic communication) post-pandemic to increase efficiency and opportunity for collaboration with families. For example, the district often has a goal to share summaries of students' behavioral data (e.g., intervention data, office discipline referral data) with secure links sent via text message for family members to access on their cell phones. Administrators are working toward setting up the systems to do this efficiently and in compliance with privacy regulations.

Funding, Alignment, and Policy

Support for PBIS is coordinated and funded by the district's Special Education Department. Resources were devoted to teachers to spend time engaging in outreach. Specifically, district leadership dedicated one hour in teachers' day for family outreach activities (e.g., calling families, sharing resources, and communicating student progress updates). In addition, targeted family outreach aims to support school attendance lead by each school's wellness team. This team typically includes a social worker, administrator, general and special education teacher, and school counselor. The team works alongside the school PBIS team and also meets monthly with the district attendance coordinator to review relevant data and discuss individual students with attendance concerns. The district coordinator for attendance attends all the school-level wellness team meetings and helps school connect with families to build a comprehensive plan for school engagement (e.g., intensive tutoring plan). On occasion, the district attendance coordinator will serve in an advocate role by attending court hearings and providing family-level assistance to support caregivers and students navigate social systems (e.g., courts).

In addition, Lynn Public School district leadership changed what was once known as the Parent Information Center to the Welcome Center. Initially, the Parent Information Center was a place to register children for school with no connection to any social or community support. District leadership noticed, however, that many families continued to contact individuals who first helped them enroll their child within the district with questions about services and community aid. The Welcome Center was created to respond to the need for a family hub where caregivers could access information and support to navigate school and the community successfully. Now, the Welcoming Center coordinates a variety of services for families including staff who connect authentically with families to build trust (e.g., meet with families, support families in the community [e.g., medical appointments], direct families to shelters or food banks for needed supplies). The district plans for the Welcome Center to hire more support personnel (e.g., social workers) to support students and families after registration in order to build and sustain relationships while the student is enrolled in Lynn Public Schools. The Welcome Center staff will coordinate with school-based parent liaison who support families within individual school communities.

Local Implementation Demonstration

The PBIS district leadership team recognizes the opportunity to showcase specific schools demonstrating excellence in family–school collaboration. Although this has not happened formally yet, the team sees the value of an exemplar school team showcasing other schools how family–school collaboration might be maximized to support students' social–emotional wellness and families' feelings of connectedness to school. This is a goal the team intends to integrate into its strategic plan as it continues to grow and improve its efforts as a district.

SUMMARY

School districts are complex systems in which change and sustained implementation may require sustained effort across multiple stages. However, throughout the change and implementation process, there exists the opportunity to collaborate with families. This chapter offered considerations for building capacity to promote family–school collaboration districtwide when designing and implementing MTSS, specifically PBIS. Considerations pertain to the composition of the district leadership team, the time and resources invested (inputs), the actions taken by the team (outputs) to promote positive youth outcomes, and the way in which a local demonstration site serves as a model for other stakeholders. The resources provided in the current chapter's appendices can support the actions of a collaborative district team to consider and enact change. Looking ahead, a collaborative, multistakeholder district PBIS leadership team will ideally become the rule rather than the exception. This chapter endeavored to provide guidance to teams to maximize the impact of their work together as well as support relevant and sustained change.

PBIS District Systems Fidelity Inventory (DSFI) Family–School Collaboration Self-Check

The purpose of this self-check is to generate discussion and reflection among district leaders regarding ways of partnering with families when planning district activities.

	Critical Features	Questions and Considerations
Inputs		
Leadership Teaming	Team Membership	• Does the district team include family members (or family representation) who are broadly representative of the community?
	Team Expertise	• Are there individuals on the leadership team with expertise in local family concerns and needs?
	Team Operating Procedures	• Do team operating procedures include structures and practices that prompt communication with families to ensure transparency and promote feedback?
	Action Planning	• Do family stakeholders/representatives across various cultural groups have opportunities to provide input on the district strategic plan?
	Communication with Key Stakeholders	• Does the District Leadership Team regularly engage in two-way communication with family stakeholders to solicit feedback on implementation progress with district outcomes?
Stakeholder Engagement	Stakeholder Involvement	• Is there a written process in place to actively involve families, especially underserved families and cultures, in setting goals and developing policies?
	Information Dissemination	• Have multiple pathways for communication with families been identified and utilized based on family input on preferred communication methods?
	Stakeholder Participation	• Do district leaders regularly participate in family–school collaboration events?
Funding & Alignment	Budget Plan	• Does funding support family–school collaboration and capacity building activities?
	Community Agency Alignment	• Does the district reach out to community agencies that work closely with families (e.g., pediatric practices, mental health providers, afterschool programs, youth organizations) to develop partnerships, align practices, and coordinate supports?
	Alignment to District Outcomes	• Does the district facilitate input from families on district outcome or improvement goals? • Are improvement goals and progress data communicated with families through multiple methods?
	Alignment to Initiatives	• Is there a clear description that aligns key district initiatives with the goals and structures supporting family–school partnerships?
	Initiative Adoption Procedures	• Is a process followed to incorporate input and feedback from families on initiatives?

(continued)

	Critical Features	Questions and Considerations
Policy	*Vision/Mission Statement*	• Does the statement include support for culturally responsive, strengths-based approaches to family engagement, and is it endorsed by family representatives?
	Discipline Policy Review	• Does the District Leadership Team regularly review discipline policies with families and include their input?
	Discipline Guides	• Are district discipline policy and procedural guides shared annually with all families in languages and formats that are accessible?
	Transition System	• Does the district obtain input from families when developing systems to support student transitions (e.g., new student, school to school)? . • Is information on transition supports shared with all families in accessible languages and formats?
Workforce Capacity	*Hiring/Promotion*	• Does the District Leadership Team include knowledge of PBIS in hiring criteria, recruitment, promotion, job descriptions, and performance evaluations of family support personnel?
Outputs Training	*District Professional Development Plan*	• Does the District Leadership Team include input from families and/or family representatives when designing a 3- to 5-year professional development plan? • Does the professional development plan include training for staff in family engagement strategies?
	District Professional Development Calendar	• Is the professional development calendar shared with families to support family member involvement?
	Professional Development Alignment	• Are PBIS professional development materials and practices aligned with the goals of family support personnel?
	Ongoing Professional Development	• Does district professional development include ongoing opportunities for families on how PBIS efforts support common family routines? • Are family engagement strategies integrated within the PBIS framework across tiers to support school-site practices?
	Communities of Practice Internal Professional Development	• Are families invited to and regularly access in-district networking opportunities focused on PBIS? • Do families have access to professional development on supports available to their child at Tiers 1, 2, and 3 as well as information on supporting their child across the tiers or on requesting assistance if they have concerns?

(continued)

	Critical Features	Questions and Considerations
Coaching	*Coaching*	• Do coaches at the school and district level have expertise in coordinating with families and engaging them in decision-making?
	Implementation Process	• Is there a written process in place for orienting family support personnel to tiered interventions and information for requesting ongoing assistance or coaching?
Evaluation	*Evaluation Plan*	• Does the District Leadership Team complete a 3- to 5-year evaluation plan that includes input from families (e.g., through surveys, focus groups)?
	Data Collection Systems	• Do district and school level data systems include mechanisms for assessing family engagement and collecting information on family perceptions?
	Evaluation Feedback Loop	• Is there a district evaluation schedule that ensures feedback from families is collected as part of a broader evaluation and shared with internal coaches for problem solving and action planning?
	Student Identification Data	• Does the district provide schools with written guidelines supporting data-decision rules to identify students for Advanced Tiers supports include parent referral/request for assistance? • Do data indicate families are familiar with the referral process?
	Student Performance Data	• Does the District Leadership Team track the proportion of students accessing and making progress with Tier 2 and Tier 3 supports and share this information in aggregate with families?
	Annual Evaluation	• Are annual progress reports on the activities and outcomes related to PBIS (e.g., fidelity, student outcomes) shared annually with families?
	Acknowledgement of Progress	• Do families receive information on district outcomes and accomplishment related to PBIS goals, at least quarterly, and are they solicited for feedback?
Local Implementation Demonstration	*Site Selection*	• Does the district's formal site selection process for chosing initial PBIS pilot schools and expanding to new schools include soliciting input from families and family representatives on needs, interest in involvement, and implementation considerations?
	Model Demonstrations	• Does the district criteria for identifying model demonstration schools include family engagement and active partnership at all levels of decision making?

CHAPTER 10

From Theory to Practice
Successful Family–School Collaboration in Schools

Shelby Cook, Imad Zaheer, Julie Fogt, Laura Casey,
and Misty Lewis

The purpose of this chapter is to provide examples of advancing family–school collaboration. The chapter begins with an overview of the primary frameworks and practices central to the examples. The examples include suggestions and ideas for promoting two-way communication and shared decision making with families and also articulate ways to share data with families and proactively support student social behavior. Finally, program evaluation examples highlight ways to promote a two-way dialogue with families about continual improvement.

MTSS is a proactive schoolwide approach to promote a positive school climate and culture. The MTSS framework combines the tenets of RTI, a tiered service delivery model designed originally for academic progress monitoring and remediation at varying levels of intensity (Burns & Coolong-Chaffin, 2006), and PBIS, which is the identification and promotion of desired behavior across a continuum. According to Sugai et al. (1999), PBIS is "a general term that refers to the application of positive behavioral interventions and systems to achieve socially important behavior change" (p. 7). Both RTI and PBIS use a systemic, multileveled approach to prevention and intervention based on student need. The systematic approach considers four main contexts in which practices and processes are applied:

Shelby Cook, LMSW, is a master's-level clinician for the SMART Center at the University of Memphis.

Imad Zaheer, PhD, is Associate Director for School Mental Health at the Child Help Partnership, St. John's University, Flushing, New York.

Julie Fogt, PhD, is Director of the Centennial School at Lehigh University, Allentown, Pennsylvania.

Laura Casey, PhD, is Professor of Instruction Curriculum Leadership at the University of Memphis.

Misty Lewis, EdD, is a school counselor at Community Montessori School in the Jackson–Madison County School System, Jackson, Mississippi.

schoolwide, in classroom, outside of classroom, and by individual student to leverage common resources (Colvin & Fernadez, 2000).

Leveraging resources across contexts includes garnering family and community engagement, whether for consent or bilateral partnering, as referenced in the Individual with Disabilities Education Act (IDEA; IDEA, 2004) and Every Student Succeeds Act of 2015 (ESSA; Von Ravensberg & Blakely, 2017). In addition, professional organizations, such as the Council for Exceptional Children (CEC), recognize collaboration with families as a high-leverage practice (McLeskey, 2017). Further, the Center on MTSS at the American Institutes for Research (AIR) endorses family engagement in their MTSS fidelity rubric by emphasizing the core role of the family within MTSS (Center on MTSS, 2021). To assist schools in their efforts to engage families within and across the MTSS tiers, the Center on PBIS published a concept and strategies piece that is free and accessible to all, thus allowing stakeholders to complete the circle from the theory of family involvement to the actual practice of families acting as equal partners (Weist et al., 2017). The goal of family–school partnership is to ensure that all families, regardless of socioeconomic status, race, gender, or status of employment, are an integral part of all decision making and are fully able to play a meaningful role in their child's academic and behavioral journey, from creating open lines of communication to facilitating a shared vision to evaluating progress at their individual child's level (Garbacz et al., 2021). This chapter seeks to provide the story of a living, working relationship of family and community engagement within an MTSS model by presenting two school-level case studies that demonstrate successes, learning opportunities, and areas of improvement experienced along the way.

CASE STUDY: WEST TENNESSEE SCHOOL, TENNESSEE

The Tennessee Behavior Supports Project (TBSP) was a grant project funded by the Tennessee Department of Education (fiscal year 2015–2021) to provide training and technical support to Tennessee public schools on the implementation of Response to Instruction and Intervention—Behavior (RTI²-B), Tennessee's model for PBIS. In the 2018–2019 school year, the TBSP piloted an effort to enhance family and community engagement (FACE) within PBIS. This pilot project involved one rural district, West Tennessee Rural School District, consisting of three schools. This district was selected as the site for the TBSP FACE pilot program due to their strong history of districtwide PBIS implementation fidelity and a demonstrated prioritization of increasing FACE across the district. West Tennessee School (WTS, a pseudonym) was one of these three schools and was selected for this case study due to the staff's exemplary efforts during the FACE pilot project. In addition, the WTS school counselor was integral in the facilitation of the FACE pilot program for her school and district.

School History and Demographics

WTS is a public school in rural West Tennessee serving second through sixth grade. In the 2018–2019 school year, student enrollment was 440 with 74% Black, 20% White, and

6% Hispanic. The gender breakdown of the students was 51% female and 49% male. More than half of students (66%) qualified as economically disadvantaged and were eligible for a free or reduced-price lunch, and 13% of students were identified as having one or more disabilities. WTS was designated as a Targeted Support and Improvement School, as they fall in the bottom 5% of schools statewide based on their accountability scores for certain enrollment subgroups (Tennessee Department of Education, 2020).

The WTS administration has consistently demonstrated a high level of commitment to PBIS. WTS received Tier 1 PBIS training in 2016–2017, Tier 2 training in 2017–2018, and Tier 3 Training in 2018–2019. WTS has been repeatedly recognized by the TBSP as a Model of Demonstration (MOD) School, a statewide designation for schools demonstrating exemplary implementation of PBIS. Schools with MOD designation serve as model sites for schools across the state that are interested in enhancing their implementation of PBIS. Each level of designation indicates a higher level of PBIS implementation: Bronze recognizes Tier 1 implementation; Silver recognizes Tiers 1 and 2; and Gold, the highest level of achievement, recognizes implementation at all three tiers. WTS was designated a Bronze Model of Demonstration School in 2017–2018, a Silver Model of Demonstration School in 2018–2019, and a Gold Model of Demonstration School in both 2019–2020 and 2020–2021.

TBSP FACE Pilot Project

The FACE pilot project, supported by the TBSP, involved the formation of FACE teams at each school. These teams functioned similarly to and alongside schoolwide PBIS leadership teams and were tasked with building family and community engagement in the schools throughout the district. The TBSP designed a training and implementation protocol for schools and districts to follow and piloted this protocol within the West Tennessee Rural School District.

Prior to attending FACE training, teams were required by the TBSP to complete a FACE Leadership Team agreement (Appendix 10.A). This agreement was designed to secure administrative support prior to training and required early identification of school team members. The school administrator was required to sign the form to indicate political and financial support, including promoting visibility of the effort and establishing capacity for training, coaching, and evaluation. In Fall 2018, the FACE teams attended a day and a half of workshop-based training to develop plans for facilitating collaboration with families and community partners within the schools and the district. The FACE team training covered the best practices in family and community engagement, such as acknowledging cultural sensitivity (Garcia et al., 2016a), addressing core beliefs (Burgess & Frierson, 2018; Garcia et al., 2016a; Henderson et al., 2007), engaging in strengths-based problem solving (Garcia et al., 2016b), building trust (Garcia et al., 2016c), developing cross-cultural communication strategies (Garcia et al., 2016c), and sharing decision making (Garcia et al., 2016d). The team was allowed time to develop plans and products for a FACE implementation manual, including products to guide schoolwide initiatives to promote family–school–community partnerships and products to encourage the use of PBIS strategies at home. This manual was integrated into the schoolwide PBIS manual and allowed space for ongoing record-keeping to ensure sustainability of shared decision making. To guide implementation planning at training and to later assess fidelity, the FACE teams utilized the TBSP's Tiered Fidelity Inventory—Family and Community Engagement (Cook, 2018), which was modeled after the schoolwide PBIS Tiered Fidelity Inventory (Algozzine et al., 2014).

After the first day of FACE training, the school teams administered the Family and Community Engagement Survey for Families (FACERS-F) and the Family and Community Engagement Survey for Educators (FACERS-E), which measured a variety of indicators related to family engagement, including family and educator perceptions of family–school relationships and family preferences for communication (Cook et al., 2022). These surveys were developed by the TBSP to provide a pre- and posttest measure for stakeholder feedback and voice throughout the FACE pilot project. The surveys allowed teams to tailor their efforts and strategies over time, based on the input received from families and educators. Surveys were administered digitally to all educators. The family surveys were delivered in a variety of formats. Initially, the surveys were sent out via email and posted on the school portal, and responses were few. To accommodate the needs of families, surveys were then sent out in hard copies. The school also allowed many families to complete the survey in the computer lab during the back-to-school night. Although this approach created more work when synthesizing the data, the completion rate was well worth it. On the second day of training, teams reviewed the survey results and adjusted their plans accordingly.

After completing training, the teams implemented their plans, meeting monthly to assess fidelity and adjust plans as indicated by data sources. Team meeting minutes were stored alongside the FACE manual. The team utilized an action planning process to ensure that they were regularly adjusting plans based on gathered family feedback. To promote schoolwide implementation of FACE principles, the team conducted professional development with the full faculty and staff to share about what they learned and planned throughout the course of the TBSP FACE team training. The FACE manual developed at training served as a resource for staff members to regularly review the team's plans. The FACE team coaches were also encouraged to attend the monthly PBIS district coaching meetings, which provided district support and accountability to coaches and allowed for problem-solving conversations and districtwide collaboration.

FACE Team Development

The FACE team process was designed to enhance shared decision making across stakeholders. However, the process of building the WTS FACE team was gradual. At the onset of training, only four members were identified for the team, and all of them were school employees. Initially, staff members stated that they did not have anyone that would be able to serve on this team outside of school staff. After some critical thinking, the team reevaluated their process to identify team members and gradually grew over the next several months. Team memebers began paying attention to who serves in the school community and makes donations to the school. An intentional effort was made to invite representatives from different groups across the community, to provide an avenue for each group to have a voice and provide feedback to the FACE team process. Despite the team having some fear about inviting people to serve on the team, everyone they asked was delighted to join.

The initial team of four grew to thirteen by the end of the 2018–2019 school year, consisting of five school faculty members, three school staff members, and five family/community members. The school faculty was represented on the team by the school counselor, principal, instructional coach, and two grade-level teachers. Next, cafeteria staff and bus monitors were invited to join the team. These individuals expressed feeling honored to be included, as these roles are often excluded from school leadership efforts. Their participation was especially valuable to the team because they were long-standing members of the community and had many community connections, specifically with harder to reach families. Several students' parents came aboard the team as well, serving in dual roles as family members and employees at local businesses and nonprofit organizations. The police chief and a representative from a local mental health agency also joined the effort.

Similar to the PBIS leadership team process, FACE teams were encouraged to set expectations and roles early. The WTS team decided to allow each team member to define their own role to encourage buy-in and to maximize use of that individual's skills. Their identified team roles included a facilitator, note-taker, student needs coordinator, outreach and event coordinator, community involvement liaison, safety and community concerns liaison, family and staff ideas liaison, teacher representative, student services representative, local nonprofit (Helping Hand) representative, and local business (American Woodmark) representative. As demonstrated in these team roles, specific members were delegated as liaisons to continually discuss school initiatives within the community and to bring informal feedback to the team at each monthly meeting. As a creative solution for scheduling issues, team members agreed to send a friend or spouse in their place if they had to miss a meeting, which allowed further exposure of the team's work within the school community. Other team norms included using a structured agenda for all meetings and sending out meeting minutes within 48 hours of meeting. A team member term commitment of one school year was also established. If unable to complete their term, members were expected to recommend another person to serve in their place.

For schools without a FACE team, we recommend including at least one family and community representative on the schoolwide PBIS leadership team (see Table 10.1 to develop clear expectations for this role). A role description can help mediate fears commonly expressed by both families and educators related to family engagement and shared

TABLE 10.1. Family/Community Member Role Description for PBIS Leadership Teams

Purpose of the role:	*[School Name] values the input of families and communities. For that reason, we would like to include family and community members on our PBIS leadership teams. These members will serve as a liaison between the community and the PBIS leadership team, providing integral feedback and input to the team.*
Key responsibilities:	• Act as a representative of family and/or community voice. • Gather feedback from families and community members about PBIS. • Attend regular PBIS leadership team meetings. • Ask the facilitator to add feedback to the agenda. • Share feedback and questions with team. • Guide discussion to develop plan to address feedback/questions. • Disseminate information from meetings to the community.

decision making. When identifying family and community members to invite, one should review the process followed by the WTS team outlined previously in this chapter. Look for natural leaders already serving in the school community and evaluate existing school–community partnerships to identify potential stakeholders. During this process, be sure to consider individuals that are representative of the student population.

FACE Team Initiatives: Year 1

After training, the team began the work of facilitating family–school–community partnerships within PBIS. To introduce families to PBIS concepts, the team shared at open house about the schoolwide expectations, acknowledgments, and discipline plans using a PowerPoint presentation. The team also created a flyer with 10 tips for supporting PBIS at home. Additional tips for implementing PBIS at home were incorporated into the monthly family newsletter. Families were encouraged to use a PBIS Home Matrix that reflected the schoolwide expectations and outlines how they could be implemented at home. The FACE team also sent out a monthly family newsletter with a variety of information about academics and behavior. Teachers were asked to make a minimum of two family contacts per month with a positive message about each of their students. While it was permissible to send these messages via Class Dojo or an agenda note, phone calls were encouraged as they would allow space for further conversation and relationship building. Additionally, students who received a ticket for positive behavior had a duplicate sent home in their daily agenda book to notify the family of the student's accomplishment. If students were eligible to participate in behavior parties, families received a letter. A calendar with reward events was sent home monthly.

Families could also engage in two-way communication with educators at family–teacher conferences and at a variety of family night events organized by the FACE team. The team scheduled designated days for families to join students at lunch, providing an additional opportunity to build relationships between educators and families. Teachers were encouraged to regularly communicate with families via text message and email to ensure the lines of communication remained open. Families could also engage in communication on the school's Facebook page. The school principal often hosted live videos on the platform discussing school updates, allowing families to respond and ask questions in real time.

In Fall 2018, the team decided to systematically call all students' families to gather additional feedback about families' knowledge of and experiences with the school's PBIS implementation to guide further decision making and initiative planning. The FACE team recruited the school wide PBIS team to help make the calls, assembling a team of five faculty and staff members. The school roster and phone number list were utilized to divide the student body evenly among members in alphabetical order. At the time, there were approximately 500 students at WTS, but many of them had siblings also attending the school. The staff members checked through their individual lists and noted sibling groups to ensure that each family received only one phone call. In the end, each individual had 75–100 families to call. To make the task manageable, team members committed to making five phone calls each day for around a month. The team agreed to attempt one call to each family and had a scripted voicemail message to leave if there was no answer. If family member did answer, the following script was used:

> "Hello, this is [name of faculty/staff member] calling from [name of school].
>
> "We are working very hard to contact families of our students to find out things you love about our school and to find out about things we could improve. Could I ask you five questions about your family's experience with our school?
>
>> "You are the family of (name of student and siblings) correct?
>>
>> "Have you had an opportunity to meet with or talk to your child's teacher this school year?
>>
>> "How do you get updates about what is going on at school (website, papers sent home, school newspaper, etc.)?
>>
>> "What kinds of things do you enjoy coming to do or see at our school (lunches, class parties, awards programs, holiday programs, etc.)?
>>
>> "What is one thing that you can think of that would make our school better?
>>
>> "Thank you so much for your time and help with this!"

At the next monthly meeting, the team compiled the data in an excel spreadsheet to compare answers and look for trends. Around 30–40 percent of the families were reached through this effort, and although the numbers were lower than desired, two important insights were gained through this process. First, there was a disconnect in communication. Many families had not yet met or spoken to a teacher. Families stated they did not always know what was going on at the school. Second, there were not many suggestions of things to change or ways to make the school better. Team members sensed feelings of skepticism and mistrust from families in these conversations. Through these insights, the team realized they needed to immediately begin working on the relationship between the school and the community. Identified areas of growth included adding more family and community members to the FACE team and increasing more personal interaction from teachers and staff members with families to build a sense of shared community. During the next meeting, the team brainstormed new members to add to the team and discussed ways to be more familiar to students' families. Building positive home–school relationships became the first priority.

This process led to a team reset in the spring of 2019. At this point, the team had grown significantly, from a team of four school faculty members to a comprehensive and diverse team of five school faculty members, three school staff members, and five family/community members (as described previously in this chapter). The FACE team coach recognized a need to reset the team to ensure a shared vision, given that most of the team members were not present at the initial training where most of the team building and initiative planning took place. At the next meeting, the FACE team developed the following vision statement: *To strengthen relationships in all aspects of the school community.* To meet this vision, short- and long-term goals were established. In the short term, the team wanted the school staff to become more familiar to families, to educate families on the resources available to them, and to show the positive climate and culture that they had been working to build within the building for years in hopes of changing perceptions about the school. In the long term, they wanted to become a central hub for community resources, serve students and families with a more holistic approach, and improve their Family and Community Engagement Survey (FACERS) results, which were used as a tool for progress monitoring and data-based decision making.

The work to meet these goals began through a variety of social media campaigns. The team began posting regularly about their PBIS initiatives such as student of the week and good behavior parties. These posts allowed the community behind-the-scenes access into what was happening at school every day, and team members worked to facilitate a more positive outlook on school operations. Further, the team regularly posted student and staff "shout-outs" to recognize the great work of students and staff and to build a sense of positivity and community. The staff shout-outs included a picture of the staff member and a few words about them, such as where they went to college or what were their special interests, in addition to their role at the school and why they were selected for the shout-out. The student shout-outs featured a photo of the student with an administrator and specific mention of how the student demonstrated the schoolwide expectations.

When planning these posts, the team was intentional about featuring all staff, including cafeteria workers, bus drivers, and custodians. It was important to the team to include these staff members, as they had realized in their team-building process that these individuals were often undervalued. One of their highest performing posts recognized the school's crossing guard, who garnered 74 comments, 48 shares, and reached over 3,500 people. Turning the spotlight to different stakeholders brought new pockets of the community into the fold. The team also found that these positive spotlight postings were more likely to be shared and engaged with than the simple announcements that are typically posted by schools. These posts allowed the social media platforms to grow followers, allowing even more families and community members to see the school in this positive light. To reach individuals in the community who did not have social media accounts or access to the internet, the team partnered with the local newspaper and television station to spotlight positive initiatives and events occurring at the school as often as possible.

Year 1 Evaluation

According to their TFI-FACE scores and FACERS surveys, the diligent work of the FACE team contributed to a more collaborative school environment where families, community members, and school staff became engaged in working towards the common goal of student achievement and wellness. As demonstrated in Figure 10.1, the team has gradually increased their TFI-FACE scores since initial implementation in Fall 2018, indicating the progressive expansion of their efforts to enhance family and community engagement within the school.

At the end of the first year of implementation, the FACERS-F and FACERS-E measured changes in perceptions after FACE implementation. The survey data suggest that the efforts of the FACE team have had some success in enhancing family engagement within the school. More families reported that behavioral expectations were clear at the school, more families also reported that they were asked to provide input on PBIS and

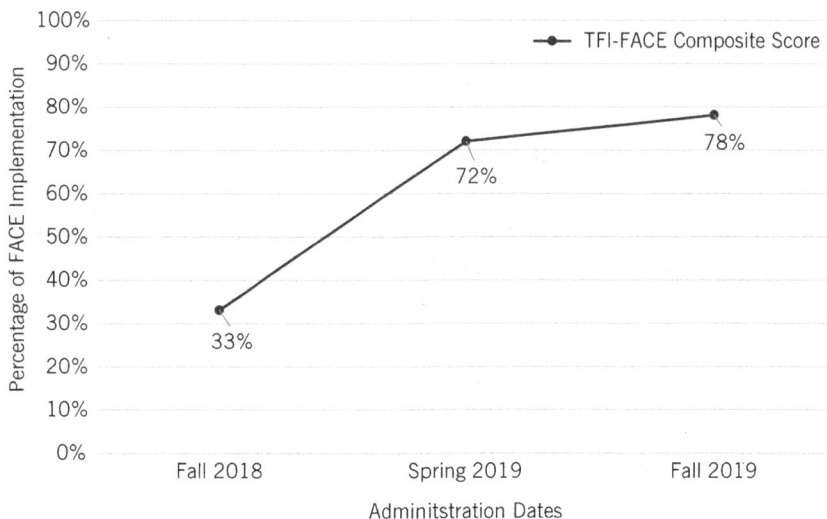

FIGURE 10.1. West Tennessee School's TFI-FACE scores. West Tennessee School gradually increased its Tiered Fidelity Inventory—Family and Community Engagement (TFI-FACE) composite score throughout the pilot program, indicating increasing implementation of family and community engagement practices.

family engagement plans. Families reported higher levels of educator contacts for positive behavior. Family reports of receiving and utilizing information about implementing PBIS at home also increased (Table 10.2). While the family surveys did not reflect positive changes in family–educator relationships, the educator surveys did. Educators reported having more positive relationships with families and higher levels of trust and respect in their relationships (Table 10.3). We hypothesize that the increase of professional development related to family engagement and cultural responsiveness has helped to shift educator core beliefs related to families, thus leading them to having more positive perceptions of their relationships with families. As perceptions and relationships take time to change, we hope that shifts in these relational indicators will be positively reflected on the family surveys in the future, as the shifts in educator core beliefs begin to permeate their behaviors and their relationships with their students' families. Further, the annual school report card indicated 90% teacher retention from 2018–2019 to 2019–2020 (Tennessee Department of Education, 2020). Although we cannot link the work of the FACE team directly to teacher retention, their work was one of many initiatives to support a more positive school climate.

Year 2 FACE Team Adaptations and Initiatives

After a year of growth and assessment, the FACE team set out with strong plans for the 2019–2020 year. In Fall 2019, the FACE team organized an Open House Community Event, where the success of their efforts was demonstrated due to high attendance numbers. Instead of a classic back-to-school night, the team capitalized on this opportunity to provide an avenue for community collaboration. The theme of the night surrounded a love

TABLE 10.2. Family and Community Engagement Survey for Families (FACERS-F) Responses

	Response to question (%)	
	Pretest (N = 373)	Posttest (N = 356)
"The staff is clear about the behavior expectations at my child's school."		
Strongly agree	57%	63%
Slightly agree	17%	21%
Undecided or neutral	20%	12%
Slightly disagree	3%	2%
Strongly disagree	3%	2%
"I have been asked to provide input on family and community engagement within the RTI²-B (PBIS) program."		
Yes	12%	19%
No	88%	81%
"I have been asked to provide input on family and community engagement within the RTI2-B (PBIS) program."		
Yes	14%	20%
No	85%	80%
"Someone at my child's school has contacted me about my child behaving well."		
Yes	42%	49%
No	58%	51%
"I have received information from my school on how to use the same behavioral expectations at home that are used at school."		
Yes, I have received it, and I always use it at home.	15%	17%
Yes, I have received it, and I sometimes use it at home.	8%	12%
Yes, I have received it, but I never use it at home.	3%	6%
No, I have not received it.	73%	64%
"I have received information from my school about how to use an acknowledgment system at home like the one used at school."		
Yes, I have received it, and I always use it at home.	14%	16%
Yes, I have received it, and I sometimes use it at home.	8%	13%
Yes, I have received it, but I never use it at home.	5%	5%
No, I have not received it.	74%	65%
"I have received training from my school on how to use appropriate consequences to problem behavior at home."		
Yes, I have received it, and I always use it at home.	10%	13%
Yes, I have received it, and I sometimes use it at home.	6%	9%
Yes, I have received it, but I never use it at home.	2%	4%
No, I have not received it.	82%	73%

for the school district, including a photo booth where families could pose for a photo with a dry erase board where they had written why they love the school district. The photos were later used as part of a Facebook campaign during behavior kickoff week (described below). The team invited a variety of vendors to attend and set up booths throughout the cafeteria. School booths included the FACE team, Coordinated School Health, Title I, After-School

TABLE 10.3. Family and Community Engagement Survey for Educators (FACERS-E) Responses

	Response to question (%)	
	Pretest ($N = 36$)	Posttest ($N = 40$)
"Families at my school respect me"	61%	70%
Slightly Agree	23%	22%
Undecided or Neutral	10%	5%
Slightly Disagree	7%	0%
Strongly Disagree	0%	2%
"My student's families trust me."		
Strongly Agree	48%	75%
Slightly Agree	45%	19%
Undecided or Neutral	7%	3%
Slightly Disagree	0%	3%
Strongly Disagree	0%	0%
Strongly Agree	48%	75%
"I have a positive relationship with the families of my students."		
Strongly Agree	65%	73%
Slightly Agree	35%	22%
Undecided or Neutral	0%	3%
Slightly Disagree	0%	3%
Strongly Disagree	0%	0%

Programs, and Transportation. Community booths included Arise2Read, Alpha Kappa Alpha Sorority, Fire Department, Police Department, Girl Scouts, Health Connect America (local mental and behavioral health provider), Public Library, American Woodmark (local business), and Helping Hand (local nonprofit). Several community agency booths gave out free school supplies.

For years, WTS has held a behavior kickoff week at the beginning of the year to introduce the students to the components of the PBIS plan. During the 2019–2020 behavior kickoff week, the FACE team partnered with the PBIS team to integrate families into the behavior kickoff experience through a social media campaign. Each day of the week had a focus area for the social media posting that went along with the activities they were being done in the school to teach the PBIS expectations. Videos of students explaining the schoolwide expectations were created and used as a teaching tool within the school and shared on social media. These videos not only provided positive recognition for these students that their families could see, but they also allowed families to learn about the schoolwide PBIS program and encouraged them to reinforce those expectations at home.

Next Steps

As this team continues to build upon their work, several next steps focus primarily on equity. First, the team plans to focus more on informing the school's behavior policies, ensuring that family voice is considered in the discipline plan. They would like to use the knowledge gathered from their family and community partnerships to enhance trauma-informed discipline practices and to address policies that may be contributing to disparities in discipline. Moreover, they have not yet ensured that representation on this team includes input from families experiencing disproportionate discipline, and plans to address disproportionate discipline need to be expanded. The team also hopes to be more intentional in the future about equitable representation through the shared decision-making processes. While the FACE team does reflect the school's demographics, we currently have not been tracking demographic information of survey participants. A simple fix would be to add a question to the FACER surveys regarding the student's enrollment subgroups to ensure that feedback is representative and proportionate to the entire student body.

CASE STUDY: PENN SCHOOL, PENNSYLVANIA

Penn School (a pseudonym), an Approved Private School, is funded through the Pennsylvania Department of Education and governed by a university in Pennsylvania. The school provides educational programming as specified in the IEPs of children and youth ages 6–21 with behavioral disorders and autism. As the laboratory school of the university's College of Education, Penn School also serves as a training center for aspiring individuals pursuing careers in special education and related fields. Penn School's teacher residency model deploys graduate students as teacher associates who receive robust mentoring from masters-level educators with exceptional skills in teaching students with challenging behaviors and employing evidence-based practices.

Student enrollment at the school mirrors the demographics of students with behavioral disorders and autism in the local community (U.S. Census Bureau, n.d.). The ethnicity make-up of the 72 students who attend the school are White (79%), Hispanic (10%), Black (6%), multiracial (3%), American Indian (1%), and Asian (1%). The gender breakdown is 88% male and 12% female. The students' primary disabilities under the IDEA include emotional disturbance (51%), autism (38%), other health impairments (5.6%), specific learning disability (2.8%), and intellectual disability (2.8%). Half (50%) of the students are considered economically disadvantaged and are eligible for free and reduced lunch.

Penn School's multi-tiered PBIS framework was established over 20 years ago. The framework began with creating a shared vision, establishing buildingwide student expectations, and implementing evidence-based practices aimed at reducing and eliminating the use of physical restraint, seclusionary time-out procedures, and out-of-school suspensions (Fogt & Piripavel, 2002). During the initial implementation year, the use of physical restraints, compared to the previous year, declined by 69% (George et al., 2013); the use of seclusionary time-out decreased from an average of 782 to 181 minutes per day (Miller et al., 2005); and out-of-school suspensions were curbed by 16%. Twenty years later, Penn School's PBIS framework continues to achieve impressive results. For example, data from the 2018–2019 school year affirm 100% reductions in the use of physical restraint and seclusionary time-out procedures, and a 97% curtailment in out-of-school suspensions compared to the 1997–1998 school year.

Strong, authentic, and prosperous family–school relationships are the bedrock of Penn's positive school culture. Penn School's philosophy about the decisive role of families in their child's education is codified in the staff Policy and Procedure Handbook. It states:

> Cultivating parent support begins with the recognition that parents are the experts on their children. Parents know much more about their children and have gained that information over a longer period of time than we, as school officials, ever could hope to do. As educators we must show great respect for parent's opinions, privacy, background, dignity and their natural desire, just like ours, to grow. Part of that understanding comes from an awareness of who we are and what we value but a large part of it comes from the understanding that others may have profoundly different but equally decent and ethical guidance mechanisms. (Penn School, 2021)

Additionally, the skillful execution of Penn School's philosophy is realized through stated job expectations, staff training, and mentoring opportunities. These critical organizational features connect Penn's philosophy to meaningful structures and supports that guide teacher and staff behavior.

It is the recognition that the quality of home–school relationships mediates the effectiveness of Penn School's PBIS model that steers many of the programmatic decisions at the school. Teachers are trained how to positively interact with families in school activities such as strength-based intake procedures, case management, and IEPs. During the intake meeting, Penn School staff gain insight into student and family strengths rather than rehash the negative behaviors that are well documented in the school records. With the identification of student and family strengths, staff can leverage these positive characteristics to develop successful programming for each student. Penn School staff also elicit family and student perspectives about the student's aspirations and long-term goals and explore the role that Penn School could play in helping the student achieve those goals. Expectations for collaboration and open communication are also discussed at the intake meeting. Case management expectations require teachers to establish ongoing communication (i.e., weekly) with the families of students assigned to their caseload. The predominant method of communication is by telephone; however, some families prefer email correspondence.

Regardless of the method used, the purpose of weekly communication with families is to promote an equal partnership where teachers discuss academic and behavioral progress, and families are provided with an opportunity to share concerns and receive support. When discussing behavioral issues, teachers are taught to focus on the interventions and supports they are using and describe their child's performance in relation to those interventions rather than simply recount the topography of the child's aberrant behaviors. Communication centered around interventions designed to assist their child likely conveys a message to families that teachers are systematically and proactively taking meaningful action to help their child improve their school performance. Teachers are expected to document all communications with families, school district representatives, and other professionals in a Communication Log (Appendix 10.B). The IEP process is another activity where family engagement and collaboration are highly encouraged and supported. Teachers work closely with families to identify appropriate IEP goals and discuss ensuing support and services.

In addition to weekly phone conferences, teachers communicate with families daily via a brief written progress note on the student's point sheet. Penn School students carry point sheets and have the opportunity to earn points for meeting school and classroom expectations. Teachers provide ratings of a 0, 1, or 2 on each behavioral goal and specific feedback to the student after every period. The assumption is that students begin every period with zero points. Students do not lose points for inappropriate behavior. Rather, they earn points for appropriate behaviors. A student who clearly meets classroom expectations earns two points; a student who performs close to classroom expectations earns one point; and a student who performs below expectations earns no points. Earned points are exchanged for backup reinforcers, such as additional privileges, special school events, and school store items.

Teachers encourage families to use the point sheet as a communication tool. The point sheet contains a space for teachers to write notes to families and a space for families to respond. Teachers are taught to write progress notes that are positive and affirming, pointing out areas in the day where the student excelled or demonstrated growth. These affirming statements can also be used to help structure conversations between the family and their child about the school day. Teachers ask that families begin the conversation by discussing the positive aspects of their child's day by identifying a time in the school day where their child has earned most of their points. Teachers also recommend families to not admonish their child for not earning points, viz. receiving a zero on their point sheet, as their child already received private, corrective feedback about their performance from their teacher. Students who return their point sheets the following day are awarded bonus points that can be exchanged at the school store (i.e., 25 bonus points for a family signature and 50 bonus points for a signature and a brief note from their family member).

Penn School teachers regularly share student academic and behavior data with families to keep them apprised of progress. At the elementary and middle school levels, teachers and students, under teacher supervision, use the Seesaw application (*https://web.seesaw.me*) to post digital content, including student work samples, on a daily basis. Seesaw is a learning platform where students can post their work and complete activities assigned by teachers. Through a family log-in, Seesaw makes it easy for parents to view their student's work, leave feedback for their student, and send and receive private messages with their student's teacher. Teachers can organize student's work in folders by content area or class. When families respond through Seesaw, it provides their child with another opportunity for acknowledgment and praise. Anecdotally, families reported favorable reviews of the Seesaw app since they appreciated viewing their child's assignments, both photographs and videos, and interacting with their child by "liking" and commenting on their posts. Families also disclosed that seeing work samples in real time deepens their conversations about school with their child.

Weekly academic reports, listing the student's current grade in each class, are sent home with the point sheet. Additionally, teachers discuss the academic performance of students assigned to their caseload during weekly telephone conferences with their families. Student behavioral data are graphed and shared with families monthly. Examining monthly graphs encourages families to view behavioral change as a process of growth rather than a "good" or "bad" day. Progress reports on IEP goals are given to families on a quarterly basis.

In lieu of traditional family–teacher conferences, Penn School hosts two family nights, one in fall and one in spring, as another channel for family–school collaboration. The students, their family members, and invited guests (e.g., friends, wraparound staff) enjoy speaking with Penn School teachers and staff, eating a meal, perusing the bookfair, and participating in family and student raffles for attendance at the event. Families often seek guidance from Penn School staff to troubleshoot issues emerging at home and in the community, such as managing conflicts with siblings, structuring visits with extended family members and friends, and setting behavioral expectations for their child in community settings. Families report that family night feels more like a family reunion as they appreciate interacting in a supportive atmosphere with families of other students who often have experienced similar educational challenges in the past. Families receive support from other families thereby creating a network of support and resources.

One of Penn School's tenets is the steadfast commitment to treating families as partners in their child's education and engaging in shared decision making with them. Penn School staff recognize the value of family voice in decision making, seek to procure a greater number of perspectives, and desire to learn from families. Penn School staff verbalize their commitment to actively listening and learning from families at the onset of opportunities to partner with families. Family input ultimately yields higher quality decisions because it possesses child's information that is often not known to teachers including physical, developmental, medical, social, and family histories. Usually, families who have a voice in the decision will have a greater commitment to the course of action. A number of Penn School practices rely on this collaborative approach including the IEP process and the petitioning process.

Penn School staff treat the IEP process with reverence and encourage families to participate in every aspect of IEP development. First, teachers must acknowledge the negative school experiences some families endured prior to coming to entering Penn School. These negative experiences may contribute to families feeling unwelcome, disconnected, or resented. Teachers strive to heal acrimonious relationships and restore trust in school officials by proactively establishing rapport with them, honoring their needs and values, and actively listening to concerns voiced by families. Penn School policies and governed practices at the school require teachers to help families take an active role and support their involvement in the IEP process. Conversations with parents about their ideas for their child's IEP begin weeks before the scheduled meeting during weekly telephone conferences. To facilitate family involvement and participation, teachers schedule the IEP meeting at a preferred time identified by the family member to accommodate their schedule. During the IEP meeting, teachers welcome all family contributions and seek to include their input in the document. Teachers are trained to invite family contributions, check for understanding, and facilitate familial agreement as each section of the IEP is discussed to ensure that the family's voice is heard, respected, and included.

Another collaborative practice that supports family engagement at Penn School is the petitioning process, the means by which middle and high school students advance through Penn School's level system (i.e., Steps to Success program). Students who achieve specified criteria at one step apply to the Petitioning Committee for advancement to the next step.

The process begins when the student completes the "Petition to Advance" packet (Appendix 10.C) , if necessary, with assistance from the homeroom teacher and submits it to the program coordinator. In addition to completing the required form, the student and homeroom teacher must schedule a Petition Meeting with the program coordinator. Families often serve on the Petitioning Committee and attend the Petition Meeting. The decision to move a student through the step system is based on data that reflect the student's performance in the program. At the Petition Meeting, the committee members use the "Student Performance Scale" in the Petition to Advance packet to rate the student's performance at Penn School. There are two possible outcomes of the Petitioning Process: (1) advancement to the next step or (2) retention at the present step. If the student is denied advancement to the next step, the committee clearly stipulates their expectations for the student and works with the student to develop a plan to improve any areas of concern. Another meeting is scheduled for the committee to review the student's progress toward the plan and inform the student of his or her advancement to the next step.

Shared decision making also extends to the disciplinary practices at the school. The benefits of family engagement in their child's education, both in academic achievement and behavioral outcomes, is well documented (Henderson & Mapp, 2002). Penn School staff believe families play a critical role in resolving discipline issues with their children and seek to involve them in constructive ways. During the intake meeting, Penn School's proactive disciplinary approach is described, and the role of families in resolving behavior problems at school is discussed. Family involvement in rectifying behavioral issues, ranging from employing prevention strategies through aiding with intervention support, is based on family preference, availability during the school day, and the student's response to their family's assistance.

Penn School practices aimed at supporting student behavior are intentionally proactive and instructional by design. Penn School's PBIS framework uses a direct instruction approach to behavioral expectations (e.g., modeling and teaching expectations, monitoring student performance, and providing immediate and specific feedback) across all school settings to prevent the occurrence of problem behavior (Miller et al., 2005). Additionally, teachers are taught to view student behavior through a trauma-informed lens by working to develop nurturing and trusting relationships with their students, creating a physically and psychologically safe learning environment, and engaging in culturally responsive teaching practices. Teachers also rely on differential reinforcement to weaken challenging behaviors and strengthen replacement behaviors and are encouraged to use only positive and neutral statements to shape student behavior in the classroom. When low-level problem behaviors in the classroom escalate, teachers employ a gradation of interventions to prevent the occurrence of more severe forms of misbehavior. At times, teachers may prompt students to use a pre-taught strategy referred to as "problem solving." As an instructional approach to discipline, problem solving focuses on skill development rather than punishment like most traditional disciplinary procedures. Penn School's problem-solving strategy, adapted from Glasser's reality therapy (1965), consists of four steps: (1) problem identification, (2) prevention, (3) a plan, and (4) a commitment. Consistent with reality therapy, problem solving is a solutions-oriented strategy that helps students focus on healthy choice making, acceptance of responsibility, accountability for behavior, and a willingness to change antisocial behaviors to get their needs met. With an emphasis on solving current issues rather than delving into past experiences, the purpose of problem solving is to teach students to use respectful words and actions (i.e., use of replacement behaviors to resolve problems instead of aggressive or violent behaviors) to mend relationships, communicate their desires, and create an actionable plan that will remedy the present situation. As appropriate, families will assist during the problem-solving process by talking with their child about possible action plan steps or discussing salient variables with staff. Penn's commitment to engaging in shared equitable disciplinary practices requires unguarded transparency and ongoing communication with each student's parents or caregivers.

As a laboratory school, a commitment to continual learning and growth among all school community members is embedded in Penn School's ethos. Families are essential members of the learning community. Learning activities vary in format and length, including written policies and procedures (e.g., student and parent handbooks), weekly family–teacher telephone conferences, and workshops. Penn School offers training via workshops to assist families with a multitude of needs including cultivating positive communication with their child, establishing home expectations, managing low-level behavior at home, supporting positive conversations about point sheets, and preventing and managing low-level behavior in the community. For example, Penn School staff, Heintzelman and Spradlin (2018), conducted a series of virtual training sessions on family-generated topics. One of the topics was preparing for summer camp (Appendix 10.D). The training focused on before-, during-, and after-camp activities and strategies that families could employ to promote a successful camp experience for their child. The training also included a handout for the camp counselors about the child's strengths, positive interventions, and things to avoid.

Teachers are also important members of Penn School's learning community and as a laboratory school, the staff development program is extensive and robust. The aim of the Penn School staff development program is to prepare teachers in fundamental practices that support student educational gains (George et al., 2013). Staff development episodes are held weekly for 2½ hours and cover many topics related to strengthening family school collaboration. Teachers also participate in weekly team meetings and mentoring time which provide additional opportunities for teachers to learn about cultivating professional and productive relationships with families.

Program evaluation is an important component of effective programs. Penn School provides families with informal and formal opportunities to provide feedback to the school. Informal feedback is offered during weekly conferences, family night events, and other activities held at the school. Formally, Penn School solicits feedback via a parent survey. The survey attempts to engage families in planning how they would like to be involved in their child's education and solicits feedback about some of the prominent features of Penn School's PBIS program (Appendix 10.E). For example, to gauge the school's efforts to work collaboratively with families, the survey asks parents, "Do you feel that your child's teacher contacts you too often, just enough, or too little?" Other survey items ask parents to share how their child's experience and how their experience with Penn School can be improved. Collected data are analyzed at the building level to determine effective communication strategies and conducive parent training and support topics.

SUMMARY

As stated at the beginning of this chapter, family–school collaboration has been recognized as a central component to school based MTSS and RTI processes to address academic and behavioral needs of students. Unfortunately, in practice, there is a sizable gap between best practices as highlighted in research and how those strategies are carried out in schools with fidelity (Balu et al., 2015). To help fill the need for improving family–school collaboration in practice, the TFI-FSC was created to highlight, track, and monitor family–school collaboration practices across six key domains of (1) positive home–school relationships, (2) two-way communication, (3) shared decision making, (4) family voice for equitable discipline, (5) training and support for family–school collaboration, and (6) evaluation.

For each of these domains, the TFI-FSC provides specific examples and criteria that can give broad direction for schools regarding what their current system looks like and what areas are identified for growth. However, to provide additional practical guidance, this chapter detailed two exemplar MTSS systems that incorporate practices that address all six domains on the TFI-FSC, serving as real-world proof of concept for how the different domains within the TFI-FSC have been and can be addressed within varying school contexts from public to alternative school settings. In addition, for each school, examples and templates of forms and activities used to further family–school collaboration are provided as potential resources for schools who might be interested in using similar procedures and strategies at their site.

For readers considering using the TFI-FSC in their own family, school, and community context to establish collaborations across systems, we hope these case studies illustrate two concrete school-level exemplars of family–school collaboration practices featured in TFI-FSC. However, we want to caution readers and practitioners to not to directly adopt the practices but rather consider the local context and needs of your school and determine which of the practices highlighted here would best serve the community. For example, some of the strategies highlight the use of technology like the Seesaw app to have more elaborate ongoing bidirectional communication with families. However, depending on preferences of families and school staff, other apps or modalities may be preferred ways to establish bidirectional communication. Furthermore, we recommend that wherever possible, using a single strategy that works to address multiple domains of family–school collaboration as highlighted on the TFI-FSC tool in order to minimize effort and maximize the impact of the work. This would increase the chances of successful implementation by using a small core set of practices that address multiple domains of family–school collaboration.

Family and Community Engagement (FACE)
Leadership Team Agreement

SCHOOL NAME: _____ DISTRICT: _____ DATE: _____

The following checklist is a list of factors that will facilitate systems change for family and community engagement (FACE). The list is based on components that promote outcomes and sustainability for effective FACE. This agreement is to ensure positive outcomes for all key players in the implementation process.

ITEMS TO COMPLETE

FACE LEADERSHIP TEAM

A FACE Leadership Team of no more than eight members will be established. These individuals should have a strong understanding of a multi-tiered systems approach. At least one member of the FACE team should also be on the leadership team for the schools multi-tiered system as well as one member from the district. Other members may include school faculty and staff, community members, family members, and students (when age-appropriate). Appropriate community members may be identified by considering community stakeholders and agencies with a strong presence in the school and in the life of students (after-school programs, mental health agencies, local government, etc.).

TEAM MEMBERS		
NAME	**TITLE**	**EMAIL ADDRESS**

The FACE Leadership Team commits to meeting at least six to nine times per academic year. The team will evaluate the effectiveness of implementation of FACE goals, analyze and problem-solve FACE data, collaborate with tiered leadership teams on FACE needs and goals, and regularly provide FACE updates through faculty meetings.

VISIBILITY

Entire school faculty will participate in an awareness presentation of the FACE initiative.

A majority of the school faculty (80%), staff, and 100% of administrator(s) support the implementation of FACE.

FACE is disseminated through media (i.e. newsletter, school web site, social media).

It is recommended that FACE be an agenda item at all RTI2-B Tier 1/2/3 Leadership Team meetings and faculty meetings.

(continued)

Family and Community Engagement (FACE)
Leadership Team Agreement *(page 2 of 2)*

POLITICAL SUPPORT
Strong family and community engagement will be one of the top school plan goals.
School will provide a letter of support signed by the principal to school staff that commits to the integration of FACE, lists and encourages participation in ongoing training opportunities, and commits to a systems change process.
School will provide an annual letter of support signed by the principal to school staff on the importance of FACE and a strong commitment to families and the community.

POLICY
School leaders as well as family and community members will be informed and involved in adopting policies and practices pertaining to FACE.

TRAINING CAPACITY
The principal will allow 1.5 days of training for the school's FACE team.
The FACE Team will actively participate in all trainings and implementation activities.
Following FACE team training, principal will allocate time for training of all school personnel in the philosophy, strategies, and process of FACE and provide for follow-up coaching as needed with individual staff members.
The FACE Team will develop action plans that initiate faculty trainings and identify individuals who can assume faculty training responsibilities of FACE implementation.
The school administrator or designee will actively participate in all trainings, school meetings, and engage in additional work as needed in order to fully implement and sustain FACE.

COACHING CAPACITY
Each school will assign a FACE coach to oversee implementation of FACE, communicate regularly with a FACE Site Consultant, maintain up-to-date with best practices in the FACE program, and facilitate FACE team meetings.

FAMILY AND COMMUNITY MEMBERS
The team will commit to integrating family and community voice into the FACE team. Ideally, the team will consist of several family and community members who are able to attend all FACE trainings and meetings. However, adjustments can be made to include family and community voice if these members are unable to attend all trainings and meetings.

EVALUATION CAPACITY
School agrees to participate in surveys regarding beliefs about family and community engagement in order to provide data for FACE goal setting and monitoring.
FACE team agrees to hold meetings at least six to nine times per academic year to discuss FACE action planning and implementation.
FACE team agrees to annually assess FACE outcomes using tools approved by the district, the West Tennessee Behavior Supports Project, and the Tennessee Department of Education.

_____ _____

PRINCIPAL SIGNATURE   **DATE**

Communication Log

Student First and Last Name _____				
Date	Time	People Involved	Type	Notes or Screenshot of Communication

Petition to Advance

Student Information	
Name:	Date:
Grade: Age:	Teachers:
Current Step: Day:	Coordinator:

Committee Members				
Name	Title	Signature	Date	Recommendation to Accept Petition (Yes / No)
	HR Teacher*			
	Coordinator*			
	Staff Advocate			
	Parent			
	Student Member**			
	Teachers***			
	Teachers***			
	Support Teachers*			

Note. At least three (3) committee members are required to review student's petition.
* = Required member
** = Student advocate invited by petitioning student
*** = All of student's teachers must sign and issue recommendation

Petition Status and Decision	
Date of Committee Meeting:	Petition Granted: ☐ Yes ☐ No
Petition Granted	**Petition Rejected**
Step Status: | Day:	Review Date:
	List reason:
	List reconsideration criteria:

(continued)

Student Performance Scale – Teacher Version

Name:	Date:	
Homeroom:	Current Step:	Day:

Rating Scale
1 = Unacceptable   2 = Needs Improvement   3 = Average   4 = Above Average   5 = Excellent

Results of Observations and Anecdotal Reports	1	2	3	4	5
Observation 1 Date:					
Observation 2 Date:					
Behavioral Competency	**1**	**2**	**3**	**4**	**5**
Bus Behavior					
In-class Behavior					
Transition / Between Class Behavior					
Free / Break Time Behavior					
Identify Triggers and Use an Anger Management or Coping Strategy					
Attendance (e.g., truancies, suspensions)					
Academic Competency	**1**	**2**	**3**	**4**	**5**
Staying On-task					
Completing In-class Assignments					
Completing Homework					
Report Card and Overall Progress					

Narrative

Provide brief description of the student's progress on IEP goals and current Step.

Data Summary

Please attach graphs, daily data sheets, or written summaries of the student's progress. Be sure to include daily percentages attained on this Step as well as individual goal information. PLEASE BRING CURRENT POINT SHEET TO REVIEW GOALS.

(continued)

Student Competency Report – Student Version

Name:	Date:	
Homeroom:	Current Step:	Day:

Rating Scale
1 = Unacceptable   2 = Needs Improvement   3 = Average   4 = Above Average   5 = Excellent

List three (3) positive statements about yourself and your performance at school.	1	2	3	4	5
1.					
2.					
3.					

Rate your overall performance on your step.	1	2	3	4	5
Be There, Be Ready					
Be Responsible					
Be Respectful					
Keep Hands and Feet to Self / Maintain Personal Space					
Follow Directions					
Additional IEP GOAL 1:					
Personal Hygiene					
Bus Behavior					
Identify Triggers and Use an Anger Management or Coping Strategy					
Attendance (e.g., truancies, suspensions)					
Assignment Sheet / Book Filled Out					
Completing In-class Assignments					
Quality of Work					
Report Card and Overall Progress					

Student Narrative: List the ways in which you are demonstrating the ability needed to advance to the next step. How do we know you can handle it?	1	2	3	4	5
1.					
2.					
3.					

Note to Student

The committee will be listening carefully for these qualities: 1) Ability to accept responsibility for your own actions; 2) honesty; and 3) ability to express how your behavior has changed – past behavior, present behavior, how you handle difficult situations and how this shows positive change, and what you think you still need to learn.

Preparing for Summer Camp

Before Camp
- Visit the camp.
- Connect with the counselors to learn about a typical camp day schedule.
- Copy the PBSP from your child's IEP and provide the counselors with a copy.
- Find a place at camp where your child can take time.
- Practice a camp day schedule—wake up, drive, walk in, see camp space, practice going to the place where they can take time, drive home.
- Discuss lunch choice options.
- Setup reinforcers based on clear, attainable criteria.

During Camp

Car Ride to Camp
- State expectations during the car ride and as you approach the camp.
- Remind your child to use strategies if upset and the location at camp to take time.
- Tell your child you love him/her and you have confidence he will have a great day.

If problems arise...
- Acknowledge your child is upset.
- Determine what your child needed in the moment where the problem occurred.
- Talk to your child about what he can do in a similar situation if it happens again.
- Speak to the counselors about what they observed during the problem.
- Determine if the action plan can be followed by your child and the camp counselors.

Car Ride Home from Camp
- Praise your child for completing a day of camp.
- Prompt your child to share one thing that went well throughout the day.
- Celebrate the successes from the day.
- State expectations for snacks when your child gets home.
- Review the schedule for the remainder of the day.

After Camp
- Thank the counselors.
- Debrief with your child to determine if this camp is a good option for next year.
- Make note for yourself about how the camp went; whether the child had good counselor experience; and what you did to have a successful camp experience.
- Mark in your calendar to look at camps next February.

(continued)

Getting to Know _____

Strengths:
-
-
-

What works well for me:
- Speaking kindly
- Stating clear expectations that are worded positively to tell me what I should do (e.g., tell me to walk, instead of don't run)
- Giving me space when I am upset. Identify a location where I can go to be alone safely
- Earning reinforcers
- Providing choices
- Sticking with a schedule and telling me if there are changes
- Recognizing my feelings

What doesn't work well for me:
- Raising your voice
- Entering my personal space
- Putting your hands on me
- Using a disrespectful tone of voice
- Threatening me
- Taking away privileges

When I am upset, you can:
- In a calm, polite tone of voice, say,
  - "I am here to help you. Would you like me to find a space where you can be alone?"
  - "Please put your head down and take time."
  - "I see you are upset. How can I help you?"
  - "Would you like to talk to your mom or dad? I would be happy to get them on the phone for you."
  - "Take some deep breaths."
  - "Use your words to tell me how I can help you."

Parent Survey

Dear Parent,

We are seeking your feedback to better understand your satisfaction with _____ School's policies and procedures. We will use your input to work toward enhancing your child's experience at _____ School. All responses are anonymous. Thank you for sharing your thoughts and completing this survey.

At _____ School, we set clear expectations, follow policies and procedures, and use effective, positive commands in our school settings (e.g., classrooms, hallways, library, bathroom, gym) so that students know what is expected of them.

1. Do you use these strategies in your home?   YES   NO

a. **IF YES,** how helpful are these strategies?	**Not at all helpful**		**Helpful**	**Very helpful**	
	1	2	3	4	5

    b. **IF NO,** would you like training in how to use these strategies?   YES   NO

At _____ School, students are **praised for positive behavior**; on the other hand, **challenging behavior that does not harm the student or others is often ignored.**

2. Do you use these strategies in your home?   YES   NO

    a. **IF YES,** how helpful are these strategies?

Not at all helpful		Helpful	Very helpful	
1	2	3	4	5

    b. **IF NO,** would you like training in how to use these strategies?   YES   NO

At _____, we value **family involvement and collaboration.**

3. Do you feel that your child's teacher contacts you **too often** or **too little**?

Too little		Just Enough		Too often
1	2	3	4	5

4. How would you prefer to be contacted? (Please select the **best** way to contact you)
_____ Mail   _____ E-mail   _____ Phone

(continued)

Compared to **MY CHILD's experience** at his previous school, **MY CHILD's experience** at _____, is:

Worse		The Same		Better
1	2	3	4	5

Compared to **MY experience** with my child's previous school, **MY experience** with_____, is:

Worse		The Same		Better
1	2	3	4	5

    a. How can **your child's** experience be improved?:

    b. How can **YOUR** experience be improved?:

1) How would you like to be involved in:
   a) Your student's academic success?

   b) Your student's behavioral success?

Thank you so much for completing this survey! ☺

References

Adams, K. S., & Christenson, S. L. (1998). Differences in parent and teacher trust levels: Implications for creating collaborative family–school relationships. *Special Services in the Schools, 14*, 1–22.

Adams, K. S., & Christenson, S. L. (2000). Trust and the family–school relationship examination of parent–teacher differences in elementary and secondary grades. *Journal of School Psychology, 38*(5), 477–497. *https://doi.org/10.1016/S0022-4405(00)00048-0*

Adkins-Sharif, J. (2017, September 1). Beginning again with marginalized parents. ASCD Blog. *www.ascd.org/el/articles/beginning-again-with-marginalized-parents*

Algozzine, R. F., Barrett, S., Eber, L., George, H., Horner, R. H., Lewis, T. J., et al. (2014). *SWPBIS Tiered Fidelity Inventory.* Positive Behavioral Interventions & Supports (PBIS). *www.pbis.org*

Algozzine, R. F., Barrett, S., Eber, L., George, H., Lewis, T., Putnam, B., et al. (2019, April 1). *SWPBIS Tiered Fidelity Inventory. Version 2.1.* Positive Behavioral Interventions & Supports (PBIS). *www.pbis.org/resource/tfi*

Allen, A., Scott, L. M., & Lewis, C. W. (2013). Racial microaggressions and African American and Hispanic students in urban schools: A call for culturally affirming education. *Interdisciplinary Journal of Teaching and Learning, 3*(2), 117–129.

Allen, S. F., & Tracy, E. M. (2004). Revitalizing the role of home visiting by school social workers. *Children & Schools, 26*(4), 197–208. *https://doi.org/10.1093/cs/26.4.197*

Amaro-Jiménez, C., Hungerford-Kresser, H., Esquivel, S., Doddy, M., & Daniel, B. (2021). Partnering for change: Lessons from college access efforts for culturally and linguistically diverse students and families. *School Community Journal, 30*(2), 105–120.

Anderson, C. M., & Borgmeier, C. (2010). Tier II interventions within the framework of school-wide positive behavior support: Essential features for design, implementation, and maintenance. *Behavior Analysis in Practice, 3*(1), 33–45. *https://doi.org/10.1007/BF03391756*

Anderson, C. M., Lewis-Palmer, T., Todd, A. W., Horner, R. H., Sugai, G., & Sampson, N. K. (2012). *Individual student systems evaluation tool (Version 3.0).* University of Oregon, Educational and Community Supports.

Andis, P., Cashman, J., Praschil, R., Oglesby, D., Adelman, H., Taylor, L., & Weist, M. D. (2002). A strategic and shared agenda to advance mental health in schools through family and system partnerships. *International Journal of Mental Health Promotion, 4*(4), 28–35. *doi.org/10.1080 /14623730.2002.9721886*

Artiles, A. J. (2003). Special education's changing identity: Paradoxes and dilemmas in views of culture and space. *Harvard Educational Review, 73*(2), 164–202. *doi.org/10.17763/haer.73.2.j78t573x377j7106*

Artiles A. J. (2013). Untangling the racialization of disabilities: An intersectionality critique across disability models. *Du Bois Review: Social Science Research on Race, 10*(2), 329–347. *doi:10.1017 /S1742058X13000271*

Artiles, A. J. (2019). Fourteenth annual Brown lecture in education research: Reenvisioning equity research: Disability identification disparities as a case in point. *Educational Researcher, 48*(6), 325–335. *doi.org/10.3102/0013189X1987194*

Auerbach, S. (2009). Walking the walk: Portraits in leadership for family engagement in urban schools. *School Community Journal, 19*(1), 9–31.

Bacher-Hicks, A., Billings, S. B., & Deming, D. J. (2019). *The School to Prison Pipeline: Long-Run Impacts of School Suspensions on Adult Crime* (NBER Working Paper No. 26257). National Bureau of Economic Research. *https://scholar.harvard.edu/sites/scholar.harvard.edu/files/ddeming /files/w26257.pdf*

Bailey, T. R., Colpo, A., & Foley, A. (2020). *Assessment Practices Within a Multi-Tiered System of Supports* (Document No. IC-18). Collaboration for Effective Educator, Development, Accountability, and Reform Center. *https://ceedar.education.ufl.edu/wp-content/uploads/2020/12/As sessment-Practices-Within-a-Multi-Tiered-System-of-Supports-2.pdf*

Baker, T. L., Wise, J., Kelley, G., & Skiba, R. J. (2016). Identifying barriers: Creating solutions to improve family engagement. *School Community Journal, 26*(2), 161–184.

Bal, A. (2011). *Culturally responsive school-wide positive behavioral interventions and supports framework.* Wisconsin Department of Public Instruction.

Bal, A. (2016). From intervention to innovation: A cultural-historical approach to the racialization of school discipline. *Interchange: A Quarterly Review of Education, 47*, 409–427.

Bal, A. (2017). System of disability. *Critical Education, 8*(6), 1–27. *https://dm.education.wisc.edu/abal /intellcont/System%20of%20Disability_Bal_2017-1.pdf*

Bal, A. (2018). Culturally responsive positive behavioral interventions and supports: A process-oriented framework for systemic transformation. *Review of Education, Pedagogy, and Cultural Studies, 40*(2), 144–174. *doi.org/10.1080/10714413.2017.1417579*

Bal, A., Afacan, K., & Cakir, H. I. (2018). Culturally responsive school discipline: Implementing learning lab at a high school for systemic transformation. *American Educational Research Journal, 55*(5), 1007–1050. *doi.org/10.3102/0002831218768796*

Bal, A., & Perzigian, A. B. (2013). Evidence-based interventions for immigrant students experiencing behavioral and academic problems: A systematic review of the literature. *Education and Treatment of Children, 34*(4), 5–28.

Bal, A., Schrader, E. M., Afacan, K., & Mawene, D. (2016). Using learning labs for culturally responsive positive behavioral interventions and supports. *Intervention in School and Clinic, 52*(2), 122–128. *doi.org/10.1177/1053451216636*

Balu, R., Zhu, P., Doolittle, F., Schiller, E., Jenkins, J., & Gersten, R. (2015). *Evaluation of Response to Intervention practices for elementary school reading. NCEE 2016-4000.* National Center for Education Evaluation and Regional Assistance, Institute of Education Sciences, U.S. Department of Education. *https://files.eric.ed.gov/fulltext/ED560820.pdf*

Bang, M., Faber, L., Gurneau, J., Marin, A., & Cynthia, S. (2016). Community-based design research: Learning across generations and strategic transformations of institutional relations toward axiological innovations. *Mind, Culture, and Activity, 23*(1), 28–41. *doi.org/10.1080/10749039.2015.1087572*

Bang, M., & Vossoughi, S. (2016). Participatory design research and educational justice: Studying learning and relations within social change making. *Cognition and Instruction, 34*(3), 173–193. *doi.org/10.1080/07370008.2016.1181879*

Barajas-López, F., & Ishimaru, A. M. (2016). "Darles el lugar": A place for nondominant family knowing in educational equity. *Urban Education, 55*(1), 38–65. *doi.org/10.1177/0042085916652179*

Barger, M., Kim, E., Kuncel, N., & Pomerantz, E. (2019). The relation between parents' involvement in children's schooling and children's adjustment: A meta-analysis. *Psychological Bulletin, 145*(9), 855–890. *doi.org/10.1037/bul0000201*

Barrett, S., Eber, L., & Weist, M. D. (2013). *Advancing education effectiveness: An interconnected systems framework for Positive Behavioral Interventions and Supports (PBIS) and school mental health.* Center for Positive Behavioral Interventions and Supports. *https://cdn. prod.website-files.com/5d3725188825e071f1670246/5d76c6a8344facab50085275_final-monograph.pdf*

Batsche, Elliott, J., Graden, J., Grimes, J., Kovaleski, J., Prasse, D., et al. (2005). *Response to intervention: Policy considerations and implementation.* National Association of State Directors of Special Education.

Baquedano-López, P., Alexander, R. A., & Hernandez, S. J. (2013). Equity issues in parental and community involvement in schools: What teacher educators need to know. *Review of Research in Education, 37*(1), 149–182. *doi.org/10.3102/0091732X12459718*

Bernadel, S. (2021). *Seriously, don't touch our hair!: NWLC files amicus brief supporting students challenging race-based discipline and harassment.* National Women's Law Center. *https://nwlc .org/seriously-dont-touch-our-hair-nwlc-files-amicus-brief-supporting-students-challenging -race-based-discipline-and-harassment*

Bertram, R. M., Blase, K. A., & Fixsen, D. L. (2015). Improving programs and outcomes: Implementation frameworks and organization change. *Research on Social Work Practice, 25*(4), 477–487. *doi.org/10.1177/1049731514537687*

Bertrand, M., & Rodela, K. C. (2018). A framework for rethinking educational leadership in the margins: Implications for social justice leadership preparation. *Journal of Research on Leadership Education, 13*(1), 10–37. *doi.org/10.1177/1942775117739414*

Blase, K. A., Van Dyke, M., Fixsen, D. L., & Bailey, F. W. (2012). Implementation science: Key concepts, themes, and evidence for practitioners in educational psychology. In B. Kelly & D. F. Perkins (Eds.), *Handbook of implementation science for psychology in education* (pp. 13–34). Cambridge University Press.

Bohanon, H., Flannery, K. B., Malloy, J., & Fenning, P. (2009). Utilizing positive behavior supports in high school settings to improve school completion rates for students with high incidence conditions. *Exceptionality, 17*(1), 30–44. *doi.org/10.1080/09362830802590193*

Boone, B., Pizzuti, A., Peachock, M., Wellman, M., O'Leen, E., Offredo, M., & Jordan, E. (2018). PBIS: Tier 2 family engagement rubric guide. The Ohio State University. *https://ohiofamiliesengage. osu.edu*

Burgess, P. W., & Frierson, T. (2018, June 12). *Growing the capacity for parent leadership & school support organizations* [Conference session]. Tennessee Department of Education Family Engagement Conference, Murfreesboro, TN.

Burns, M., & Coolong-Chaffin, M. (2006). Response to intervention: The role of and effect on school psychology. *School Psychology Forum: Research in Practice, 1*(1), 3–15.

Bradshaw, C. P., Koth, C. W., Bevans, K. B., Ialongo, N., & Leaf, P. J. (2008). The impact of schoolwide positive behavioral interventions and supports (PBIS) on the organizational health of elementary schools. *School Psychology Quarterly, 23*(4), 462. *doi.org/10.1037/a0012883*

Bradshaw, C. P., Mitchell, M. M., & Leaf, P. J. (2010). Examining the effects of schoolwide positive behavioral interventions and supports on student outcomes: Results from a randomized controlled effectiveness trial in elementary schools. *Journal of Positive Behavior Interventions, 12*(3), 133–148. *doi.org/10.1177/1098300709334798*

Bronfenbrenner, U. (1979). *The ecology of human development: Experiments by nature and design.* Harvard University Press.

Brooks, S. K., Smith, L. E., Webster, R. K., Weston, D., Woodland, L., Hall, I., & Rubin, G. J. (2020). The impact of unplanned school closure on children's social contact: Rapid evidence review. *Eurosurveillance, 25*(13), 2000188. *doi.org/10.2807/1560-7917.ES.2020.25.13.2000188*

Brown v. Board of Education. (2007). *All hands in: An interactive resource guide.* Center on Culture, Race & Equity at Bank Street College (2017). *https://educate.bankstreet.edu/cgi/view content.cgi?article=1041&context=faculty-staff&_ga=2.15292918.1973567214.1663427700 -1952201627.1663427700*

Bruhn, A. L., & Hirsch, S. E. (2017). From good intentions to great implementation. *Report on Emotional & Behavioral Disorders in Youth, 17*(3), 64–70.

Bruhn, A. L., Lane, K. L., & Hirsch, S. E. (2014). A review of tier 2 interventions conducted within multitiered models of behavioral prevention. *Journal of Emotional and Behavioral Disorders, 22*(3), 171–189. *doi.org/10.1177/1063426613476092*

Byrom, N. (2018). An evaluation of a peer support intervention for student mental health. *Journal of Mental Health, 27*(3), 240–246. *doi.org/10.1080/09638237.2018.1437605*

Burns, M., & Coolong-Chaffin, M. (2006). Response to intervention: The role of and effect on school psychology. *School Psychology Forum: Research in Practice, 1*, 3–15.

Cakir, H. I. (2020). *Contradictions, transformative agency, and collective design: Facilitating inclusive problem-solving and systemic design at an urban middle school for addressing racial disparities in school discipline* [Doctoral dissertation]. University of Wisconsin–Madison.

Carlson, R., Hock, R., George, M. Kumpiene, G. Yell, M., McCartney, E., Riddle, D., & Weist, M. D. (2020). Relational factors influencing parents' engagement in special education for high school youth with emotional/behavioral disorders. *Behavioral Disorders, 45*(2),103–116. *doi.org/10 .1177/0198742919883276*

Cashman, J., Linehan, P., Purcell, L., Rosser, M., Schultz, S., & Skalski, S. (2014). *Leading by convening: A blueprint for authentic engagement.* National Association of State Directors of Special Education.

Castillo, J. M., Batsche, G. M., Curtis, M. J., Stockslager, K., March, A., Minch, D., & Hines, C. (2016). *Problem Solving/Response to Intervention evaluation tool technical assistance manual—revised 2016.* University of South Florida.

Center on Culture, Race & Equity at Bank Street College. (2017). Culture, race and equity. Available at *www.bankstreet.edu/our-work-with-schools-and-communities/bank-street-education-center/ culture-race-equity*

Center on Multi-Tiered System of Supports. (2021). *Multi-tiered System of Supports (MTSS) Fidelity of Implementation Rubric.* American Institutes for Research. *https://mtss4success.org/sites /default/files/2021-04/MTSS-IntegRubricMarch2021-508.pdf*

Center on Positive Behavioral Interventions and Supports (2016). *Stakeholder Input and Satisfaction Survey-Family (SISS Family)–Pilot version 0.1.* University of Oregon. *www.dropbox.com/s /1f2x8ljyta69dim/SISS%20Family%20survey%202016-08-10.pdf?dl=0*

Center on Positive Behavioral Interventions and Supports (PBIS, 2017). SWPBS implementation blueprint (Revised). *https//pbis.org*

Center on Positive Behavioral Interventions and Supports (2020). Positive Behavioral Interventions and Supports District Systems Fidelity Inventory (DSFI) (Revised). *https//pbis.org*

Cherng, H.-Y. (2016). Is all classroom conduct equal? Teacher contact with parents of racial/ethnic minority and immigrant adolescents. *Teachers College Record: The Voice of Scholarship in Education, 118*(11), 1–36. *doi.org/10.1177/016146811611801104*

Christenson, S. L. (2004). The family–school partnership: An opportunity to promote the learning competence of all students. *School Psychology Review, 33*, 83–104.

Christenson, S. L., Rounds, T., & Franklin, M. J. (1992). Home–school collaboration: Effects, issues, and opportunities. In S. L. Christenson & J. C. Conoley (Ed.), *Home–school collaboration: enhancing children's academic and social competence* (pp. 19–51). National Association of School Psychologists.

Christenson, S. L., & Sheridan, S. M. (2001). *Schools and families: Creating essential connections for learning.* Guilford Press.

Christianakis, M. (2011). Parents as "help labor": Inner-city teachers' narratives of parent involvement. *Teacher Education Quarterly, 38*(4), 157–178.

Clauss-Ehlers, C., Carpio, M. G., & Weist, M. D. (2020). Mental health literacy: A strategy for global mental health promotion. *Adolescent Psychiatry, 10*(2), 73–83. *doi.org/10.2174/221067661066 6200204104429*

Collier, T., & Rizzardi, V. (2020). Improving schoolwide approaches in school behavioral health. In Weist, M. D., Franke, K., & Stevens, R. (Eds.), *School behavioral health: Interconnecting comprehensive school mental health and positive behavior support* (pp. 21–34). Springer.

Colvin, G., & Fernandez, E. (2000). Sustaining effective behavior support systems in an elementary school. *Journal of Positive Behavior Interventions, 2*(4), 251–253. *doi.org/10.1177/1098300 70000200414*

Conduct Problems Prevention Research Group. (2007). Fast track randomized controlled trial to prevent externalizing psychiatric disorders: Findings from grades 3 to 9. *Journal of the American Academy of Child & Adolescent Psychiatry, 46*(10), 1250–1262. *doi.org// 10.1097/chi.0b013e31813e5d39*

Cook, S. (2018). *Tiered Fidelity Inventory-Family and Community Engagement (TFI-FACE): A Tool for Evaluating Family and Community Engagement within Positive Behavioral Interventions and Supports (PBIS).* Tennessee Behavior Supports Project at the University of Memphis Lambuth.

Cook, S., Casey, L., Lewis, M., & Hunter, W. (2022). Building a Framework for Family and Community Engagement in Positive Behavior Interventions and Supports: Tennessee's First Steps [Manuscript in review]. *International Journal of Positive Behavior Support.*

Cooper, C. W. (2009). Parent involvement, African American mothers, and the politics of educational care. *Equity and Excellence in Education, 42*(4), 379–394. *doi.org/10.1080/10665680903228389*

Council for Exceptional Children. (2015). *What every special educator must know: Professional ethics & standards* (7th ed.). Author.

Cox, D. D. (2005). Evidence-based interventions using home–school collaboration. *School Psychology Quarterly, 20*(4), 473–497. *doi.org/10.1521/scpq.2005.20.4.473*

Crone, D. A., Hawken, L. S., Horner, R. H. (2010). *Responding to Problem Behavior in Schools, Second Edition: The Behavior Education Program.* Guilford Press.

Darling-Hammond, L. (2015). *The flat world and education: How America's commitment to equity will determine our future.* Teachers College Press.

DeMatthews, D. (2018). School leadership, social capital, and community engagement: A case study of an elementary school in ciudad Juárez, Mexico. *School Community Journal, 28*(1), 167–194. *https://www.adi.org/journal/2018ss/DeMatthewsSpring2018.pdf*

Dewey, J. (1997). *Democracy and education: An introduction to the philosophy of education.* Free Press.

Dishion, T. J., Kavanagh, K., Schneiger, A., Nelson, S., & Kaufman, N. K. (2002). Preventing early adolescent substance use: A family-centered strategy for the public middle school. *Prevention Science, 3*(3), 191–201. *doi.org/10.1023/a:1019994500301*

Dishion, T. J., & Patterson, G. R. (2016). The development and ecology of antisocial behavior: linking etiology, prevention, and treatment. *Developmental Psychopathology, 3*, 1–32. *doi.org/10.1002 /9780470939406.ch13*

Dishion, T. J., & Stormshak, E. (2007). *Intervening in children's lives: An ecological, family-centered approach to mental health care.* American Psychological Association.

Domitrovich, C. E., Bradshaw, C. P., Greenberg, M. T., Embry, D., Poduska, J. M., & Ialongo, N. S. (2010). Integrated models of school-based prevention: Logic and theory. *Psychology in the Schools, 47*(1), 71–88. *doi.org/10.1002/pits.20452*

Domitrovich, C. E., Bradshaw, C. P., Poduska, J. M., Hoagwood, K., Buckley, J. A., Olin, S., et al. (2008). Maximizing the implementation quality of evidence-based preventive interventions in schools: A conceptual framework. *Advances in School Mental Health Promotion, 1*(3), 6–28. *doi .org/10.1080/1754730x.2008.9715730*

Donovan, S. M., & Cross, C. T. (Eds.). (2002). *Minority students in special and gifted education.* National Academy Press, Division of Behavioral and Social Sciences.

Dumas, M. J. (2014). 'Losing an arm': Schooling as a site of black suffering. *Race Ethnicity and Education, 17*(1), 1–29. *doi.org/10.1080/13613324.2013.850412*

Dumka, L. E., Gonzales N. A., & Bonds, D. (2008). Academic success of Mexican origin adolescent boys and girls: The role of mothers' and fathers' parenting and cultural orientation. *Sex Roles, 60*(7–8), 588–599. *doi.org/10.1007/s11199-008-9518-z*

Drummond, K. V., & Stipek, D. (2004). Low-income parents' beliefs about their role in children's academic learning. *The Elementary School Journal, 104*(3), 197–213.

Dunn, L. M. (1968). Special education for the mildly retarded: Is much of it justifiable? Exceptional Children, 35, 5–22.

Dutch International Mental Health Hub. (2021, March). *An international perspective on the impact of the COVID-19 pandemic on child and youth mental health and future directions* [Webinar]. *www.rug.nl/gmw/expertisecentrum-gmcp/agenda/210223-webinar*

Eagle, J. W., Dowd-Eagle, S. E., Snyder, A., & Holtzman, E. G. (2015). Implementing a multi-tiered system of support (MTSS): Collaboration between school psychologists and administrators to promote systems-level change. *Journal of Educational and Psychological Consultation, 25*(2–3), 160–177. *doi.org/10.1080/10474412.2014.929960*

Eber, L., Barrett, S., Perales, K., Jeffrey-Pearsall, J., Pohlman, K., Putnam, R, et al. (2019). *Advancing Education Effectiveness: Interconnecting School Mental Health and School-Wide PBIS, Volume 2: An Implementation Guide.* Center for Positive Behavior Interventions and Supports. *https://cdn.prod.website-files.com/5d3725188825e071f1670246/5f6914a88117c9834d0638f8 _ISF%20v2%20Implementation%20Guide.pdf*

Eber, L., Scherder, E., Raulson, C., Abshier, D., Perales, K., & Weist, M. D. (2021). *Installing an Interconnected Systems Framework at the school level: Recommendations and examples to guide school leadership teams, practitioners and coaches.* Center on Positive Behavioral Interventions and Supports. *https://cdn.prod.website-files.com/5d3725188825e071f1670246/602 ff0a2995a3f8ac1067813_Installing%20an%20Interconnected%20Systems%20Framework%20 at%20the%20School%20Level.pdf*

Eber, L., Sugai, G., Smith, C. R., & Scott, T. M. (2002). Wraparound and positive behavioral interventions and supports in the schools. *Journal of Emotional and Behavioral Disorders, 10*(3), 171–180. *doi.org/10.1177/10634266020100030501*

Engeström, Y. (2011). From design experiments to formative interventions. *Theory & Psychology, 21*(5), 598–628. *doi.org/10.1177/0959354311419252*

Engeström, Y. (2008). *From teams to knots: Activity-theoretical studies of collaboration and learning at work.* Cambridge University Press.

Engeström, Y., & Sannino, A. (2010). Studies of expansive learning: Foundations, findings, and future challenges. *Educational Research Review, 5,* 1–24. *doi.org/10.1016/j.edurev.2009.12.002*

Eppley, K., & Shannon, P. (2017). Practice-based evidence: Intelligent action inquiry for complex problems. *Literacy Research: Theory, Method, and Practice, 66*(1), 389–405. *doi.org/10.1177 /2381336917719685*

Eppley, K., Shannon, P., Azano, A. P., & Brenner, D. (2018). What Counts as Evidence in Rural Schools? Evidence-Based Practice and Practice-Based Evidence for Diverse Settings. *Rural Educator, 39*(2), 35–39. *doi.org/10.35608/ruraled.v39i2.208*

Epstein, J. L. (1996). Perspectives and previews on research and policy for school, family, and community partnerships. In A. Booth & J. F. Dunn (Eds.), *Family–school links: How do they affect educational outcomes* (pp. 209–246). Routledge.

Epstein, J. L., Galindo, C. L., & Sheldon, S. B. (2011). Levels of leadership: Effects of district and school leaders on the quality of school programs of family and community engagement. *Educational Administration Quarterly, 47*(3), 462–495. *doi.org/10.1177/0013161X10396929*

Every Student Succeeds Act, 20 U.S.C. § 6301 (2015). *www.congress.gov/bill/114th-congress/senate-bill/1177*

Fallon, L. M., Kurtz, K. D., & Mueller, M. R. (2018). Direct training to improve educators' treatment integrity: A systematic review of single-case design studies. *School Psychology Quarterly, 33*(2), 169–181. *doi.org/10.1037/spq0000210*

Fallon, L. M., & Mueller, M. R. (2017). Culturally responsive wraparound supports: Collaborating with families to promote students' behavior regulation across settings. *Contemporary School Psychology, 21*, 201–210.

Fallon, L. M., Veiga, M., & Sugai, G. (2021). Strengthening MTSS for behavior (MTSS-B) to promote racial equity. *School Psychology Review, 52*(5), 518–533. *doi.org/10.1080/2372966X.2021.1972333*

Family–School–Community Alliance (FSCA, 2019). *Model for family-school collaboration. www.fscalliance.org.*

Fan, X., & Chen, M. (2001). Parental involvement and students' academic achievement: A meta-analysis. *Educational Psychology Review, 13*(1), 1–22. *doi.org/10.1023/A:1009048817385*

Fantuzzo, J., Tighe, E., & Childs, S. (2000). Family Involvement Questionnaire: A multivariate assessment of family participation in early childhood education. *Journal of Educational Psychology, 9*(2), 367–376. *doi.org/10.1037/0022-0663.92.2.367*

Fefer, S. A., Donnelly, M., & Santana, Z. A. (2021). Pilot Implementation of School-Based Behavioral Parent Training: Outcomes and Acceptability. *Journal of Child and Family Studies, 31*(2), 1–16. *doi.org/10.1007/s10826-021-02117-9*

Fefer, S. A., Hieneman, M., Virga, C., Thoma, A., & Donnelly, M. (2020). Evaluating the Effect of Positive Parent Contact on Elementary Students' On-Task Behavior. *Journal of Positive Behavior Interventions, 22*(4), 234–245.

Fehrer, K. (2019). *Oakland Unified School District full-service community schools outcomes: A retrospective: Shifting school culture & relationships with families and the broader community.* John W. Gardner Center for Youth and Their Communities. *https://files.eric.ed.gov/fulltext/ED604095.pdf*

Feil, E. G., Frey, A. J., Walker, H. M., Small, J. W., Seeley, J. R., Golly, A., & Forness, S. R. (2014). The efficacy of a home–school intervention for preschoolers with challenging behaviors: A randomized controlled trial of preschool first step to success. *Journal of Early Intervention, 36*(3), 151–170.

Feinberg, A., Fefer, S., & Vatland, C. (2020, October 21–23). *Using family data to inform home–school communication and collaboration within PBIS* [Conference session]. Virtual PBIS Leadership Forum. YouTube. *www.youtube.com/watch?v=_Nz1BgHaU-s*

Ferguson, C., Jordan, C., & Baldwin, M (2010). *Working systematically in action: Engaging family and community.* SEDL.

Fien, H., Nelson, N. J., Smolkowski, K., Kosty, D., Pilger, M., Baker, S. K., & Smith, J. L. M. (2021). A conceptual replication study of the Enhanced Core Reading Instruction MTSS-reading model. *Exceptional Children, 87*(3), 265–288. *doi.org/10.1177/0014402920953763*

Ferguson, C. (2005). *Reaching Out to Diverse Populations: What Can Schools Do to Foster Family-School Connections?* Southwest Educational Development Laboratory. *https://sedl.org/connections/resources/rb/rb5-diverse.pdf*

Fix, R. L., Mayworm, A., Lawson, G. M., Becker, K. D., Lever, N. A., Hoover, S. (2017). Strategies for effective family engagement in elementary and middle schools. In M. D. Weist, S. A. Garbacz, K. L. Lane, & D. Kincaid (Eds.), *Aligning and integrating family engagement in Positive Behavioral Interventions and Supports (PBIS): Concepts and strategies for families and schools in key contexts* (pp. 98–119). Center for Positive Behavioral Interventions and Supports. *https:// pbis.org*

Fixsen, D. L., Blasé, K., Metz, A., & Van Dyke, M. (2013). Statewide implementation of evidence-based programs. *Exceptional Children, 79*(3), 213–230. *doi.org/10.1177/001440291307900206*

Fixsen, D. L., Naoon, S. F., Blasé, K. A., Friedman, R. M., & Wallace, F. (2005). Implementation research: A synthesis of the literature. The National Implementation Research Network.

Flamboyan Foundation. (n.d.). Classroom Family Engagement Rubric. *https://assets-global.web site-files.com/5d3725188825e071f1670246/5d8507aea2d3aa3c7bc14ac3_Classroom-Family -Engagement-Rubric-V4-VF-3.pdf*

Flores, O. J., Kyere, E. (2021). Advancing equity-based school leadership: The importance of family–school relationships. *Urban Review, 53*(1), 127–144.

Florida Problem-Solving/Response to Intervention Project. (2011). *MTSS Myths & Truths. https:// floridarti.usf.edu/resources/myths/educators/Myths%20and%20Truths%20Educators.pdf*

Fogt, J. B., & Piripavel, C. M. (2002). Positive school-wide interventions for eliminating physical restraint and exclusion. *Reclaiming Children and Youth, 10*(4), 227–232.

Fox, L., & Swett, J. (2017). Implementing partnerships with families to promote social and emotional competence of young children. In M. D. Weist, S. A. Garbacz, K. L. Lane, & D. Kincaid (Eds.), *Aligning and integrating family engagement in positive behavioral interventions and supports (PBIS): Concepts and strategies for families and schools in key contexts* (pp. 84–97). Center for Positive Behavioral Interventions and Supports.

Freeman, J., Sugai, G., Simonsen, B., & Everett, S. (2017). MTSS coaching: Bridging knowing to doing. *Theory Into Practice, 56*(1), 29–37. *doi.org/10.1080/00405841.2016.1241946*

Freire, P. (2000). *Pedagogy of the oppressed.* Continuum.

Fullan, M. (2007). *Leading in a culture of change.* Wiley.

Gandhi, L. (2021, September 14). *Black girls are fighting back against discriminatory school dress codes.* PRISM. *https://prismreports.org/2021/09/14/bipoc-girls-are-fighting-back-against-dis criminatory-school-dress-codes*

Garbacz, S. A. (2019). Enhancing family engagement in schoolwide positive behavioral interventions and supports. *Intervention in School and Clinic, 54*(4), 195–203. *doi.org/10.1177/105345 1218782428*

Garbacz, S. A., Beattie, T., Masser, J., & DeGarmo, D. (2019). Initial validation of an elementary version of the positive family support strengths and needs assessment. *Assessment for Effective Intervention, 45*(1), 73–80. *doi.org/10.1177/1534508418793514*

Garbacz, S. A., Bolt, D. M., Seeley, J. R., Stormshak, E. A., & Smolkowski, K. (2020). Examining school proactive outreach to families in public middle schools. *School Psychology Review, 49*(4), 493–509. *doi.org/10.1080/2372966X.2020.1787081*

Garbacz, S. A., Herman, K. C., Thompson, A. M., & Reinke, W. M. (2017). Family engagement in education and intervention: Implementation and evaluation to maximize family,school, and student outcomes. *Journal of School Psychology, 62*, 1–10. *doi.org/10.1016/j.jsp.2017.04.002*

Garbacz, S. A., Hirano, K., & McIntosh, K., Eagle, J. W., Minch, D., Vatland, C. (2018). Family engagement in schoolwide positive behavioral interventions and supports: Barriers and facilitators to implementation. *School Psychology Quarterly, 33*(3), 448–459. *doi.org/10.1037/spq0000216*

Garbacz, S. A., Kelly, K., & Albers, C. (2021). Theoretical foundations of school psychology research and practice. In K. K. Kelly, S. A. Garbacz, & C. A. Albers (Eds.), *Theories of School Psychology: Critical Perspectives* (1st ed., pp. 1–21). Routledge.

Garbacz, S. A., Lee, Y., Hall, G. J., Stormshak, E. A., & McIntyre, L. L. (2021). Initiating family–school collaboration in school mental health through a proactive and positive strengths and needs assessment. *School Mental Health, 13*(4), 667–679.

Garbacz, S. A., McIntosh, K., & Eagle, J. W. (2014). *Family–school practices survey—School teams (Version1.1).* Educational and Community Supports, University of Oregon. *https://bit.ly/2WwNonX*

Garbacz, S. A., McIntosh, K., Eagle, J. W., Dowd-Eagle, S. E., Hirano, K. A., & Ruppert, T. (2016). Family engagement within schoolwide positive behavioral interventions and supports. *Preventing School Failure: Alternative Education for Children and Youth, 60*(1), 60–69. *doi.org/10.1080/1045988X.2014.976809*

Garbacz, S. A., McIntosh, K., Vatland, C. H., Minch, D. R., & Eagle, J. W. (2018). Identifying and examining school approaches to family engagement within schoolwide positive behavioral interventions and supports. *Journal of Positive Behavior Interventions, 20*(3), 127–137. *doi.org/10.1177/1098300717752318*

Garbacz, S. A., Minch, D., & Cook, S. (2019). *Tiered Fidelity Inventory—Family–School Collaboration (TFI-FSC). www.fscalliance.org.*

Garbacz, S. A., Minch, D., Cook, S., McIntosh, K., Weist, M., & Eagle, J. (2019). *Family–School Collaboration: Tiered Fidelity Inventory.* Unpublished tool, Family School Community Alliance and OSEP Technical Assistance Center on Positive Behavioral Interventions and Supports.

Garbacz, S. A., Minch, D., Jordan, P., Young, K., & Weist, M. D. (2020). Moving towards meaningful and significant family partnerships in education. *Adolescent Psychiatry, 10*(2), 110–122. *doi.org/10.2174/2210676610666200324113209*

Garbacz, S. A., Rose, J. J., Weist, M. D., & McIntosh, K. (2018). Defining and promoting family engagement in schoolwide positive behavioral interventions and supports. *2017 National PBIS Forum Roundtable/Discussion/Question-Answer (RDQ) Practice Brief.* Center for Positive Behavioral Interventions and Supports.

Garbacz, S. A., Stormshak, E. A., McIntyre, L. L., & Kosty, D. (2019). Examining family–school engagement in a randomized controlled trial of the family check-up. *School Psychology, 34*(4), 433–443. *doi.org/10.1037/spq0000284*

Garbacz, S. A., & Weist, M. D. (2019). *Family–school collaboration in Positive Behavioral Interventions and Supports: Creating a school atmosphere to promote collaboration.* 2018 National PBIS Forum Roundtable/Discussion/Question-Answer (RDQ) Practice Brief. Center for Positive Behavioral Interventions and Supports.

Garbacz, S. A., Witte, A. L., & Houck, S. N. (2017). Family engagement foundations: supporting children and families. In M. Weist, S. A. Garbacz, K. Lane, & D. Kincaid (Eds.), *Aligning and integrating family engagement in positive behavioral interventions and supports (PBIS): Concepts and strategies for families and schools in key contexts* (pp. 9–30). Center for Positive Behavioral Interventions and Supports.

Garcia, M. E., Frunzi, K., Dean, C. B., Flores, N., & Miller, K. B. (2016a). *Toolkit of Resources for Engaging Families and the Community as Partners in Education: Part 1: Building an understanding of family and community engagement. REL 2016–148.* U.S. Department of Education, Institute of Education Sciences, National Center for Education Evaluation and Regional Assistance, Regional Educational Laboratory Pacific. *https://files.eric.ed.gov/fulltext/ED569110.pdf*

Garcia, M. E., Frunzi, K., Dean, C. B., Flores, N., & Miller, K. B. (2016b). *Toolkit of Resources for Engaging Families and the Community as Partners in Education: Part 2: Building a cultural bridge. REL 2016–151.* U.S. Department of Education, Institute of Education Sciences, National Center for Education Evaluation and Regional Assistance, Regional Educational Laboratory Pacific. *https://files.eric.ed.gov/fulltext/ED569111.pdf*

Garcia, M. E., Frunzi, K., Dean, C. B., Flores, N., & Miller, K. B. (2016c). *Toolkit of Resources for Engaging Families and the Community as Partners in Education: Part 3:Building trusting relationships with families and the community through effective communication. REL 2016– 152.* U.S. Department of Education, Institute of Education Sciences, National Center for Education Evaluation and Regional Assistance, Regional Educational Laboratory Pacific. *https:// nces.gov/pubsearch/pubsinfo.asp?pubid=REL2016152*

Garcia, M. E., Frunzi, K., Dean, C. B., Flores, N., & Miller, K. B. (2016d). *Toolkit of Resources for Engaging Families and the Community as Partners in Education: Part 4: Engaging all in data conversations. REL 2016–153.* U.S. Department of Education, Institute of Education Sciences, National Center for Education Evaluation and Regional Assistance, Regional Educational Laboratory Pacific. *https://ies.ed.gov/ncee/edlabs/projects/project.asp?projectID=4509*

Garcia-Reid, P. (2007). Examining social capital as a mechanism for improving school engagement among low income Hispanic girls. *Youth & Society, 39*(2), 164–181. *doi.org/10.1177/0044118 X07303263*

George, H. P., Cox, K. E., Minch, D., & Sandomierski, T. (2018). District practices associated with successful SWPBIS implementation. *Behavioral Disorders, 43*(3), 393–406. *doi.org/10.1177 /0198742917753612*

George, M. P., George, N. L., Kern, L., & Fogt, J. B. (2013). Three-tiered support for students with EBD: Highlights of the universal tier. *Education and Treatment of Children. 36*(3), 47–62. *doi .org/10.1353/ETC.2013.0022*

Georgis, R., Gokiert, R. J., Ford, D. M., & Ali, M. (2014). Creating inclusive parent engagement practices: Lessons learned from a school community collaborative supporting newcomer refugee families. *Multicultural Education, 21*(3/4), 23–27.

Gibbons, K., Brown, S., & Niebling, B. C. (2019). *Effective universal instruction: An action-oriented approach to improving Tier 1.* Guilford Press.

Gillborn, D. (2005). Education as an act of white supremacy: Whiteness, critical race theory, and education reform. *Journal of Educational Policy, 20*(4), 485–505. *doi.org/10.1080/02680930500132346*

Glasser, W. (1965). *Reality therapy: A new approach to psychiatry.* Harper & Row.

Goddard, R. D. (2003). Relational networks, social trust, and norms: A social capital perspective on students' chances of academic success. *Educational Evaluation and Policy Analysis, 25*(1), 59–74. *doi.org/10.3102/01623737025001059*

Goldman, S. E., Sanderson, K. A., Lloyd, B. P., & Barton, E. E. (2019). Effects of school–home communication with parent-implemented reinforcement on off-task behavior for students with ASD. *Intellectual and Developmental Disabilities, 57*(2), 95–111, 172, 174. *doi.org/10.1352/1934 -9556-57.2.95*

Gonzalez, R. (2020). *The Spectrum of Family and Community Engagement for Educational Equity.* Facilitating Power. *https://movementstrategy.org/wp-content/uploads/2021/08/Spectrum-of -Family-Community-Engagement-for-Educational-Equity.pdf*

Gonzales, S. M., & Gabel, S. L. (2017). Exploring involvement expectations for culturally and Linguistically diverse parents: What we need to know in teacher education. *International Journal of Multicultural Education, 19*(2), 61–81. *https://files.eric.ed.gov/fulltext/EJ1148047.pdf*

Gopalan, G., Jung Lee, S., Harris, R., & Acri, M. (2017). Utilization of peers in services for youth with emotional and behavioral challenges: A scoping review. *Journal of Adolescence, 55*(1), 88–115. *doi.org/10.1016/j.adolescence.2016.12.011*

Grant, K. B., & Ray, J. (2019). *Home, school, and community collaboration: Culturally responsive family engagement* (4th ed.). SAGE.

Grasley-Boy, N. M., Gage, N. A., Reichow, B., MacSuga-Gage, A. S., & Lane, H. (2020). A conceptual replication of targeted professional development to increase teachers' behavior-specific praise. *School Psychology Review, 52*(1), 1–15. *doi.org/10.1080/2372966X.2020.1853486*

Gregory, A., Skiba, R. J., & Noguera, P. A. (2010). The achievement gap and the discipline gap: Two sides of the same coin? *Educational Researcher, 39*(1), 59–68. *doi.org/10.3102/0013189X09 357621*

Hambacher, E. (2018). Resisting punitive school discipline: Perspectives and practices of exemplary urban elementary teachers. *International Journal of Qualitative Studies in Education, 31*(2), 102–118. *doi.org/10.1080/09518398.2017.1349958*

Hammond, Z. (2018). Culturally Responsive Teaching Puts Rigor at the Center: Q&A with Zaretta Hammond. *Learning Professional, 39*(5), 40–43. *https://learningforward.org/wp-content/uploads /2018/10/culturally-responsive-teaching-puts-rigor-at-the-center.pdf*

Harry, B. (1992). Restructuring the participation of African-American parents in special education. *Exceptional Children, 59*(2), 123–131. *doi.org/10.1177/001440299205900205*

Harry, B. (2008). Collaboration with culturally and linguistically diverse families: Ideal versus reality. *Exceptional Children, 74*(3), 372–388. *doi.org/10.1177/001440290807400306*

Harry, B., & Klingner, J. (2014). *Why are so many minority students in special education?* Teachers College Press.

Hastings, O. (2018). Less equal, less trusting? Longitudinal and cross-sectional effects of income equality on trust in the U.S. States, 1973–2002. *Social Sciences Research, 74,* 77–95. *doi.org/10 .1016/j.ssresearch.2018.04.005*

Hawken, L. S., Adolphson, S. L., Macleod, K. S., & Schumann, J. (2009). Secondary-tier interventions and supports. In W. Sailor, G. Dunlop, G. Sugai, & R. Horner (Eds.), *Handbook of Positive Behavior Support* (pp. 395–420). Springer.

Hawken, L. S., Crone, D. A., Bundock, K., & Horner, R. H. (2021). *Responding to Problem Behavior in Schools: The check-in, check-out intervention* (3rd ed.). Guilford Press.

Hawken, L. S., Sandra MacLeod, K., & Rawlings, L. (2007). Effects of the Behavior Education Program (BEP) on Office Discipline Referrals of Elementary School Students. *Journal of Positive Behavior Interventions, 9*(2), 94–101. *doi.org/10.1177/10983007070090020601*

Hedwig, L., Esposito, M., Edwards, F., Chun, Y., & Grinstein-Weiss, M. (2020). *The demographics of racial inequity in the United States.* Brookings. *www.brookings.edu/blog/up-front/2020/07/27 /the-demographics-of-racial-inequality-in-the-united-states*

Heintzelman, S., & Spradlin, K. (2018, June 4). *Preparing for summer camp* [Presentation handout]. Centennial School Virtual Parent Training.

Henderson, A. T., & Mapp, K. L. (2002). *A New Wave of Evidence: The Impact of School, Family and Community Connections on Student Achievement.* Southwest Educational Development Laboratory. *https://sedl.org/connections/resources/evidence.pdf*

Henderson, A. T., Mapp, K. L., Johnson, V. R., & Davies, D. (2007). *Beyond the bake sale: The essential guide to family–school partnerships.* New Press.

Hendricker, E., Bender, S. L., & Ouye, J. (2017). Family involvement in school-based behavioral screening: A review of six school psychology journals from 2004–2014. *Contemporary School Psychology, 22*(3), 344–354. *doi.org/10.1007/s40688-017-0163-9*

Herman, K. C., Reinke, W. M., & Frey, A. J. (2020). *Motivational interviewing in schools: Strategies for engaging parents, teachers, and students* (2nd ed.). Springer.

Hertz, M. F., & Barrios, L. C. (2021). Adolescent mental health, COVID-19, and the value of school-community partnerships. *Injury Prevention, 27*(1), 85–86. *doi.org/10.1136/injuryprev-2020-044050*

Hicklen House, S. (2020). Implementing culturally responsive practices in family–school partnership programs. In S. A. Garbacz (Ed.), *Establishing family–school partnerships in school psychology: Critical skills* (pp. 135–151). Routledge.

Hill, N. E., & Tyson, D. F. (2009). Parental involvement in middle school: A meta-analytic assessment of the strategies that promote achievement. *Developmental Psychology, 45*(3), 740–763. *doi.org/10.1037/a0015362*

Ho, P., & Cherng, H. S. (2018). How far can the apple fall? Differences in teacher perceptions of minority and immigrant parents and their impact on academic outcomes. *Social Science Research, 74,* 132–145. doi: 10.1016/j.ssresearch.2018.05.001. Epub 2018 May 7. PMID: 29961480.

Ho, P., & Hua-Yu, S. C. (2018). How far can the apple fall? Differences in teacher perceptions on minority and immigrant parents and their impact on academic outcomes. *Social Sciences Research, 74,* 132–145. *doi.org/10.1016/j.ssresearch.2018.05.001*

Holmes, S., Smith, T., & Garbacz, A. (2020). Theories and frameworks that underlie family–school partnerships. In K. K. Kelly, S. A. Garbacz, & C. A. Albers (Eds.), *Theories of school psychology: Critical perspectives* (pp. 273–294). Routledge.

hooks, b. (1989). Choosing the margin as a space of radical openness. *The Journal of Cinema and Media. 36,* 15–23.

Hoover-Dempsey, K. V., Walker, J. M. T., Jones, K. P., & Reed, R. P. (2002). Teachers involving parents (TIP): Results of an in-service teacher education program for enhancing parental involvement. *Teaching and Teacher Education, 18*(7), 843–867. *doi.org/10.1016/S0742-051X(02)00047-1*

Hoover-Dempsey, K. V., Walker, J. M. T., Sandler, H. M., Whetsel, D., Green, C. L., Wilkens, A. S., & Closson, K. (2005). Why do parents become involved? Research findings implications. *The Elementary School Journal, 106*(2), 105–130. *doi.org/10.1086/499194*

Horner, R. H., & Day, H. M. (1991). The effects of response efficiency on functionally equivalent competing behaviors. *Journal of Applied Behavior Analysis, 24*(4), 719–732. *doi.org/10.1901 /jaba.1991.24-719*

Horner, R. H., Kincaid, D., Sugai, G., Lewis, T., Eber, L., Barrett, S., et al. (2014). Scaling up school-wide positive behavioral interventions and supports: Experiences of seven states with documented success. *Journal of Positive Behavior Interventions, 16*(4), 197–208. *doi.org/10.1177/109 8300713503685*

Horner, R. H., Sugai, G., & Fixsen, D. L. (2017). Implementing effective educational practices at scales of social importance. *Clinical Child and Family Psychology Review, 20*(1), 25–35. *doi .org/10.1007/s10567-017-0224-7*

Horner, R. H., Sugai, G., Smolkowski, K., Eber, L., Nakasato, J., Todd, A. W., & Esperanza, J. (2009). A randomized, wait-list controlled effectiveness trial assessing school-wide positive behavior support in elementary schools. *Journal of Positive Behavior Interventions, 11*(3), 133–144. *doi .org/10.1177/1098300709332067*

Horner, R., Sugai, G., & Vincent, C. (2005). School-wide positive behavior support: Investing in student success. *Impact, 18*(2), 4–5.

Houri, A. K., Thayer, A. J., & Cook, C. R. (2019). Targeting parent trust to enhance engagement in a school–home communication system: A double-blind experiment of a parental wise feedback intervention. *School Psychology, 34*(4), 421–432. *doi.org/10.1037/spq0000318*

Hrastinski, S. (2021). Teachers as developers of local evidence to improve digital course design. *Interactive Learning Environments, 29*(4), 648–654. *doi.org/10.1080/10494820.2019.1594959*

Huffman, R., Krueger, F., Collins, D., & Weist, M. D. (2021, April). *Family engagement in school mental health: Key themes and strategies for improvement.* Paper presented at the Southeastern School Behavioral Health Conference, Myrtle Beach, SC.

Hussar, B., Zhang, J., Hein, S., Wang, K., Roberts, A., Cui, J., Smith, M., Bullock Mann, F., Barmer, A., & Dilig, R. (2020). *The Condition of Education 2020 (NCES 2020-144).* U.S. Department of Education, National Center for Education Statistics. *https://nces.ed.gov/pubsearch/pubsinfo .asp?pubid=2020144*

Individuals with Disabilities Education Act, 20 U.S.C. § 1400 (2004).

Iruka, I. Curenton, S., Durden, T., & Escayg, K-A. (2020). *Don't look away: Embracing Antibias Classrooms.* Gryphon House.

Ishimaru, A. M. (2020). *Just Schools: Building Equitable Collaborations with Families and Communities (Multicultural Education Series).* Teachers College Press.

Jeynes, W. H. (2003). A meta-analysis: The effects of parental involvement on minority children's academic achievement. *Education and Urban Society, 35*(2), 202–218. *doi:10.1177/0013124502239392*

Jeynes, W. H. (2007). The relationship between parental involvement and urban secondary school student academic achievement: A meta-analysis. *Urban Education, 42*(1), 82–110. *doi.org/10.1177/0042085906293818*

Jeynes, W. (2010). The salience of the subtle aspects of parental involvement and encouraging that involvement: Implications for school-based programs. *Teachers College Record: The Voice of Scholarship in Education, 112*(3), 747–774. *doi.org/10.1177/016146811011200311*

Jeynes, W. (2012). A meta-analysis of the efficacy of different types of parental involvement programs for urban students. *Urban Education, 47*(4), 706–742. *doi.org/10.1177/0042085912445643*

Jimerson, S. R., Burns, M. K., & Van Der Heyden, A. M. (2016). From response to intervention to multi-tiered systems of support: Advances in the science and practice of assessment and intervention. *Handbook of Response to Intervention* (pp. 1–6). Springer.

Jodl, K. M., Michael, A., Malanchuk, O., Eccles, J. S., & Sameroff, A. (2001). Parents' roles in shaping early adolescents' occupational aspirations. *Child Development, 72*(4), 1247–1266. *doi.org/10.1111/1467-8624.00345*

Jones, C. (2022). The purpose of parents: School personnel perceptions of the role of parents in secondary schools. *School Community Journal, 32*(1), 85–104.

Joussemet, M., Mageau, G. A., Larose, M. P., Briand, M., & Vitaro, F. (2018). How to talk so kids will listen & listen so kids will talk: A randomized controlled trial evaluating the efficacy of the how-to parenting program on children's mental health compared to a wait-list control group. *BMC Pediatrics, 18*(1), 1–16. *doi.org/10.1186/s12887-018-1227-3*

Kalyanpur, M., & Harry, B. (1999). *Culture in special education: building reciprocal family-professional relationships.* Brookes.

Kaplan, L. S., & Owings, W. A. (2021). Countering the furor around Critical Race Theory. *NASSP Bulletin, 105*(3), 200–218. *doi.org/10.1177/01926365211045457*

Kendall, P. C. (1994). Treating anxiety disorders in children: Results of a randomized clinical trial. *Journal of Consulting and Clinical Psychology, 62*(1), 100–110. *doi.org/10.1037/0022-006x.62.1.100*

Kincaid, D., & Horner, R. (2017). Changing systems to scale up an evidence-based educational intervention. *Evidence-Based Communication Assessment and Intervention, 11*(3–4), 99–113. *doi.org/10.1080/17489539.2017.1376383*

Kincheloe, J. L., & Mclaren, P. (2011). Rethinking critical theory and qualitative research. In K. Hayes, S. R. Steinberg, & K. Tobin (Eds.), *Key works in critical pedagogy* (pp. 285–326). Springer.

King-Thorius, K. A., Rodriguez, E. M., & Bal, A. (2014). *Equity by design: Remediating the role of school-family partnerships in systemic change within culturally responsive positive behavior interventions and supports.* Culturally Responsive Positive Behavioral Interventions and Supports. *http://crpbis.org*

Kittelman, A., McIntosh, K., & Hoselton, R. (2019). Adoption of PBIS within school districts. *Journal of School Psychology, 76*, 159–167. *doi.org/10.1016/j.jsp.2019.03.007*

Ko, D. (2020). *Transformative agency toward tribal prolepsis: Culturally decolonizing positive behavioral interventions and supports.* [Doctoral dissertation]. University of Wisconsin–Madison.

Ko, D., Bal, A., Cakir, H. I., & Kim, H. (2021). Expanding transformative agency: Learning Lab as a social change intervention for racial equity in school discipline. *Teachers College Record: The Voice of Scholarship in Education, 123*(2). *www.tcrecord.org*

Kramarczuk Voulgarides, C., Aylward, A., & Noguera, P. A. (2014). The elusive quest for equity: An Analysis of how contextual factors contribute to the likelihood of school districts being legally cited for racial disproportionality in special education. *Journal of Law in Society, 15*, 241–273.

Krijnen, E., Van steensel, R., Meeuwisse, M., & Severiens, S. (2022). Aiming for educational partnership between parents and professionals: Shared vision development in a professional learning community. *School Community Journal, 32*(1), 265–300.

Kutcher, S., Wei, Y., & Morgan, C. (2015). Successful application of a Canadian mental health curriculum resource by usual classroom teachers in significantly and sustainably improving student mental health literacy. *Canadian Journal of Psychiatry, 60*(12), 580–586. *doi.org/10.1177 /070674371506001209*

Lac, V. T., & Cumings Mansfield, K. (2018). What do students have to do with educational leadership? Making a case for centering student voice. *Journal of Research on Leadership Education, 13*(1), 38–58. *doi.org/10.1177/1942775117743748*

Ladson-Billings, G., & Tate, W. F. (1995). Toward a critical race theory of education. *Teachers College Record: The Voice of Scholarship in Education, 97*(1), 47–68. *doi.org/10.1177/016146819509700104*

Ladson-Billings, G., & Tate, W. F. (2006). *Education research in the public interest.* Teachers College.

La Salle, T. P., Wang, C., Wu, C., & Rocha Neves, J. (2020). Racial mismatch among minoritized students and white teachers: Implications and recommendations for moving forward. *Journal of Educational and Psychological Consultation, 30*(3), 314–343. *doi.org/10.1080/10474412.201 9.1673759*

Lassen, S. R., Steele, M. M., & Sailor, W. (2006). The relationship of school-wide positive behavior support to academic achievement in an urban middle school. *Psychology in the Schools, 43*(6), 701–712. *doi.org/10.1002/pits.20177*

Learning Forward (2013). *Standards into practice: School-system roles. Innovation configuration maps for standards for professional learning.* Oxford University Press. *https://learningforward .org/wp-content/uploads/2017/09/standards-into-practice-central-office-ic-maps.pdf*

Lee, A., & Gage, N. A. (2020). Updating and expanding systematic reviews and meta-analyses on the effects of school-wide positive behavior interventions and supports. *Psychology in the Schools, 57*(5), 783–804. *doi.org/10.1002/pits.22336*

Lever, N. A., Adelsheim, S., Prodente, C., Christodulu, K. V., Ambrose, M. G., Schlitt, J., & Weist, M. D. (2003). System, agency and stakeholder collaboration to advance mental health programs in schools. In M. D. Weist, S. W. Evans, & N. A. Lever (Eds.), *Handbook of school mental health: Advancing practice and research* (pp. 149–162). Springer.

Leverson, M., Smith, K., McIntosh, K., Rose, J., & Pinkelman, S. (2021). *PBIS Cultural Responsiveness Field Guide: Resources for Trainers and Coaches.* Center for Positive Behavioral Interventions and Supports. *https://pbis.org*

Lewis, T. J., Barrett, S., Sugai, G., & Horner, R. H., Mitchell, B. S., & Starkey, D. (2016). *Training and professional development blueprint for positive behavioral interventions and supports.* Center for Positive Behavioral Interventions and Supports. *https://pbis.org*

Lewis, T. J., McIntosh, K., Simonsen, B., Mitchell, B. S., & Hatton, H. L. (2017). Schoolwide systems of positive behavior support: Implications for students at risk and with emotional/behavioral disorders. *AERA Open, 3*(2), 1–11. *doi.org/10.1177/2332858417711428*

Losen, D. J., & Martinez, P. (2020). *Lost opportunities: How disparate school discipline continues to drive differences in the opportunity to learn.* Learning Policy Institute; Center for Civil Rights Remedies at the Civil Rights Project.

Lyon, A. R., Coifman, J., Cook, H., McRee, E., Liu, F. F., Ludwig, K., et al. (2021). The cognitive walkthrough for implementation strategies (CWIS): A pragmatic method for assessing implementation strategy usability. *Implementation Science Communications, 2*(78). *doi.org/10.1186 /s43058-021-00183-0*

Manz, P. H., Fantuzzo, J. W., & Power, T. J. (2004). Multidimensional assessment of family involvement among urban elementary students. *Journal of School Psychology, 42*(6), 461–475. *doi.org /10.1016/j.jsp.2004.08.002*

Mapp, K., & Kuttner, P. (2013). *Dual capacity-building framework for family–school partnerships.* U.S. Department of Education.

Martin, K. S., Nantais, M., & Harms, A. (2015). *Reading Tiered Fidelity Inventory* (2nd ed.). Michigan Department of Education, Michigan's Integrated Behavior and Learning Support Initiative.

Massachusetts Department of Elementary and Secondary Education. (2020). Lynn Public School District profile. *https://profiles.doe.mass.edu/general/general.aspx?topNavID=1&leftNavId=1 00&orgcode=01630000&orgtypecode=5*

Masten, A. S., & Cicchetti, D. (2010). Developmental cascades. *Development and Psychopathology, 22*(3), 491–495. *doi.org/10.1017/S0954579410000222*

Mawene, D. (2021). *Examining racial disproportionality in special education and school discipline in a suburban community* [Doctoral dissertation]. University of Wisconsin–Madison.

Mawene, D., & Bal, A. (2020). Spatial othering: Examining residential areas, school attendance zones, and school discipline in an urbanizing school district. *Education Policy Analysis Archives, 28*(91). *doi.org/10.14507/epaa.28.4676*

McCutcheon, K. D., George, M. W., Mancil, E., Taylor, L. K., Paternite, C., & Weist, M. D. (2014). Partnering with youth in school mental health: Recommendations from students. In M. Weist, N. Lever, C. Bradshaw, & J. Owens (Eds.), *Handbook of school mental health: Research, training, practice and policy* (2nd ed., pp. 185–194). Springer.

McDaniel, H., Schiele, B., Taylor, L. K., Haak, J., & Weist, M. D. (2014). Strengthening the components and processes of family involvement in school mental health. In M. Weist, N. Lever, C. Bradshaw, & J. Owens (Eds.), *Handbook of school mental health: Research, training, practice, and policy* (2nd ed., pp. 195–208). Springer.

McDaniel, S. C., & Bruhn, A. L. (2016). Using a changing-criterion design to evaluate the effects of check-in/check-out with goal modification. *Journal of Positive Behavior Interventions, 18*(4), 197–208. *doi.org/10.1177/1098300715588263*

McEachern, A. D., Dishion, T. J., Weaver C. M., Shaw, D. S., Wilson, M. N., & Gardner, F. (2012). Parenting young children (PARYC): Validation of a self-report parenting measure. *Journal of Child and Family Studies, 21*(3), 498–511. *doi.org/10.1007/s10826-011-9503-y*

McIntosh, K., Girvan, E. J., Fairbanks Falcon, S., McDaniel, S. C., Smolkowski, K., Bastable, E., et al. (2021). Equity-focused PBIS approach reduces racial inequities in school discipline: A randomized controlled trial. *School Psychology, 36*(6), 433–444. *doi.org/10.1037/spq0000466*

McIntosh, K., Girvan, E. J., Horner, R. H., Smolkowski, K., & Sugai, G. (2018). *A 5-point intervention approach for enhancing equity in school discipline.* Center on Positive Behavioral Interventions and Supports. *https://pbis.org*

McIntosh, K., & Goodman, S. (2016). *Integrated multi-tiered systems of support: Blending RTI and PBIS.* Guilford Press.

McIntosh, K., Mercer, S. H., Hume, A. E., Frank, J. L., Turri, M. G., & Mathews, S. (2013). Factors related to sustained implementation of schoolwide positive behavior support. *Exceptional Children, 79*(3), 293–311.

McIntosh, K., Predy, L. K., Upreti, G., Hume, A. E., Turri, M. G., & Mathews, S. (2014). Perceptions of contextual features related to implementation and sustainability of school-wide positive behavior support. *Journal of Positive Behavior Interventions, 16*(1), 31–43. *doi.org/10.1177/1098300712470723*

McIntosh, K., Ty, S. V., Horner, R. H., & Sugai, G. (2013). School-wide positive behavior interventions and supports and academic achievement. In J. Hattie & E. M. Anderman (Eds.), *International guide to student achievement* (pp. 146–148). Taylor and Francis.

McKinley, B., & Brayboy, J. (2005). Toward a tribal critical race theory in education. *The Urban Review, 37*(5), 425–446. *doi.org/10.1007/s11256-005-0018-y*

McLeskey, J., Barringer, M-D., Billingsley, B., Brownell, M., Jackson, D., Kennedy, M., et al. (2017). *High-leverage practices in special education.* Council for Exceptional Children & CEEDAR Center. *https://ceedar.education.ufl.edu/wpcontent/uploads/2017/07/CEC-HLP-Web.pdf*

McMahon, R. J., & Forehand, R. L. (2005). *Helping the noncompliant child: Family-based treatment for oppositional behavior.* Guilford Press.

Means, D. R., Blackmon, S., Drake, E., Lawrence, P., Jackson, A., Strickland, A., & Willis, J. (2020). We have something to say: Youth participatory action research as a promising practice to address problems of practice in rural schools. *The Rural Educator, 41*(3), 43–54.

Metzler, C. W., Biglan, A., Ary, D. V., & Li, F. (1998). The stability and validity of early adolescents' reports of parenting constructs. *Journal of Family Psychology, 12*(4), 600–619. *doi.org/10.1037/0893-3200.12.4.600*

Miller, A. L. (2019). (Re)conceptualizing family–school partnerships with and for culturally and linguistically diverse families. *Race Ethnicity and Education, 22*(6), 746–766. *doi.org/10.1080/13613324.2019.1599339*

Minch, D. R. (2012). *A preliminary investigation of family engagement practices in schools implementing problem-solving/response to intervention (PS/RtI)* [Doctoral dissertation, University of South Florida Tampa]. Digital Commons @ University of South Flordia. *https://scholarcommons.usf.edu/etd/4373*

Minch, D. R. (2016). Tools to Measure Family Engagement. In J. M. Castillo *Problem Solving/Response to Intervention evaluation tool technical assistance manual-revised 2016* (Chapter 5). University of South Florida.

Minch, D. R., Garbacz, S. A., Kern, L., & Baton, E. (2023). Assessing and Evaluating Family School Collaboration in Schools. In S. W. Evans, J. S. Owens, C. P. Bradshaw, & M. D. Weist (Eds.), *Handbook of school mental health: Innovations in science and practice* (3rd ed., pp. 169–185). Springer.

Minch, D. R., Garbacz, S. A., & Weist, M. (2019, October). *Implementing and assessing family–school collaboration.* Presentation at the Positive Behavioral Interventions and Supports National Leadership Forum, Chicago, IL.

Minch, D. R., Garbacz, S. A., & Weist, M. (2020). *Advancing family–school collaboration in positive behavior interventions and supports through the Family–School–Community Alliance.* OSEP Technical Assistance Center on Positive Behavioral Interventions and Supports. *https://pbis.org*

Minch, D. R., Vatland, C., Winneker, A., Gaunt, B., & Williams, H. (2017). *School-level family and community engagement in MTSS innovation configuration.* Florida's Positive Behavior Support Project. *www.flpbis.org*

Minch, D. R., Webster, R., & Jackson, C. (2018, September). *PBIS forum 2018–Using Family & Student Voice to Inform Equitable PBIS Implementation* [Video]. YouTube. *https://www.youtube.com/watch?v=Fu231Y9x6yE*

Miller, D. N., George, M. P., & Fogt, J. B. (2005). Establishing and sustaining research-based practice at Centennial School: A descriptive case study of systemic change. *Psychology in the Schools, 42*(5), 553–567. *doi.org/10.1002/pits.20091*

Milner, H. R. (2013). Analyzing poverty, learning, and teaching through a critical race theory lens. *Review of Research in Education, 37*(1), 1–53. *doi.org/10.3102/0091732X12459720*

Minke, K. M., Sheridan, S. M., Kim, E. M., Ryoo, J. H., & Koziol, N. A. (2014). Congruence in parent–teacher relationships: The role of shared perceptions. *The Elementary School Journal, 114*(4), 527–546. *doi.org/10.1086/675637*

Missouri PBIS Center (2017). *Progress Monitoring for Tier 2. https://pbismissouri.org/wp-content/uploads/2017/05/2H_STI2016.pdf*

Moore, K. J., Garbacz, S. A., Gau, J. M., Dishion, T. J., Brown, K. L., Stormshak, E. A., & Seeley, J. R. (2016). Proactive parent engagement in public schools: Using a brief strength and needs assessment in a multiple-gating risk management strategy. *Journal of Positive Behavior Interventions, 18*(4), 230–240. *doi.org/10.1177/1098300716632590*

Murray, M., & Curran, E. (2008). Learning together with parents of children with disabilities: Bringing parent–professional partnership education to a new level. *Teacher Education and Special Education, 31*(1), 59–63. *doi.org/10.1177/088840640803100106*

Murray, B., & McCrone, S. (2014). An integrative review of promoting trust in the patient-primary care provider relationship. *Journal of Advance Nursing, 71*(1), 3–23. *doi.org/10.1111/jan.12502*

Murray, M., Munger, M. H., Colwell, W. B., & Claussen, A. J. (2018). Building capacity in special education: A statewide initiative to improve student outcomes through Parent–Teacher partnerships. *School Community Journal, 28*(1), 91–105.

National Association of School Psychologists. (NASP, 2013). *Promoting Just Special Education Identification and School Discipline Practices* [Position statement]. *www.nasponline.org/x26829.xml*

National Association of School Psychologists. (NASP, 2020). *NASP 2020 Professional Standards Adopted. www.nasponline.org/standards-and-certification/nasp-2020-professional-standards-adopted*

National Center for Education Statistics. (NCES, 2020). *Lynn Public Schools. Education Demographic and Geographic Estimates. https://nces.ed.gov/Programs/Edge/ACSDashboard/2507110*

National Center for Education Statistics. (NCES, 2021). *Racial/Ethnic Enrollment in Public Schools. https://nces.ed.gov/programs/coe/indicator/cge*

National Women's Law Center. (NWLC, 2018a, April 24). *Dress coded: Black girls, bodies and bias in D.C. schools. https://nwlc.org/resource/dresscoded*

National Women's Law Center. (NWLC, 2018b, May 17). *Five reasons why American schools are still separate and unequal 64 years after Brown v. Board. https://nwlc.org/five-reasons-why-american-schools-are-still-separate-and-unequal-64-years-after-brown-v-board*

National Women's Law Center. (NWLC, 2018c). *Let her learn: A toolkit to stop push out for girls of color. https://nwlc.org/wp-content/uploads/2016/11/final_nwlc_NOVO2016Toolkit.pdf*

National Women's Law Center. (NWLC, 2019, September 14). *Dress coded II: Protest, progress and power in D.C. schools. https://nwlc.org/resource/dresscoded-ii*

No Child Left Behind Act of 2001, Public Law 107-110, 20 U.S.C. § 6319 (2002).

North Carolina Partnership for Children Inc. (NCPC, 2021a). *Family Engagement and Leadership Overview. www.smartstart.org/wp-content/uploads/2021/11/Family-Engagement-and-Leadership.pdf*

North Carolina Partnership for Children Inc. (NCPC, 2021b). *Supporting and Empowering Family Leaders. www.smartstart.org/wp-content/uploads/2021/11/Supporting-Empowering-Family-Leaders.pdf*

North Carolina Partnership for Children Inc. (NCPC, 2021c). *Checklist for Pre-Planning for Effective Family Leadership & Engagement. www.smartstart.org/wp-content/uploads/2021/11/Checklist-Preplanning-for-Effective-Family-Leaders.pdf*

Oakland Unified School District. (2020). *Student and family engagement theory of action. https://learningpolicyinstitute.org/media/3936/download?inline&file=csf_theory_of_action_community_school_transformation.pdf*

Overstreet, S., Devine, J., Bevans, K., & Efreom, Y. (2005). Predicting parental involvement in children's schooling within an economically disadvantaged African American sample. *Psychology in the Schools, 42*(1), 101–111. *doi:10.1002/pits.20028*

Park, E. Y., & Blair, K. S. C. (2020). Check-in/Check-out implementation in schools: A meta-analysis of group design studies. *Education and Treatment of Children, 43,* 361–375.

Park, S., & Holloway, S. (2018). Parental involvement in adolescents' education: An examination of the interplay among school factors, parental role construction, and family income. *School Community Journal, 28*(1), 9–36.

Patrikakou, E. N., & Weissberg, R. P. (2000). Parents' perceptions of teacher outreach and parent involvement in children's education. *Journal of Prevention and Intervention in the Community, 20*(1–2), 103–119. *doi.org/10.1300/J005v20n01_08*

Pearce, L. R. (2009). Helping children with emotional difficulties: A response to intervention investigation. *The Rural Educator, 30*(2), 34–46.

Penn School (pseudonym). (2021). *Penn School Policy and Procedure Handbook.* Author.

Perales, K., Eber, L., Barrett, S., Quell, A., Ulker, A., & Weist, M. D. (2017). Promoting family engagement in schools through interconnected PBIS and school mental health. In M. Weist, A. Garbacz, K. Lane, & D. Kincaid (Eds.), *Aligning and integrating family engagement in Positive Behavioral Interventions and Supports (PBIS): Concepts and strategies for families and schools in key contexts* (pp. 71–83). Center for Positive Behavioral Interventions and Supports.

Pham, A. V., N. Goforth, A., N. Aguilar, L., Burt, I., Bastian, R., & Diaków, D. M. (2021). Dismantling systemic inequities in school psychology: cultural humility as a foundational approach to social justice. *School Psychology Review, 51*, 692–709. *doi.org/10.1080/2372966X.2021.1941245*

Phelan, P., Davidson, A. L., & Cao, H. T. (1991). Students' multiple worlds: Negotiating the boundaries of family, peer, and school cultures. *Anthropology & Education Quarterly, 22*(3), 224–250. *https://doi.org/10.1525/aeq.1991.22.3.05x1051k*

Pinkelman, S. E., McIntosh, K., Rasplica, C. K., Berg, T., & Strickland-Cohen, M. K. (2015). Perceived enablers and barriers related to sustainability of school-wide positive behavioral interventions and supports. *Behavioral Disorders, 40*(3), 171–183. *doi.org/10.17988/0198-7429-40.3.171*

Pitre, A. (2021, June 23). *A conversation about Critical Race Theory in education with Dr. Abul Pitre* [Video]. YouTube. *https://youtu.be/YdcFLCt7a6s*

Pogrow, S. (2017). The failure of the U.S. education research establishment to identify effective practices: Beware effective practices policies. *Education Policy Analysis Archives, 25*(5), 1–22. *doi.org/10.14507/epaa.25.2517*

Powell, T., & Coles, J. A. (2021). 'We still here': Black mothers' personal narratives of sense making and resisting antiblackness and the suspensions of their Black children. *Race Ethnicity and Education, 24*(1), 76–95. *doi.org/10.1080/13613324.2020.1718076*

Proctor, S. L. (2016). Introduction to the special issue: Encouraging racial and social justice throughout the pre-K to graduate school pipeline. *School Psychology Forum: Research in Practice, 10*, 233–236.

Proctor, S. L., Williams, B., Scherr, T., & Li, K. (2017). Intersectionality and school psychology: Implications for practice. *National Association of School Psychology, 46*(4), 1–21.

Pushor, D., & Amendt, T. (2018). Leading an examination of beliefs and assumptions about parents. *School Leadership & Management, 38*(2), 202–221. *doi.org/10.1080/13632434.2018.1439466*

Putnam, R., McCart, A., Griggs, P., & Choi, J. H. (2009) Implementation of schoolwide positive behavior support in urban settings. In W. Sailor, G. Dunlap, G. Sugai, & R. Horner (Eds.), *Handbook of positive behavior support* (pp. 443–643). Springer.

Race Matters Institute. (n.d.). Equity Impact Assessment. *www.mdcinc.org/projects/race-matters-institute*

Raffaele, L. M., & Knoff, H. M. (1999). Improving homeschool collaboration with disadvantaged families: Organizational principles, perspectives, and approaches. *School Psychology Review, 28*(3), 448–466. *doi.org/10.1080/02796015.1999.12085977*

Raffaele, L. M., Ogg, J., Loker, T., & Fefer, S. (2013). Including parents in the continuum of school-based mental health services: A systematic review of intervention program research from 1994–2010. *Journal of Applied School Psychology, 29*(1), 1–36. *doi.org/10.1080/15377903.2012.725580*

Rao, S., & Kalyanpur, M. (2002). Promoting home–school collaboration in positive behavior support. In J. M. Lucyshyn, G. Dunlap, & R. W. Albin (Ed.), *Families and positive behavior support* (pp. 219–239). Brookes.

Ray, S., & Gibbons, A. (2021, November). *Why are states banning critical race theory?* Fixgov Blog. Brookings. *www.brookings.edu/blog/fixgov/2021/07/02/why-are-states-banning-critical-race -theory.*

Reilly, K. (2022, April 22). *Florida's Governor just signed the 'stop woke act': Here's what it means for schools and businesses.* Time Blog. *https://time.com/6168753/florida-stop-woke-law*

Reschly, A. L., & Christenson, S. L. (2012). Moving from "context matters" to engaged partnerships with families. *Journal of Educational and Psychological Consultation, 22*(1–2), 62–78. *doi.org /10.1080/10474412.2011.649650*

Reynolds, S., Wilson, C., Austin, J., & Hooper, L. (2012). Effects of psychotherapy for anxiety in children and adolescents: A meta-analytic review. *Clinical Psychology Review, 32*(4), 251–262. *doi.org/10.1016/j.cpr.2012.01.005*

Rispoli, K. M., Mathes, N. E., & Malcolm, A. L. (2019). Characterizing the parent role in school-based interventions for autism: A systematic literature review. *School Psychology, 34*(4), 444–457. *doi .org/10.1037/spq0000283*

Ritblatt, S. N., Beatty, J. R., Cronan, T. A., & Ochoa, A. M. (2002). Relationships among perceptions of parent involvement, time allocation, and demographic characteristics: Implication for policy reformation. *Journal of Community Psychology, 30*(5), 519–549. *https://doi.org/10.1002/jcop.10018*

Rodriguez, L., & Welsh, R. O. (2022). The dimensions of school discipline: Toward a comprehensive framework for measuring discipline patterns and outcomes in schools. *AERA Open, 8*(1), 1–23. *doi.org/10.1177/23328584221083669*

Roth, R. A., Suldo, S. M., Ferron, J. M., & Dowdy, E. (2017). Improving middle school students' subjective well-being: Efficacy of a multicomponent positive psychology intervention targeting small groups of youth. *School Psychology Review, 46*(1), 21–41. *doi.org/10.1080/02796015 .2017.12087610*

Sabnis, S. V., & Proctor, S. L. (2021). Use of critical theory to develop a conceptual framework for critical school psychology. *School Psychology Review, 51*, 661–675. *doi.org/10.1080/2372966X .2021.1949248*

Sanders, M. G. (2012). Achieving scale at the district level: A longitudinal multiple case study of partnership reform. *Educational Administration Quarterly, 48*(1), 154–186. *doi.org/10.1177 /0013161X11417432*

Sandomierski, T., Martinez, S., Webster, R., Winneker, A., & Minch, D. (2021). From "quick fix" to lasting commitment: Using root cause analysis to address disproportionate discipline outcomes. *Preventing School Failure: Alternative Education for Children and Youth, 66*(1), 1–13. *https:// doi.org/10.1080/1045988X.2021.1937025*

Sanetti, L. H. M., Collier-Meek, M. A., Long, A. C. J., Byron, J., & Kratochwill, T. R. (2014). Increasing teacher treatment integrity of behavior support plans through consultant and implementation planning. *Journal of School Psychology, 53*(3), 209–229. *doi: 10.1016/j.jsp.2015.03.002*

Santiago, R. T., Garbacz, S. A., Beattie, T., & Moore, C. L. (2016). Parent–teacher relationships in elementary school: An examination of parent–teacher trust. *Psychology in the Schools, 53*(10), 1003–1017. *https://doi.org/10.1002/pits.21971*

Schanding, G. T., Strait, G. G., Morgan, V. R., Short, R. J., Enderwitz, M., Babu, J., & Templeton, M. A. (2021). Who's included? diversity, equity, and inclusion of students in school psychology literature over the last decade. *School Psychology Review, 52*, 408–420. *doi.org/10.1080/2372966X .2021.1927831*

Schwartz, S. (2021, June 11). *Map: Where Critical Race Theory is under attack.* Education Week. *www.edweek.org/leadership/map-where-critical-race-theory-is-under-attack/2021/06*

Scott T. M., Anderson C., Mancil, R., & Alter P. (2009). Function-based supports for individual students in school settings. In W. Sailor, G. Dunlap, G. Sugai, R. Horner (Eds.), *Handbook of positive behavior support* (pp. 421–441). Springer.

Seitsinger, A. M., Felner, R. D., Brand, S., & Burns, A. (2008). A large-scale examination of the nature and efficacy of teachers' practices to engage parents: Assessment, parental contact, and student-level impact. *Journal of School Psychology, 46*(4), 477–505. *doi: 10.1016/j.jsp.2007.11.001*

Semega, J., Kollar, M., Shrider, E. A., & Creamer, J. (2019). *Income and poverty in the United States: 2019* (Report No. P60-270) U.S. Census Bureau. *www.census.gov/library/publications/2020 /demo/p60-270.html*

Sénéchal, M., & Young, L. (2008). The effect of family literacy interventions on children's acquisition of reading from kindergarten to grade 3: A meta-analytic review. *Review of Educational Research, 78*(4), 880–907.

Serpell, Z. N., & Mashburn, A. J. (2011). Family–school connectedness and children's early social development. *Social Development, 21*(1), 21–46. *doi.org/10.1111/j.1467-9507.2011.00623.x*

Sheldon, S. B. (2002). Parents' social networks and beliefs as predictors of parent involvement. *The Elementary School Journal, 102*(4), 301–316. *doi.org/10.1086/499705*

Sheridan, S. M. (2014a). *Teachers and parents as partners.* Ancora.

Sheridan, S. M. (2014b). *The tough kid: Teachers and parents as partners.* Pacific Northwest Publishers.

Sheridan, S. M., & Eastberg, S. (2020). Targeting student concerns through family–school programs: Individualized Tier 3 supports engaging parents as partners. In A. Garbacz (Eds.), *Establishing family–school partnerships in school psychology: Critical skills* (pp. 111–134). Routledge.

Sheridan, S. M., Kim, E. M., Coutts, M. J., Sjuts, T. M., Holmes, S. R., Ransom, K. A., & Garbacz, S. A. (2012). *Clarifying parent involvement and family–school partnership intervention research: A preliminary synthesis. CYFS Working Paper No. 2012–4.* Nebraska Center for Research on Children, Youth, Families and Schools. *https://files.eric.ed.gov/fulltext/ED537845.pdf*

Sheridan, S. M., & Kratochwill, T. R. (2008). *Conjoint behavioral consultation: Promoting family–school connections and interventions.* Springer.

Sheridan, S. M., Smith, T. E., Moorman Kim, E., Beretvas, S. N., & Park, S. (2019). A meta-analysis of family–school interventions and children's social–emotional functioning: Moderators and components of efficacy. *Review of Educational Research, 89*(2), 296–332. *doi.org/10.3102 /0034654318825437*

Sheridan, S. M., Witte, A. L., Holmes, S. R., Coutts, M. J., Dent, A. L., Kunz, G. M., & Wu, C. (2017). A randomized trial examining the effects of Conjoint Behavioral Consultation in rural schools: Student outcomes and the mediating role of the teacher–parent relationship. *Journal of School Psychology, 61*, 33–53. *doi.org/10.1016/j.jsp.2016.12.002*

Shogren, K. A., Wehmeyer, M. L., Lane, K. L., & Quirk, C. (2017). Multitiered systems of supports. In M. L. Wehmeyer & K. A. Shogren (Eds.), *Handbook of research-based practices for educating students with intellectual disability* (pp. 185–198). Routledge.

Simonsen, B., Eber, L., Black, A. C., Sugai, G., Lewandowski, H., Sims, B., & Myers, D. (2012). Illinois statewide positive behavioral interventions and supports: Evolutions and impact on student outcomes across years. *Journal of Positive Behavior Interventions, 14*(1), 5–16. *https:// doi.org/10.1177/1098300711412601*

Smith, T. E., Holmes, S. R., Sheridan, S. M., Cooper, J. M., Bloomfield, B., & Preast, J. (2020). The effects of consultation-based family–school engagement on student and parent outcomes: A meta-analysis. *Journal of Educational and Psychological Consultation, 31*(3), 278–306. *doi.org /10.1080/10474412.2020.1749062*

Smith, T. E., Reinke, W. M., Herman, K. C., & Huang, F. (2019). Understanding family–school engagement across and within elementary-and middle-school contexts. *School Psychology, 34*(4), 363–375. *doi.org/10.1037/spq0000290*

Smith, T. E., & Sheridan, S. (2019). The effects of teacher training on teachers' family-engagement practices, attitudes, and knowledge: A meta-analysis. *Journal of Educational and Psychological Consultation, 29*(2), 128–157. *doi.org/10.1080/10474412.2018.1460725*

Smith, T. E., Sheridan, S. M., Kim, E. M., Park, S., & Beretvas, S. N. (2020). The effects of family–school partnership interventions on academic and social–emotional functioning: A meta-analysis exploring what works for whom. *Educational Psychology Review, 32*(2), 511–544. *doi.org/10.1007/s10648-019-09509-w*

Smith, J. L. M., Nelson, N. J., Fien, H., Smolkowski, K., Kosty, D., & Baker, S. K. (2016). Examining the efficacy of a multitiered intervention for at-risk readers in grade 1. *The Elementary School Journal, 116*(4), 549–573.

Smolkowski, K., Seeley, J. R., Gau, J. M., Dishion, T. J., Stormshak, E. A., Moore, K. J., & Falkenstein, C. A., et al. (2017). Effectiveness evaluation of the Positive Family Support intervention: A three-tiered public health delivery model for middle schools. *Journal of School Psychology, 62*, 103–125. *doi.org/10.1016/j.jsp.2017.03.004*

Snow, C. E. (2016). The role of relevance in education research, as viewed by former presidents. *Educational Researcher, 45*(2), 64–68. *doi.org/10.3102/0013189X16638325*

Spencer, M. B., Dupree, D., & Hartmann, T. (1997). A phenomenological variant of ecological systems theory (PVST): A self-organization perspective in context. *Developmental and Psychopathology, 9*(4), 817–833. *doi.org/10.1017/s0954579497001454*

Splett, J. W., Perales, K., Al-Khatib, A., Raborn, A., & Weist, M. D. (2020). Preliminary development and validation of the Interconnected Systems Framework Implementation Inventory (ISF-II), *School Psychology, 35*(4), 255–266. *doi.org/10.1037/spq0000369*

Splett, J. W., Perales, K., Halliday-Boykins, C. A., Gilchrest, C., Gibson, N., & Weist, M. D. (2017). Best practices for teaming and collaboration in the Interconnected Systems Framework. *Journal of Applied School Psychology, 33*(4), 347–368. *doi.org/10.1080/15377903.2017.1328625*

Starr, W. (2021). Counterfactuals. In E. N. Zalta (Ed.), *The Stanford Encyclopedia of Philosophy. https://plato.stanford.edu/archives/sum2021/entries/counterfactuals*

Stattin, H., & Kerr, M. (2000). Parental monitoring: A reinterpretation. *Child Development, 71*(4), 1072–1085. *doi.org/10.1111/1467-8624.00210*

Stockslager, K., Castillo, J., Brundage, A., Childs, K., & Romer, N. (2016). *Self-Assessment of MTSS (SAM).* Florida's Problem Solving/Response to Intervention Project and Florida's Positive Behavior Intervention and Support Project.

Stormshak, E. A., Connell, A., & Dishion, T. J. (2009). An adaptive approach to family-centered intervention in schools: Linking intervention engagement to academic outcomes in middle and high school. *Prevention Science, 10*(3), 221–235. *doi.org/10.1007/s11121-009-0131-3*

Stormshak, E. A., Connell, A. M., Véronneau, M. H., Myers, M. W., Dishion, T. J., Kavanagh, K., & Caruthers, A. S. (2011). An ecological approach to promoting early adolescent mental health and social adaptation: Family-centered intervention in public middle schools. *Child Development, 82*(1), 209–225. *doi.org/10.1111/j.1467-8624.2010.01551.x*

Stormshak, E. A., DeGarmo, D., Garbacz, S. A., McIntyre, L. L., & Caruthers, A. (2020). Using motivational interviewing to improve parenting skills and prevent problem behavior during the transition to kindergarten. *Prevention Science, 22*(6), 747–757. *doi.org/10.1007/s11121-020-01102-w*

Stormshak, E. A., & Dishion, T. J., (2009). A school-based, family-centered intervention to prevent substance use: The family check-up. *The American Journal of Drug and Alcohol Abuse, 35*(4), 227–232. *doi.org/10.1080/00952990903005908*

Stormshak, E. A., & Garbacz, S. A. (2018). Family-based treatment of aggression. In T. Malti & K. H. Rubin (Eds.), *Handbook of child and adolescent aggression: Emergence, development, and intervention* (pp. 340–359). Guilford Press.

Strickland-Cohen, M. K., & Kyzar, K. B. (2019). Events that help and hinder family–teacher communication within SWPBIS: A qualitative analysis. *Journal of Positive Behavior Interventions, 21*(3), 148–158. *doi.org/10.1177/1098300718813622*

Sugai, G., & Horner, R. H. (2002a). Introduction to the special series on positive behavior supports in schools. *Journal of Emotional and Behavioral Disorders, 10*(3), 130–135. *doi.org/10.1177/10 634266020100030101*

Sugai, G., & Horner, R. H. (2002b). The evolution of discipline practices: School-wide positive behavior supports. *Child & Family Behavior Therapy, 24*(1–2), 23–50. *doi.org/10.1300/J019v24n01_03*

Sugai, G., & Horner, R. H. (2006). A promising approach for expanding and sustaining school-wide positive behavior support. *School Psychology Review, 35*(2), 245–259. *doi.org/10.1080/02796015 .2006.12087989*

Sugai, G., & Horner, R. H. (2020). Sustaining and scaling positive behavioral interventions and supports: Implementation drivers, outcomes, and considerations. *Exceptional Children, 86*(2), 120–136. *doi.org/10.1177/0014402919855331*

Sugai, G., Horner, R. H., Dunlap, G., Hieneman, M., Lewis, T. J., Nelson, C. M., et al. (1999). Applying positive behavioral support and functional behavioral assessment in schools. OSEP Technical Assistance Center on Positive Behavioral Interventions and Supports. *Journal of Positive Behavior Interventions, 2*(3). *doi:10.1177/109830070000200302*

Sugai, G., O'Keeffe, B. V., & Fallon, L. M. (2012). A contextual consideration of culture and school-wide positive behavior support. *Journal of Positive Behavior Interventions, 14*(4), 197–208. *doi .org/10.1177/1098300711426334*

Suldo, S. (2016). *Promoting student happiness: Positive psychology interventions in schools.* Guilford Press.

Sullivan, A. L., Weeks, M., Kulkarni, T., Nguyen, T., Kendrick-Dunn, T. B., & Barrett, C. (2020). Historical foundations of health disparities: A primer for school psychologists to advance social justice. *Communiqué, 49*(2), 30–32.

Sutherland, D., McHenry-Sorber, E., & Willingham, J. N. (2022). Just southern: Navigating the social construction of a rural community in the press for educational equity. *The Rural Educator, 43*(1), 37–53. *doi.org/10.35608/ruraled.v43i1.1212*

Teaching for Change. (n.d.). *Parent Organizing. www.teachingforchange.org/educator-resources /parent-organizing*

Tennessee Department of Education. (2020). *Tennessee State Report Card. https://reportcard.tnedu .gov*

Thompson, A. M., Herman, K. C., Reinke, W. M., Hawley, K., Peters, C., Ehret, A., Hobbs, A, & Elmore, R. (2021). Impact of the family access center of excellence (FACE) on behavioral and educational outcomes-A quasi-experimental study. *School Psychology Review, 50*(1), 30–35. *doi.org/10.1080/2372966X.2020.1841545*

Todd, A. W., Horner, R. H. J., Newton, J. S., Algozzine, R. F., Algozzine, K. M., & Frank, J. L. (2011). Effects of team-initiated problem solving on decision making by schoolwide behavior support teams. *Journal of Applied School Psychology, 27*(1), 42–59.

Tuck, E. (2009). Suspending damage: A letter to communities. *Harvard Educational Review, 79*(3), 409–427. *doi.org/10.17763/haer.79.3.n0016675661t3n15*

Turtura, J. E., Anderson, C. M., & Boyd, R. J. (2014). Addressing task avoidance in middle school students: Academic behavior check-in/check-out. *Journal of Positive Behavior Interventions, 16*(3), 159–167. *doi.org/10.1177/1098300713484063*

U.S. Census Bureau. (2020). Lynn City, Massachusetts. *www.census.gov/quickfacts/lynncitymassa chusetts*

U.S. Census Bureau. (n.d.). QuickFacts Lehigh County, Pennsylvania. *www.census.gov/quickfacts /lehighcountypennsylvania*

U.S. Department of Health and Human Services, Administration for Children and Families, Office of Head Start, National Center on Parent, Family, and Community Engagement. (2018). *Relationship-based competencies to support family engagement: Professional development assessment for teachers and childcare providers. https://eclkc.ohs.acf.hhs.gov/sites/default/files/pdf/no-search/rbc-sfe-pro-dev-assess-teachers.pdf*

Vickers, H. S., & Minke, K. M. (1995). Exploring parent–teacher relationships: Joining and communication to others. *School Psychology Quarterly, 10*(2), 133–150. *doi.org/10.1037/h0088300*

Vincent, C. G., & Tobin, T. J. (2011). The relationship between implementation of school-wide positive behavior support (SWPBS) and disciplinary exclusion of students from various ethnic backgrounds with and without disabilities. *Journal of Emotional & Behavioral Disorders, 19*(4), 217–232. *doi.org/10.1177/1063426610377329*

Von Ravensberg, H., & Blakely, A. (2017). *Guidance for States on ESSA State Plans: Aligning the School Climate Indicator and SW-PBIS.* OSEP Technical Assistance Center on Positive Behavioral Interventions and Supports. *https://cdn.prod.website-files.com/5d3725188825e071f1670246/5d8a8733506a9e5e3864a113_Guidance%20for%20States%20on%20ESSA%20State%20Plans.pdf*

Vygotsky, L. S. (1978). *Mind in society: The development of higher psychological processes.* Harvard University Press.

Walker, H. M., Feil, E. G., Frey, A., Small, J., Seeley, J., Golly, A., et al. (2018). First Step Next: An updated version of the first step to success early intervention program. *Perspective on Early Childhood Psychology and Education, 3*(1), 89–109.

Walker, H. M., Horner, R. H., Sugai, G., Bullis, M., Sprague, J. R., Bricker, D., & Kaufman, M. J. (1996). Integrated approaches to preventing antisocial behavior patterns among school-age children and youth. *Journal of Emotional and Behavioral Disorders, 4*(4), 194–209.

Ward, C. S., Harms, A. L., St. Martin, K., Cusumano, D., Russell, C., & Horner, R. H. (2021). Development and technical adequacy of the District Capacity Assessment. *Journal of Positive Behavior Interventions, 24*(2), *doi.org/10.1177/1098300721990911*

Ward, C. S., St. Martin, K., Horner, R., Duda, M., Ingram-West, K., Tedesco, M., et al. (2015). *District Capacity Assessment.* National Implementation Research Network. *https://nirn.fpg.unc.edu/sites/nirn.fpg.unc.edu/files/imce/documents/DCA%207.7%2010-18-19.pdf*

Warren, J. S., Edmonson, H. M., Griggs, P., Lassen, S. R., McCart, A., Turnbull, A., & Sailor, W. (2003). Urban applications of school-wide positive behavior support: Critical issues and lessons learned. *Journal of Positive Behavior Interventions, 5*(2), 80. *doi:10.1177/10983007030050020301*

Weingarten, Z., Zumeta Edmonds, R., & Arden, S. (2020). Better together: Using MTSS as a structure for building school–family partnerships. *TEACHING Exceptional Children, 53*(2), 122–130. *doi.org/10.1177/0040059920937733*

Weiss, H. B., Lopez, M. E., & Rosenberg, H. (2010). *Beyond random acts: Family, school, and community engagement as an integral part of education reform.* National Policy Forum for Family, School, & Community Engagement. Harvard Family Research Project.

Weist, M. D., Collins, D., Martinez, S., & Greenlaw, J. (2020). Furthering the advancement of school behavioral health in your community. In Weist, M. D., Franke, K., & Stevens, R. (Eds.), *School behavioral health: Interconnecting comprehensive school mental health and positive behavior support* (pp. 123–128). Springer.

Weist, M. D., Eber, L., Horner, R., Splett, J., Putnam, R., Barrett, S., et al. (2018). Improving multitiered systems of support for students with "internalizing" emotional/behavioral problems. *Journal of Positive Behavior Interventions, 20*(3), 172–184. *doi.org/10.1177/1098300717753832*

Weist, M. D., Garbacz, S. A., Lane, K. L., & Kincaid, D. (2017). *Aligning and integrating family engagement in positive behavioral interventions and supports (PBIS): Concepts and strategies for families and schools in key contexts.* Center for Positive Behavioral Interventions and Supports. *https://pbis.org*

Weist, M. D., Hoover, S., Lever, N., Youngstrom, E. A., George, M., McDaniel, H. L., & Hoagwood, K. (2019). Testing a package of evidence-based practices in school mental health. *School Mental Health: A Multidisciplinary Research and Practice Journal, 11*(4), 692–706. *doi.org/10.1007 /s12310-019-09322-4*

Weist, M. D., Mellin, E. A., Chambers, K, Lever, N. A., Haber, D., & Blaber, C. (2012). Challenges to collaboration in school mental health and strategies for overcoming them. *Journal of School Health, 82*(2) 97–105. *doi:org/10.1111/j.1746-1561.2011.00672.x*

Weist, M. D., Mellin, E., Garbacz, S. A., & Anderson-Butcher, D. (2019). Reducing the use of language that stigmatizes students. National Association of School Psychologists, *National Association of School Psychologists Communique, 47*(8), 1, 22–23.

Weist, M. D., & Paternite, C. E. (2006). Building an interconnected policy-training-practice-research agenda to advance school mental health. *Education and Treatment of Children, 29,* 173–196.

Weist, M. D., Shapiro, C., Hartley, S., Bode, A., Miller, E., Huebner, S., et al. (2019). Assuring strength- and evidence-based approaches in child, adolescent, and school mental health. In D. Osher, R. Jagers, K. Kendziora, M. Mayer, & L. Wood (Eds.), *Keeping students safe and helping them thrive: A collaborative handbook for education, safety and justice professionals, families, and communities* (Vol. 2, pp. 54–79). Praeger.

Wenger, E., McDermott, R. A., & Snyder, W. (2002). *Cultivating communities of practice: A guide to managing knowledge.* Harvard Business Press.

Whitcomb, S. A., Fefer, S., Hefter, S., & Santiago-Rosario, M. (2021). Leveraging school–university partnerships to train school psychologists in organizational consultation for PBIS. *Journal of Educational and Psychological Consultation, 31*(1), 110–127. *doi.org/10.1080/10474412.2019. 1705163*

Williamson, T., Ashby, D. I., & Webber, R. (2005). Young offenders, schools and the neighbourhood: A new approach to data-analysis for community policing. *Journal of Community & Applied Social Psychology, 15*(3), 203–228. *https://doi.org/10.1002/casp.817*

Wisconsin RtI Center. (2019). *Family interview for culturally responsive practices.* Author.

Wolfe, K., Pyle, D., Charlton, C. T., Sabey, C. V., Lund, E. M., & Ross, S. W. (2016). A systematic review of the empirical support for check-in check-out. *Journal of Positive Behavior Interventions, 18*(2), 74–88. *doi.org/10.1177/1098300715595957*

Yeager, D. S., Purdie-Vaughns, V., Garcia, J., Apfel, N., Brzustoski, P., Master, A., et al. (2014). Breaking the cycle of mistrust: Wise interventions to provide critical feedback across the racial divide. *Journal of Experimental Psychology: General, 143*(2), 804–824. *doi: 10.1037/a0033906*

Yong, M., & Cheney, D. A. (2013). Essential features of tier 2 social–behavioral interventions. *Psychology in the Schools, 50*(8), 844–861. *https://doi.org/10.1002/pits.21710*

Yull, D., Wilson, M., Murray, C., & Parham, L. (2018). Reversing the dehumanization of families of color in schools: Community-based research in a race-conscious parent engagement program. *School Community Journal, 28*(1), 319–347.

Index

Note. f or *t* following a page number indicates a figure or a table.

Ableism, 41–42
Abshier, Dama, 73–76
Academic achievement, 3, 7–9, 69, 91, 165
Accessibility, 10, 78, 97, 132, 144
Accountability, 132, 152–153
Administrators, school, 6–7, 44, 72, 117, 121, 151–152
Agencies, community, 77, 78, 130*t*, 138–139, 144, 147
Agency, 110–111, 113
    collective, 42, 44, 48
    ownership, 33
*Aligning and Integrating Family Engagement
        in Positive Behavioral Interventions and Supports*
        (Office of Special Education Programs), 69–70
Allegheny Family Network (AFN), 126
American Institutes for Research (AIR), 151
Anti-Blackness, 41–42
Anti-racism, 5, 19, 27
Anxiety, 97–98
Applied behavior analysis, 2
Arizona, 127–129
Assessments, evaluation and, 20*f*, 21*f*, 30–31, 141,
        149, 166
    FACE, 157–158, 158*f*
    FBA, 94, 97
    fidelity tools and, 54–55, 58–63, 70–72
    MTSS, 5–6, 8, 11, 52–67, 64*f*, 67*t*
    professional development and, 36, 54, 56–57, 64*f*,
        66–68, 140

self-assessment, 56, 63, 65, 67*t*
of shared decision-making processes, 54, 60,
        64*f*, 65
Tier 2, 80, 83
Tier 3, 107–111
of two-way communication, 53–54, 62, 64*f*, 65
Assimilation, forced, 46
At-risk students, 6, 69, 77, 90, 106. *See also* Tier 2,
        MTSS
Attendance, 108, 118–119, 127
Autism spectrum disorder (ASD), 90, 94, 161

B

Back-to-school night, 18, 65, 153, 158
Behavioral expectations, 15, 50, 69, 88, 114, 132,
        157–158
Behavioral Parent Training (BPT), 96, 99
Biases, 24*t*, 32, 81–82, 122
Black, Indigenous, and People of Color (BIPOC),
        37–38, 40, 43–44, 47–49
Bourdieu, Pierre, 41–42
Bronfenbrenner, U., 14
Bullying, 17
Buy-in, 50, 132, 154
    administrator, 6–7, 121
    PBIS, 71, 123–124

C

Capacity building, 81–82, 131–132, 137, 145
  in equitable family–school collaboration, 22–23,
    25t, 26t, 29t, 31–32
Caregivers. *See* parents, caregivers and
Check-In, Check-Out (CICO) intervention, 83,
    93–94, 96t, 104
  DPR, 88, 89f, 90t, 92, 100
Child welfare systems, 77, 130t
Classroom Family Engagement Rubric, 56, 65
Coaching, 12–13, 140–141, 143, 149
Cognitive-behavioral intervention, 97–98
Collaborative goals and problem solving, 21f, 22–23,
    23t, 24t, 25t, 26–27t, 28–29t, 30–31
Collective inquiry, 22–23, 26–27t, 31–33, 41
Collective learning, 10, 27, 33
Collier, T., 71
Communication, 6, 12, 57, 110, 122, 170. *See also* home-
    school communications; two-way communication
  miscommunication and, 8–9, 17
  multidirectional, 91, 108t, 112t, 113
  negative, 92, 101
  unidirectional, 121, 123
  vertical, 122, 128
Communities, community organizations and, 2, 12, 24t,
    32f, 38–39, 137, 141–142, 145–146, 154t. *See also*
    minoritized families
  agencies, 77, 78, 130t, 138–139, 144, 147
  family-run organizations in, 125–128
  school, 10, 18–19, 32, 156–157
Confidentiality, 48, 72
Controlled trials, randomized, 3, 73, 124
Coping Cat intervention, 96t, 97–98
Core variables, MTSS framework, 3–6, 4f, 6, 120
Council for Exceptional Children (CEC), 38–39, 151
COVID-19 pandemic, 54, 70, 143–144
Critical race theory (CRT), 15, 42
Critical theory, 14–15
Cross-setting support, 111, 112t, 113–114, 117
Cultural humility, 9, 10, 14–15, 24t, 99–100, 140
Culturally responsive positive behavioral interventions
    and supports (CRPBIS), 39, 42
  Learning Lab methodology, 41, 43–51, 45f
Cultural responsiveness, 5, 24t, 38–39, 82, 93, 132,
    134f, 158, 165
Curriculum, instruction and, 5–6, 81, 97, 99

D

Daily Progress Report (DPR), CICO, 88, 89f,
    90t, 92, 100
Data, 5–6, 53, 69, 77, 117, 130t, 166
  collection, 56–67, 67t
  decision-making guided by, 40, 79, 86–87
  district level, 132, 141, 144, 149
  elementary school case study, 52, 63, 64f, 65–67, 67t
  equity related, 19, 20f, 21f, 22t, 30–31
  FACE, 153, 155–156, 159t, 160t
  fidelity, 54–55

Learning Labs utilizing, 46
  qualitative, 48, 56, 71
  Tier 2 related, 80–84, 86–87, 90t, 100
  Tier 3 related, 109, 111–112, 118–119
Decision-making processes, 10, 15, 38–39, 41–42, 151
  data-driven, 40, 79, 86–87
Decision-making processes, shared, 161, 164–165
  assessing, 54, 60, 64f, 65
  equity and, 20f, 21f, 23t, 25t, 26–27t, 28t, 29–30
Demographics, 31, 37–38, 45, 53, 151–152, 161–162
Department of Education, Maryland, 126–127
Department of Education, Pennsylvania, 161
Department of Education, Tennessee, 151
Design phase, Learning Labs, 44–45, 45f
Disciplinary policies, 7, 14, 43, 69, 139, 165
  exclusionary, 16–17, 21f, 23t, 26–27t, 27–28, 28t,
    30, 37–38, 41, 47, 77
  Learning Labs addressing, 45–46
Discrimination, 14–15
District Capacity Assessment (DCA), 8
District–Community Leadership Team (DCLT),
    72, 124
District level schools, 6, 11, 20f, 59, 125–126,
    128–129, 134f
  data, 132, 141, 144, 149
  executive functions, 131, 136–140, 142, 147
  feedback at the, 137, 139–141, 144
  implementation functions, 131, 136, 140–142, 148–149
  leadership roles, 131–132, 133, 135f, 136–146
  northeast, 131, 142–146
  PBIS and, 133, 134f, 135f, 136–146, 147–150
  rural, 43, 46, 151–161
  southern, 72–73, 124
  stakeholders, 124, 132, 137–139, 143–147
  teaming processes, 72, 137, 144–145
  workforce capacity, 136–137, 139–140, 142–143, 148
District System Fidelity Inventory (DSFI), 124–125,
    136, 147–149
Distrust, 17–18, 40, 93, 156
Diversity, equity, and inclusion (DEI), 18–19
Division of labor, Learning Labs, 44–45
Dominant culture, 15, 18, 37, 41–42
Dress code policies, 14

E

Early intervention supports, 10–11, 17, 40, 55, 60, 69,
    80. *See also* Tier 1, MTSS
Eber, L., 124
Ecological systems theory, 2, 14
Economically disadvantaged students, 142, 152, 161
Educational laws, 4, 16–17, 38–39, 139
Elementary school, 3, 72, 100, 118–119, 143
  data collection and use case study, 52, 63, 64f, 64t,
    65–67, 67t
Email, 54–55, 93, 97, 100–101, 104, 153, 162
Emergency contact information, 86–87
Equity, equitable family–school collaboration and, 18
  capacity building in, 22–23, 25t, 26t, 29t, 31–32
  data relating to, 19, 20f, 21f, 22t, 30–31

exclusionary discipline and, 21*f*, 23*t*, 26–27*t*, 27–28,
    30, 37–38, 47, 78
family voices in, 20*f*, 21*f*, 23*t*, 24, 25, 25*t*, 26–27*t*, 28*t*,
    29–30, 32*f*
school staff training for, 20*f*, 21*f*, 24*t*, 26–27, 30–31
shared decision-making processes and, 20*f*, 21*f*, 23*t*,
    25*t*, 26–27*t*, 28*t*, 29–30
for Tier 2 and Tier 3, 22*t*, 23*t*, 24*t*
two-way communication and, 20*f*, 21*f*, 22*t*, 25, 25*t*,
    26–27*t*, 28*t*, 30
Evaluation. *See* assessment
Every Student Succeeds Act (ESSA), U.S., 38, 151
Evidence-based practices, 7–9, 16–17, 99
Exclusionary discipline, 16–17, 41
    equitable discipline alternatives to, 20*f*, 21*f*, 23*t*, 24,
        25, 25*t*, 26–27*t*, 28*t*, 29–30, 32*f*
    minoritized students impacted by, 27–28
Executive functions, district level, 131, 136–140,
    142, 147
Experiential knowledge, 40–41, 45, 48
Experts, 43–44, 70, 141, 147, 162

F

Facebook, 54–55, 155, 159
Families, 8–9, 11, 13–14, 43–44, 154*t*. *See also* two-way
    communication; voices, family
    clear roles for, 4*f*, 16, 22–23, 23*t*, 64*t*, 77, 87, 122, 130*t*
    engagement of, 1–2, 10, 12, 32*f*, 69–76, 79–80, 86–87,
        120–129, 130*t*, 163–166
    family-run organizations, 125–128
    historically marginalized, 10, 16–18, 29*t*, 30, 33, 42
    in leadership roles, 22–23, 25, 26–27*t*, 27, 28*t*, 34–36,
        72–76, 78, 130*t*
    minoritized and marginalized, 5, 10, 16–19, 27–28,
        30, 32*f*, 41–42
    as passive recipients, 18, 25, 43–44
    perceptions of, 53–60, 62, 141, 149
    preferences of, 21*f*, 25, 65
    training for, 20*f*, 21*f*, 23, 24*t*, 26–27*t*, 29*t*, 30–31
    White middle-class, 15–17, 18, 42, 43, 160–161
Family and Community Engagement (FACE), 151–161,
    158*f*, 159*t*, 160*t*, 168–169
Family and Community Engagement—Innovation
    Configuration (FACE-IC), 59
Family and Community Engagement Survey (FACERS),
    157–158, 158*f*
Family and Community Engagement Survey for
    Educators (FACERS-E), 153, 157, 160*t*
Family and Community Engagement Survey for
    Families (FACERS-F), 153, 157, 159*t*
Family-Based Services Association (FBSA), 125–126
Family Engagement in Problem-Solving/Response
    to Intervention Survey—Educators (FERS-E),
    57–58, 65
Family Engagement in Problem-Solving/Response to
    Intervention Survey—Family (FERS-F), 57–58
Family Interview for Culturally Responsive
    Practices, 62
Family Involvement Center (FIC), 127–128

Family Involvement Questionnaire (FIQ), 57
Family Leadership Initiative (FLI), MCF, 126
Family Matrix tool, 74–76
Family Outreach Team (FOT), 123
Family–School Collaboration. *See specific topics*
Family–School–Community Alliance (FSCA), 1–2, 20,
    20*f*, 24, 25*t*, 70
Family–school–community collaboration, 39–41, 69–78
Family–School Practices Survey—School Teams (FSPS-
    Teams), 58–59, 61
Family therapy, 111–112
Family voices, 10, 17, 64*f*, 65, 77, 130*t*
    in equitable discipline, 20*f*, 21*f*, 23*t*, 24, 25, 25*t*,
        26–27*t*, 28*t*, 29–30, 32*f*
    SISS-F and, 58
Federal education policies, 4, 38
Feedback, 21*f*, 22*t*, 50, 66, 74, 166, 176–177
    BIPOC, 43, 47
    district level, 137, 139–141, 144
    FACE, 155–156, 159*t*, 160*t*, 161
    Family and Community Engagement Survey
        for Educators, 153
    student, 12, 92
    Tier 2, 83, 88, 90*t*, 92–94, 100–101, 105
    Tier 3, 110, 113
Feedback loops, 10, 149
Fidelity tools, 20, 21*f*, 124, 129, 151. *See also*
    specific tools
    assessment, 54–55, 58–63, 70–72
First Step Next (FSN) intervention, 96*t*, 98–99
Fix, R. L., 70
Forced assimilation, 46
Formal education, 37, 50
Frequency, data collection, 60–62, 66–67, 67*t*
Functional behavioral assessment (FBA), 94, 97
Funding, 73, 117, 126–129, 130, 136–139, 144–145, 147

G

Garbacz, S. A., 117, 121
Glasser, W., 165
Goals, collaborative problem solving and, 21*f*, 22–23,
    23*t*, 24*t*, 25*t*, 26–27*t*, 28–29*t*, 30–31
Goldman, S. E., 90

H

Health fairs, 72–73
Hierarchies, 15, 39, 51, 70, 132
High school, 43–45, 50
Historically marginalized families, 10, 16–18, 29*t*,
    30, 33, 42
Home-based involvement, 53, 86, 107
Home–school communications, 25, 53–55, 57, 62,
    65, 67, 68, 117–119
    Tier 2, 80–81, 88, 90–91, 90*t*, 91, 98–105
Horizontal collaboration, 122, 128
Houri, A. K., 93
Huffman, R., 120–121

I

Identity, 14–15, 27, 32, 132
Immigrants, 40, 132, 142
Implementation functions, district level, 131, 136,
    140–142, 148–149
Income, median household, 142
Indigenous peoples, 41, 43, 46–49
Individualized education programs (IEPs), 48, 126,
    128, 161–164
Individualized supports, 6, 62, 80, 94, 100–102, 104
Individuals with Disabilities Education Act (IDEA),
    U.S., 38, 151, 161
Inequities, race/ethnicity, 10, 14–17, 37–39, 42
Institutional memory, 50
Integration, MTSS, 8, 10–11, 12
Intensive intervention supports, 55, 69, 139.
    See also Tier 3, MTSS
Interconnected systems frameworks (ISF), 5,
    72–76, 124–125
Interest convergence, 15
Intersectionality, 16, 43
Ishimaru, Anne, 18–19, 20, 22–25, 28–32

J

Juvenile justice system, 38, 77, 130*t*

K

K–12 education settings, 7
Kindergarten, 87, 101
Knowledge, experiential, 40–41, 45, 48

L

Laboratory schools, 161–166
Leadership roles, 168–169
    district level, 131–132, 133, 135*f*, 136–146
    family in, 22–23, 25, 26–27*t*, 27, 28*t*, 34–36,
        72–76, 78, 130*t*
    MTSS, 5–8, 63, 65–67, 67*t*, 69–70
    PBIS, 133, 134*f*, 138–139, 152, 154, 154*t*
    school, 5, 44–47, 58–59, 152
Learning, collective, 10, 27, 33
Learning Lab methodology, CRPBIS, 41, 43–51, 45*f*
Linguistic barriers, 40, 46, 93, 142, 144
Listening sessions, 27–28, 137, 139
Lived experiences, 14–15, 42, 125

M

Making a Plan (MAP) Team, Families as Allies, 127
Maryland, 126–127
Maryland Coalition of Families (MCF), 126
Massachusetts, 142–145
Median household income, 142
Medicaid, 127–128

Memory, institutional, 50
Mental health, 9, 17, 70–76, 77, 78, 97–99,
    125–128, 138–139
Middle school, 43–45, 91, 106
Military stakeholders, 130*t*
Minoritized families, marginalized and, 5, 10,
    16–19, 27–28, 30, 32*f*, 41–42
Minoritized students, marginalized and, 2, 142
    ethnic–racial socialization processes for, 14–15
    exclusionary discipline and, 27–28
    inequities experienced by, 16–18
Miscommunication, 8–9, 17
Mississippi, 127
Motivational interviewing, 111, 112*t*, 113
Multidimensional approaches, 81–82
Multidirectional communication, 91, 108*t*, 112*t*, 113
Multiple worlds typology, 2
Multi-tiered System of Support (MTSS) framework,
    1–6, 4*f*, 11–13, 14–19, 130*t*. *See also specific*
    interventions; specific MTSS tiers
    implementation, 7–10, 20, 23–24, 62–63, 71–72,
        80, 121–123
Mutual respect, 22*t*, 30, 33
Mutual trust, 28, 52

N

National Institute of Justice, U.S., 73
Negative behaviors, focus on, 121, 162
Negative communication, 92, 101
New Jersey, 125–126
Northeast school districts, 131, 142–146

O

Oakland Unified School District (OUSD), 132–133
Office of Special Education Programs, 69–70
Off-task behaviors, 111–112
Oppression, 132
Organizational drivers, 7–8
Outcomes, educational, 3–4, 4*f*, 7–9, 56–58, 83, 111
    racial/ethnic inequities and, 10, 14–17, 37–39, 42
Out-of-school suspensions, 46, 128, 161
Ownership agency, 33

P

Parents, caregivers and, 10, 43–44, 55, 106–113,
    127–128, 142, 162–164. *See also* families
    BPT, 96*t*, 99
    refugee, 40
    surveys of, 166, 176–177
    Tier 2 involvement, 80–85, 86–88, 89*f*,
        90–105, 90*t*, 96*t*, 97
Parent–teacher association (PTA), 17–19, 75
Parent–teacher conferences, 17–19, 164
Parent–teacher relationships, 3–5, 12, 53–59, 93,
    106–109, 108*t*, 132
Parent–Teacher Relationship Scale II (PTRS II), 56

Pennsylvania, 126, 161–166

Petitioning processes, 164–165, 171–172

Phenomenological variants, ecological systems theory, 2, 14–15

Positive behavioral interventions and supports (PBIS), 1–2, 5–7, 62, 65, 69. *See also* culturally responsive positive behavioral interventions and supports
buy-in, 71, 123–124
decision-making and, 23*t*
district level, 133–133, 134*f*, 135*f*, 136–146, 147–150
expectations, 66, 67*t*, 92, 105, 160
factors limiting, 121–124
fidelity assessments, 70–71
implementation, 21*f*, 23*t*, 24*t*, 26–27*t*, 40–41, 124, 136, 139, 141, 145, 151–161
mental health and, 70–74
Pennsylvania, 161–166
RTI and, 150–151
teaming in, 39–40
Tennessee, 151–161
training for, 24*t*, 152

Positive family–school relationship, 21*f*, 22, 22*t*, 25, 26–27*t*, 28*t*, 64*f*
Tier 2, 91–94, 96*t*, 98, 100–105

Positive Family Support—Strengths and Needs Assessment (PFS-SANA), 60–62

Positive Parent Contact (PPC), 88

Positive Parent Contact Plus (PPC+) intervention, 91–93

Power dynamics
family–educator, 17–19, 23, 29–30, 32*f*, 33, 40
racial relations and, 37–38

Problem identification, Learning Lab, 45–49

Problem solving, collaborative goals and, 21*f*, 22–23, 23*t*, 24*t*, 25*t*, 26–27*t*, 28–29*t*, 30–31

Professional development, 6, 21*f*, 56, 148, 158, 166. *See also* training
assessment and, *36*, 54, 56–57, 64*f*, 66–68, 140

Psychoeducation, 98, 101

Public health approaches, 2, 5

Q

Qualitative data, 48, 56, 71

R

Race/ethnicity
disproportionality, 38–39, 42–43, 45–47, 49
inequities, 10, 14–17, 37–39, 42

Race-neutrality, 38, 48

Racism, 14–16

Randomized controlled trials, 3, 73, 124

Reality therapy, 165–166

Refugee parents, 40

Request for assistance forms, 84–85, 86–87, 90*t*, 101, 103

Response to Instruction and Intervention—Behavior (RTI²-B), 151, 159*t*, 167

Response to intervention (RTI), 6, 8, 150–151

Responsibility, shared, 22*t*, 23, 25*t*, 26*t*, 28*t*, 30, 39–40, 109, 128, 143

Reynolds, S., 94

Rispoli, K. M., 94

Rizzardi, V., 71

Rural school districts, 43, 46, 151–161

S

Safe spaces, 48, 165

Scherder, Erin, 73–76

School atmosphere, 4, 4*f*, 27, 64*t*, 123, 134*f*, 135*f*

School community, 10, 18–19, 32, 156–157

School staff, training for, 12–13, 81, 143
equity related, 20*f*, 21*f*, 24*t*, 26–27, 30–31

Schoolwide expectations, 74–76, 80, 91–93, 102, 155, 157, 160

Seesaw application, 163, 167

Segregation, racial, 16–17

Self-assessment, 56, 63, 65, 67*t*

Service delivery models, 80–81 101, 131–132, 139, 150

Settler colonialism, 37, 41–43, 46

Sheridan, S. M., 107

Siloed frameworks, 8, 17, 39, 51, 130*t*

Social, emotional, and behavioral competencies, 2–4, 4*f*, 8–9, 106

Social capital, 10

Social justice, 14, 19, 27

Social media, 54–55, 123, 155, 157, 159

South Carolina, 129

Southern school districts, 72–73, 124

Special education services, 16, 126
racial disproportionality in, 37, 41

Stakeholder Input and Satisfaction Survey—Family (SISS-F), 57–58

Stakeholders, school, 38–39, 41, 43–44, 48, 50, 64*t*, 122–123, 128–129
district level, 124, 132, 137–139, 143–147
ISF, 74
military, 130*t*
MTSS implementation, 71

State level, schools at the, 120, 125–129, 130*t*

Stigma, 71, 77, 121–122, 130*t*

Strategic planning, 59, 63, 67*t*, 143–144

Structured meetings, 45, 108, 111–112, 112*t*

Student Assistance Program (SAP), 126

Student engagement, MTSS, 73–76, 78, 97–98, 130*t*

Student identification methods, 85–86, 100–104, 149

Students. *See also* exclusionary discipline; minoritized students
with ASD, 90, 94, 161
at-risk, 6, 69, 77, 90, 106
attendance by, 108, 118–119, 127
behavioral expectations of, 15, 50, 69, 88, 114, 132, 157–158
BIPOC, 37–38
of color, 14–15, 37–38
feedback from, 12, 92
identity development and, 14–15, 27, 32, 132
learning goals for, 24*t*, 52–53, 55, 62

Students (*continued*)
   mental health of, 9, 17, 70–76, 77, 78, 97–99,
      125–128, 138–139
   out-of-school suspensions for, 46, 128, 161
   well-being of, 4, 55–56, 62, 133
Summer camp, 166, 174–175
Surveys, 21f, 24t, 27t, 32f, 56–61, 65–67, 67t, 87,
      100–101, 166. *See also specific surveys*
   district level, 133–133
   FACE, 156–158, 159t, 160t, 161
   TSCP, 153
Suspensions, 46, 49, 128, 161
Sustainability, 6–7, 112t, 114
Systemic racism, 15
Systemic transformation, 22t, 30, 39
   Learning Labs and, 41, 47

T

Tager, Susan, 125
Teachers, educators and, 56, 81–82, 92, 106–107,
      142, 164, 166
Teachers and Parents as Partners (TAPP), 31
Teaming processes, 6, 11, 12, 32, 63–65
   CRPBIS, 50
   district level, 72, 137, 144–145
   FACE, 153–161, 154t
   MTSS, 61, 65, 75–77, 78, 123–124
   PBIS, 39–40
   Tier 3, 108–114, 108t, 109, 112t, 117–119
Team-Initiated Problem Solving (TIPS) program, 124
Tennessee, 151–161
Tennessee Behavior Supports Project (TBSP), 151
Therapy
   family, 111–112
   reality, 165–166
Tier 1, MTSS, 1, 3, 5–7, 10–12, 55, 65–66, 122
   family–school–community collaboration, 69–76,
      77, 78
   PFS-SANA in, 60
   Tier 2 and, 80, 82–84, 86, 95f, 99
   Tier 3 and, 114, 117–118
Tier 2, MTSS, 1, 5–7, 10–12, 55, 61–62, 66, 72, 122
   assessments, 80, 83
   data, 80–84, 86–87, 90t, 100
   equity considerations for, 22t, 23t, 24t
   family–school collaboration in, 79–84, 85–88, 89f,
      90–105, 90t, 95f, 96t
   feedback in, 83, 88, 90t, 92–94, 100–101, 105
   home–school communications, 80–81, 88,
      90–91, 90t, 91, 98–105
   parent and caregivers involvement at, 80–85, 86–88,
      89f, 90–105, 90t, 96t, 97
   positive family–school relationships at, 91–94,
      96t, 98, 100–105
   Tier 3 and, 95, 95f, 99, 102, 118
Tier 3, MTSS, 1, 6, 10–12, 55, 61–62, 66, 72, 75, 77, 122
   assessments, 107–111
   checklists, 114, 115f, 116f
   data, 109, 111–112, 118–119

   equity considerations for, 22t, 23t, 24t
   family–school partnerships at, 106–114, 108t, 112t,
      115–116f, 117–119
   feedback in, 110, 113
   teaming in, 108–114, 108t, 109, 112t, 117–119
   Tier 1 and, 114, 117–118
   Tier 2 and, 95, 95f, 99, 102, 118
Tiered Fidelity Inventory FACE (TFI-FACE),
      157–158, 158f
Tiered Fidelity Inventory Family–School Collaboration
      (TFI-FSC), 58, 61, 63, 64f, 70–71, 129, 167
   equitable family–school collaboration and, 20,
      20f, 22t, 23t, 24t
Tobin, T. J., 40
Tokenism, 4, 32f, 129
Training, 64t, 77, 125, 130t, 134f, 140, 143, 148.
      See also school staff, training for
   BPT, 96, *99*
   FACE, 152–153
   for families, 20f, 21f, 23, 24t, 26–27t, 29t,
      30–31, 83, 166
   PBIS, 24t, 152
Transparency, 30
Trauma, 62, 161, 165
Treaty rights, U.S., 43
Trial-and-error approaches, 10
Two-way communication, schools-families, 4, 76,
      91, 123, 167
   assessing, 53–54, 62, 64f, 65
   equity and, 20f, 21f, 22t, 25, 25t, 26–27t, 28t, 30
   FACE, 155

U

United States (U.S.), 15, 124, 142. *See also*
      specific states
   educational laws, 4, 16–17, 38–39, 139
   settler colonialism and, 37, 41–43, 46
   treaty rights, 43
Universal screening approaches, 5, 84, 86–87

V

Vertical communication, collaboration and, 122, 128
Vincent, C. G., 40
Voices. *See* family voices

W

Walker, Jane, 125
Ward, C. S., 8
Websites, 123
Weist, M., 121, 129
Well-being, student, 4, 55–56, 62, 133
Well-Being Promotion Program (WBPP), 97
White middle-class families, whiteness and, 15–17,
      18, 42, 43, 160–161
Workforce capacity, district level, 136–137, 139–140,
      142–143, 148